Following in His Steps

SOCIETY OF BIBLICAL LITERATURE

DISSERTATION SERIES
Michael V. Fox, Old Testament Editor
E. Elizabeth Johnson, New Testament Editor

Number 162
FOLLOWING IN HIS STEPS
Suffering, Community, and Christology in 1 Peter

by
Steven Richard Bechtler

Steven Richard Bechtler

FOLLOWING IN HIS STEPS
Suffering, Community, and Christology in 1 Peter

Society of Biblical Literature
Dissertation Series

Scholars Press
Atlanta, Georgia

FOLLOWING IN HIS STEPS
Suffering, Community, and Christology in 1 Peter

by
Steven Richard Bechtler

Copyright © 1998 by the Society of Biblical Literature

All rights reserved. No part of this work may be reproduced or transmitted in any form or by any means, electronic or mechanical, including photocopying and recording, or by means of any information storage or retrieval system, except as may be expressly permitted by the 1976 Copyright Act or in writing from the publisher. Requests for permission should be addressed in writing to the Rights and Permissions Office, Scholars Press, P.O. Box 15399, Atlanta, GA 30333-0399, USA.

Dedication from *Fifty Selected Songs by Schubert, Schumann, Brahms, Wolf, and Strauss,* Schirmer's Library of Musical Classics (New York/London: G. Schirmer, 1951) 50.

Library of Congress Cataloging in Publication Data
Bechtler, Steven Richard.
    Following in His steps : suffering, community, and christology in 1 Peter / Steven Richard Bechtler.
       p.   cm. — (Society of Biblical Literature dissertation series)
    Includes bibliographical references and indexes.
    ISBN 0-7885-0485-1 (alk. paper)
    1. Suffering—Biblical teaching. 2. Jesus Christ—Example—Biblical teaching. 3. Bible. N.T. Peter, 1st—Social scientific criticism. I. Title. II. Series: Dissertation series (Society of Biblical Literature)
BS2795.6S9B43 1998
227'.92067—dc21   98-8542
                                          CIP

ISBN 1-58983-439-9 (paper : alk. paper)

Printed in the United States of America
on acid-free paper

To Joy

Dass du mich liebst, macht mich mir werth,
dein Blick hat mich vor mir verklärt,
du hebst mich liebend über mich,
  mein guter Geist,
  mein bess'res Ich!
—Franz Rückert, "Widmung"

CONTENTS

Acknowledgments	ix
Abbreviations	x
Chapter 1: A HISTORY OF RESEARCH	1
From Harnack to Selwyn	1
From Lohse to Goppelt and Brox	4
From Balch and Elliott to Martin and Feldmeier	10
Conclusions	18
Chapter 2: METHODOLOGY	23
Social Sciences, Exegesis, and the Present Task	24
Sociology of Knowledge	30
The Design of the Study	39
Chapter 3: THE PROBLEM: SUFFERING AND DISGRACE	41
Authorship, Date, and Provenance	42
Authorship	43
Date	48
Provenance	52
The Social Location of the Addressees	54
Methodological Prolegomenon	54
Geographical Area	57
Ethnic Composition	61
Social Stratum	64
The Suffering of the Addressees	83
The Origin of Their Suffering	83
The Form of Their Suffering	87
Their Honor at Risk	94
Conclusions	105

Chapter 4: THE SOLUTION, PART ONE:
              THE LIMINALITY OF CHRISTIAN LIFE   109
    Symbolic-Universe Maintenance/Legitimation   109
    Christian Existence as Liminal   112
        Balch, Elliott, and Their Critics   112
        Victor Turner on Liminality   118
        Critical Appropriation of Turner's Theory   123
        Liminality in 1 Peter   126
            Temporal Liminality   127
            Metaphorical Liminality   135
                Liminal Images Evoking LXX Israel   135
                Other Images of Liminality   146
            Extracommunity Relations   156
            Intracommunity Relations   169
    Conclusions   177

Chapter 5: THE SOLUTION, PART TWO:
              CHRISTOLOGY AND HONOR   179
    1 Peter 1:3-9   181
    1 Peter 1:10–2:3   183
    1 Peter 2:4-10   186
    1 Peter 2:11-17   188
    1 Peter 2:18-25   190
    1 Peter 3:13–4:6   194
    1 Peter 4:12-19   199
    1 Peter 5:1-14   201
    Conclusions   202

Chapter 6: CONCLUSION   205

Bibliography   211
Index of Ancient Texts   227
Index of Modern Authors   237

ACKNOWLEDGMENTS

This monograph is a slightly revised version of my Ph.D. dissertation, which was originally presented to the faculty of Princeton Theological Seminary in the spring of 1996. I wish to thank my dissertation adviser, Beverly Roberts Gaventa, whose constant encouragement and incisive, lucid critiques of numerous drafts along the way have resulted in a far better work than I could have otherwise hoped to produce.

I also wish to thank the other two members of my dissertation committee: J. Christiaan Beker, my adviser during the early stages of this work and my teacher and friend throughout the course of my graduate studies; and Donald H. Juel, whose probing questions continue to stimulate my reflection on the implications of this study for understanding the faith, practices, and social situation of those called (already by the time of 1 Peter) Christians.

Thanks also go to my friend Stanley P. Saunders, who first suggested to me that the growing body of literature on the anthropological study of honor and shame in the Mediterranean world might have some relevance to the interpretation of 1 Peter.

I owe a special debt of gratitude to my parents, James C. Bechtler and Barbara Jo Bechtler, for their unfailing love and support and for introducing me to the faith.

Above all, I wish to express my profoundest gratitude to my wife, Catherine Joy Bechtler, in whose faithfulness and love God graces and ennobles my life.

ABBREVIATIONS

ANCIENT TEXTS

Aristotle
   Pol.   *Politica*
As. Mos.   *Assumption of Moses*
Barn.   *Epistle of Barnabas*
Cicero
   De Imp. Cn. Pomp.   *De Imperio Cn. Pompeii*
   Off.   *De Officiis*
   Flac.   *Pro Flacco*
1 Clem.   *First Epistle of Clement*
2 Clem.   *Second Epistle of Clement*
Clement of Alexandria
   Protr.   *Protrepticus*
Dio Chrysostom
   Or.   *Orationes*
Diodorus Siculus
   Bib. hist.   *Bibliotheca Historica*
1 Enoch   *Ethiopic Apocalypse of Enoch*
Ep. Arist.   *Epistle of Aristeas*
Epictetus
   Disc.   *Discourses*
   Ench.   *Encheiridion*
Eusebius
   Hist. eccl.   *Ecclesiastical History*
Herm. Vis.   *Shepherd of Hermas, Visions*
Ign. Phld.   Ignatius, *Letter to the Philadelphians*
Ign. Rom.   Ignatius, *Letter to the Romans*
Ign. Smyrn.   Ignatius, *Letter to the Smyrnaeans*

Josephus
  Ant.   *Antiquities of the Jews*
Juvenal
  Sat.   *Satires*
Mart. Pol.   *Martyrdom of Polycarp*
Philo
  Cher.   *De Cherubim*
  Conf.   *De Confusione Linguarum*
  Decal.   *De Decalogo*
  Ebr.   *De Ebrietate*
  Praem.   *De Praemiis et Poenis*
  Spec. leg.   *De Specialibus Legibus*
Plato
  Leg.   *Leges*
  Resp.   *Respublica*
Pliny the Younger
  Ep.   *Epistulae*
Plutarch
  Mor.   *Moralia*
Pol. Phil.   Polycarp, *Letter to the Philippians*
Pseudo-Dionysius
  Ep.   *Epistles*
Ps.-Phoc.   *Pseudo-Phocylides*
Pss. Sol.   *Psalms of Solomon*
Sib. Or.   *Sibylline Oracles*
Suetonius
  Ner.   *Nero*
Tacitus
  Ann.   *Annales*
  Hist.   *Historiae*
T. Ash.   *Testament of Asher*
T. Levi   *Testament of Levi*
Thucydides
  History   *History of the Peloponnesian War*

TITLES OF MODERN WORKS, SERIES, AND JOURNALS

AB	Anchor Bible
ABD	*Anchor Bible Dictionary*, ed. D. N. Freedman
AnBib	Analecta biblica
ANRW	*Aufstieg und Niedergang der römischen Welt*, ed. W. Hasse and H. Temporini
BAGD	Bauer, W., W. F. Arndt, F. W. Gingrich, and F. W. Danker, *A Greek-English Lexicon of the New Testament and Other Early Christian Literature*, 2d ed.
BDF	Blass, F., A. Debrunner, and R. W. Funk, *A Greek Grammar of the New Testament and Other Early Christian Literature*
BNTC	Black's New Testament Commentaries
BTB	*Biblical Theology Bulletin*
BZ	*Biblische Zeitschrift*
CBC	Cambridge Bible Commentary
CBQ	*Catholic Biblical Quarterly*
ConNT	*Coniectanea neotestamentica*
CRINT	Compendia rerum iudaicarum ad novum testamentum
CSEL	Corpus scriptorum ecclesiasticorum latinorum
DBSup	*Dictionnaire de la Bible, Supplément*, ed. L. Pirot et al.
EKKNT	Evangelisch-katholischer Kommentar zum Neuen Testament
FFNT	Foundations and Facets: New Testament
GBS	Guides to Biblical Scholarship
HNT	Handbuch zum Neuen Testament
HTKNT	Herders theologischer Kommentar zum Neuen Testament
HTR	*Harvard Theological Review*
ICC	International Critical Commentary
Int	*Interpretation*
IVPNTCS	InterVarsity Press New Testament Commentary Series

Abbreviations

JBL	*Journal of Biblical Literature*
JSNTSup	*Journal for the Study of the New Testament Supplement Series*
JSP	*Journal for the Study of the Pseudepigrapha*
JTS	*Journal of Theological Studies*
LCL	Loeb Classical Library
LD	Lectio divina
LEC	Library of Early Christianity
MeyerK	Meyer, H. A. W., *Kritisch-exegetischer Kommentar über das Neue Testament*
NABPRSSS	National Association of Baptist Professors of Religion Special Studies Series
NCB	New Century Bible
NICNT	New International Commentary on the New Testament
NovT	*Novum Testamentum*
NovTSup	Supplements to *Novum Testamentum*
NTD	Das Neue Testament Deutsch
NTS	*New Testament Studies*
OCD	*Oxford Classical Dictionary*, ed. N. G. L. Hammond and H. H. Scullard, 2d ed.
OGIS	*Orientis Graeci Inscriptiones Selectae*, ed. W. Dittenberger
PG	*Patrologiae Cursus Completus*, Series Graeca, ed. J.-P. Migne
PSTJ	*Perkins (School of Theology) Journal*
PVTG	Pseudepigrapha Veteris Testamenti graece
PW	*Paulys Real-Encyclopädie der classischen Altertumswisenschaft*, ed. G. Wissowa et al.
RAC	*Reallexikon für Antike und Christentum*, ed. T. Kauser et al.
RB	*Revue biblique*
SB	Sources bibliques
SBLDS	Society of Biblical Literature Dissertation Series
SBLMS	Society of Biblical Literature Monograph Series
SC	Sources chrétiennes
SJLA	Studies in Judaism in Late Antiquity

SNTSMS	Society for New Testament Studies Monograph Series
SVTP	Studia in Veteris Testamenti pseudepigrapha
TDNT	*Theological Dictionary of the New Testament*, ed. G. Kittel and G. Friedrich
TToday	*Theology Today*
TNTC	Tyndale New Testament Commentaries
TU	Texte und Untersuchungen
USQR	*Union Seminary Quarterly Review*
WBC	Word Biblical Commentary
WD	*Wort und Dienst*
WUNT	Wissenschaftliche Untersuchungen zum Neuen Testament
ZNW	Zeitschrift für die neutestamentliche Wissenschaft

CHAPTER 1

A HISTORY OF RESEARCH

The goal of this study is to discover how 1 Peter's references to Christ's suffering and glorification were intended to function, within the social conventions of the time, as integral parts of the letter's response to the suffering of the communities addressed. To this end, I shall focus on the interaction among four aspects of the letter: its social situation, its explicit statements about suffering, its symbolic construction of a communal self-identity for the addressees, and its references to Christ. An introductory survey of recent literature on 1 Peter, with special reference to the relationship among these four topics, will serve to clarify some of the issues involved in pursuing my objective.

From Harnack to Selwyn

Scholarship in the first half of this century was very much taken with the questions of the genre and sources of 1 Peter. Adolf von Harnack, in 1897, advanced the thesis that 1 Peter was not a letter at all but a sermon.[1] Richard Perdelwitz subsequently developed this idea in order to account for the various perspectives from which suffering seems to be viewed in the letter. Whereas in 4:12 the "fiery ordeal" (πύρωσις) appears to be a present reality, earlier in the letter (1:6; 3:13-14, 17) suffering is conceived of as merely a

---

[1] Adolf von Harnack, *Geschichte der altchristlichen Litteratur bis Eusebius*, pt. 2, vol. 1, *Die Chronologie der altchristlichen Litteratur bis Eusebius* (Leipzig: J. C. Hinrichs'sche Buchhandlung, 1897) 451.

hypothetical possibility. Furthermore, the doxology in 4:11, the earlier references to baptism and rebirth (1:3, 23; 2:2; 3:21), and indications that this baptism had only recently been received (1:6-8, 12; 2:10, 25; 3:21) seemed to Perdelwitz to indicate that 1:3–4:11 constituted a discrete entity—a baptismal homily directed to Christian initiates who had previously belonged to a mystery cult. The epistolary and hortatory material in 1:1-2 and 4:12–5:14 comprised a later document, probably written to the same community at a time when its members were undergoing persecution because of their faith. The two documents were subsequently joined together to produce what we know as 1 Peter.[2]

The thesis that 1 Peter is basically a baptismal discourse embedded in an epistolary, hortatory framework was accepted, with various modifications, by Burnett Hillman Streeter,[3] Hans Windisch,[4] Francis Wright Beare,[5] and numerous others.[6] Herbert Preisker extended the theory, arguing that 1:3–5:11 comprises an entire liturgy, 1:3–4:11 being the baptismal section and 4:12–5:11 the concluding portion for the whole congregation. Agreeing with Perdelwitz that 4:12 reflects not possible but actual, present suffering, Preisker concluded that persecution must have broken out during

---

[2]Richard Perdelwitz, *Die Mysterienreligionen und das Problem des I. Petrusbriefes: Ein literarischer und religionsgeschichtlicher Versuch* (Religionsgeschichtliche Versuche und Vorarbeiten 11/3; Giessen: Töpelmann, 1911) 16-19, 26.

[3]Burnett Hillman Streeter, *The Primitive Church: Studied with Special Reference to the Origins of the Christian Ministry* (London: Macmillan, 1929) 123-28.

[4]Hans Windisch, *Die katholischen Briefe* (HNT 15; 2d ed.; Tübingen: Mohr-Siebeck, 1930) 76-77, 82.

[5]Francis Wright Beare, *The First Epistle of Peter: The Greek Text with Introduction and Notes* (3d ed.; Oxford: Blackwell, 1970) 27.

[6]E.g., Alfred Adam, "Das Sintflutgebet in der Taufliturgie," *WD* n.s. 3 (1952) 20-21; Wilhelm Bornemann, "Der erste Petrusbrief—eine Taufrede des Silvanus?" *ZNW* 19 (1919-20) 143-65; Friedrich Hauck, *Die Briefe des Jakobus, Petrus, Judas und Johannes* (NTD 10; 5th ed.; Göttingen: Vandenhoeck & Ruprecht, 1949) 36. Bornemann's essay, written about the same time as Perdelwitz's volume but without reference to that work, defends Harnack's thesis. G. W. Beasley-Murray is convinced that Bornemann is indebted to Perdelwitz, despite the lack of any explicit citation (*Baptism in the New Testament* [London: Macmillan, 1962] 252 n. 1).

A History of Research

the composition of this liturgy.[7] F. L. Cross, in turn, expanded upon Preisker's theory. Cross attributed the repetition of the πασχ- word group in 1 Peter to the linking of πάσχω to πάσχα, as found in Melito of Sardis and Hippolytus, concluding that the letter's stress on suffering does not reflect actual suffering at all but the liturgical language of the Easter service near Passover time and the idea of the "sufferings of Christ's people in mystical union with Him."[8]

Edward Gordon Selwyn took a different approach in his 1946 commentary on 1 Peter.[9] He treats the document as an encyclical letter written by Silvanus to exhort and encourage Christians in Asia Minor in their time of trial. No intensification of suffering need be postulated to explain the πύρωσις of 4:12; throughout the letter, the trial consists not of organized imperial persecution but of episodic slander, social ostracism, mob violence, and even arrest and prosecution by local authorities.[10] Selwyn sharply criticizes Perdelwitz's view that the mystery religions provided much of the material of the letter, arguing instead that virtually all the ideas in the letter can be accounted for by recourse to OT, Jewish, and early-Christian traditions.[11] Of the latter, Selwyn discerns behind 1 Peter two distinct baptismal catechisms and a hortatory/parenetic document for persecuted Christians.[12] Although he holds to the unity of the letter,

---

[7]Herbert Preisker, in his additions to *Die katholischen Briefe*, by Hans Windisch (HNT 15; 3d ed.; Tübingen: Mohr-Siebeck, 1951) 156-62. M.-É. Boismard finds in 1 Peter not an entire liturgy, but numerous baptismal-liturgical fragments ("Une liturgie baptismale dans la Prima Petri," pts. 1-2, *RB* 63 [1956] 182-208; *RB* 64 [1957] 161-83; "Pierre [Première épître de]," *DBSup* 7.1430-48; cf. idem, *Quatre hymnes baptismales dans la première épître de Pierre* [Paris: Cerf, 1961]).

[8]F. L. Cross, *I. Peter: A Paschal Liturgy* (London: A. R. Mowbray, 1954), esp. 22. For similar views, see A. R. C. Leaney, *The Letters of Peter and Jude: A Commentary on the First Letter of Peter, a Letter of Jude and the Second Letter of Peter* (CBC; Cambridge: Cambridge University Press, 1967) 8, 15-16; and August Strobel, "Zum Verständnis von Mt 21:1-13," *NovT* 2 (1958) 210-19.

[9]Edward Gordon Selwyn, *The First Epistle of St. Peter: The Greek Text with Introduction, Notes and Essays* (London: Macmillan, 1946; 2d ed., 1947). Hereafter, page references are to the second edition, which is essentially a corrected reprint of the first.

[10]Selwyn, *Epistle of St. Peter*, 52-56, 91.

[11]Selwyn, *Epistle of St. Peter*, 305-11.

[12]Selwyn, *Epistle of St. Peter*, 363-461.

Selwyn actually presages Cross's theory by proposing that Silvanus penned the letter with the paschal baptismal celebration in mind, and that the paschal baptismal context accounts for the convergence in 1 Peter of allusions to baptism, reference to Christ as the lamb, and the prominence of Christ's suffering.[13] In the emphasis on Christ's suffering, Selwyn finds a distinctive, Petrine doctrine of atonement, which originated in Peter's personal witness of Jesus' meekness and patience in suffering, and which gave rise to the letter's ethic of subordination to others and faithful imitation of Christ's love and humble suffering.[14]

From Lohse to Goppelt and Brox

In 1954, the same year in which Cross's study appeared, Eduard Lohse published an essay that would prove to be a turning point in Petrine studies.[15] Lohse argues that the stylistic aporias Preisker observed are to be attributed not to the presence of a baptismal liturgy but to diverse traditional materials utilized by the author. Furthermore, in response to Perdelwitz, Windisch, Preisker, and Beare, Lohse points out that the references to baptism are restricted almost exclusively to 1:3–2:10, so that baptism cannot be the interpretive key to the text. First Peter is, rather, an occasional writing, a letter composed for the purpose of strengthening and comforting the congregations of Asia Minor, who are being questioned about their hope (3:15), slandered (3:16; 4:3-4, 14), and hauled into court (4:15-16). Against Selwyn, no fixed schema of catechetical instruction can be discerned within or even behind the text. Rather, the author takes up orally transmitted parenetic traditions that ultimately stemmed from many sources (including the OT, Hellenistic and Palestinian traditions, and sayings of the Lord) and subordinates them to one end: the preservation of believers in

---

[13]Selwyn, *Epistle of St. Peter*, 62.

[14]Selwyn, *Epistle of St. Peter*, 90-98.

[15]Eduard Lohse, "Paraenese und Kerygma im 1.Petrusbrief," *ZNW* 45 (1954) 68-89; ET, "Parenesis and Kerygma in 1 Peter" (trans. John Steely), *Perspectives on First Peter* (ed. Charles H. Talbert; NABPRSSS 9; Macon: Mercer University Press, 1986) 37-59. Hereafter, page references are to the English translation.

suffering. Christological traditions—confessional and hymnic pieces dealing with Christ's suffering—are also utilized alongside the parenetic materials, the former anchoring the latter so that it is the letter's christology that provides the ultimate rationale for its ethics. "Christ has suffered, and the Christians are called upon to follow in his steps."[16]

In the wake of Lohse's work, baptismal-homiletical theories tended to fall into disfavor as scholars increasingly—but by no means unanimously—accepted the literary integrity and the genuine epistolary and parenetic character of 1 Peter.[17] It was from this perspective that David Hill, in 1976, set out to clarify the role baptism plays in 1 Peter and its relationship to the theme of suffering.[18] Noting that the letter explicitly mentions baptism only once (in 3:21), Hill agrees with Lohse that baptism is subsidiary—even incidental—to the main theme of the letter, which is the conduct of Christians in the midst of suffering. First Peter is parenetic not catechetical; it is intended to encourage Christians exposed to real, physical suffering to persevere in their new way of life.[19] Baptism is invoked in 3:21, Hill explains, because baptism marked the moment of commitment to the new faith and way of life in which the recipients are now being encouraged to remain.[20]

---

[16] Lohse, "Parenesis," 59.

[17] Scholars who continue to hold to some form of the baptismal-homily theory include Beare, *Epistle of Peter*, 27, 220-26; Boismard, "Une liturgie baptismale," pts. 1-2, *RB* 63 (1956) 182-208; 64 (1957) 161-83; idem, "Pierre," 1430-48; Ralph P. Martin, "The Composition of I Peter in Recent Study," *Vox Evangelica: Biblical and Historical Essays by Members of the Faculty of the London Bible College* (London: Epworth, 1962) 40; and Bo Reicke, *The Epistles of James, Peter, and Jude: Introduction, Translation, and Notes* (AB 37; Garden City: Doubleday, 1964) 74.

[18] David Hill, "On Suffering and Baptism in I Peter," *NovT* 18 (1976) 181-89.

[19] But Hill is ambiguous about the nature and extent of this "real, physical suffering" ("On Suffering," 183): the author of 1 Peter "is concerned with *the results of an intensification of the virtually continuous harrying of Christians by local opponents which could lead* to suspicion, denial of civil rights, arrest, imprisonment and even death" (182 [emphasis mine]). Whether Hill thinks that arrest, imprisonment, and death were actual or only potential results for the author of 1 Peter is unclear.

[20] Hill, "On Suffering," 185, 189.

The year Hill's study appeared also saw the publication of Helmut Millauer's full-length monograph on suffering in 1 Peter, in which Millauer seeks to uncover the origin and tradition-historical background of the various statements about suffering that comprise 1 Peter's *Leidenstheologie*.²¹ He concludes that two great *Vorstellungskomplexe* from the tradition provide the author with most of the raw materials for the construction of this *Leidenstheologie*. First, from the election tradition of the OT and Palestinian Judaism come the notion of suffering as πειρασμός (1:6-7; 4:12), the distinction between a present time of suffering and a future time of rejoicing (1:6; 4:13b), and the idea of suffering as judgment or purification of the elect (4:17). Second, the synoptic discipleship tradition provides the conceptions of suffering as the Christian's calling (2:21), of the blessedness of the sufferer (3:24; 4:14), and of the joy of suffering (4:13a). In addition, 1 Peter employs words common to Paul and early-Christian tradition, without being directly influenced by Pauline theology (e.g., the *Leidensgemeinschaft*, συνείδησις, χάρις, δικαιοσύνη, and ἁμαρτία). Finally, the author can even employ the notion of following in someone's footsteps, embedding it in an overall theology that invests the image with a meaning quite different from that attached to it in its common usage in the Hellenistic world (2:21). On the basis of these various traditions, the letter arrives at its own idea of the significance of suffering: "Das Leiden des Erwählten in der Gemeinschaft mit Christus ist als Berufung in die Nachfolge Gnade."²²

Millauer thus views the *Leidenstheologie* of 1 Peter as the assembly of various *theological ideas* gathered from the OT, early Judaism, and early-Christian tradition. He argues that, although it is clear that the recipients are experiencing ostracism and discrimination, the letter does not provide sufficient data for a detailed description of their situation. Moreover, the letter's statements about suffering are so general that we cannot even assume that the author knows anything of any particular communities in Asia Minor.

---

²¹Helmut Millauer, *Leiden als Gnade: Eine traditionsgeschichtliche Untersuchung zur Leidenstheologie des ersten Petrusbriefes* (Europäische Hochschulschriften 23/56; Bern: Herbert Lang, 1976) 11, 185.

²²Millauer, *Leiden als Gnade*, 187.

Rather, the author addresses a general situation of widespread ostracism, fashioning a response to this situation by recourse to knowledge not of the recipients' situation but of the religious traditions at hand. "1.Petr. antwortet auf die Diskriminierung, indem er von der Tradition her das Wesen, die Situation und das daraus abzuleitende Verhalten der Christen neu bestimmt."[23] For this reason, Millauer argues, the explication of 1 Peter's statements concerning suffering is to be sought not in the vain attempt to reconstruct the historical situation but in the field of tradition history.

Leonhard Goppelt, in his 1978 commentary on 1 Peter,[24] notes that baptismal-homiletical and baptismal-liturgical theories presuppose the absence of any significant train of thought running through the letter and so lose their raison d'être when a unifying theme is demonstrated. For Goppelt, this theme is twofold: Christian existence in the midst of non-Christian society, and Christians' conquering by means of their readiness to endure repression or, in the words of 1 Peter, "to suffer."[25] The author's perspective on their situation is thoroughly kerygmatic: "The letter does not look on the situation of the Christians from the perspective of its environment as 'persecution,' but from the perspective of Christ as 'discipleship.'"[26] Despite this kerygmatic perspective, however, careful exegesis can uncover the general contours of the historical situation. For these Christians, existence within the institutions of society had become problematic. The Petrine Christians refused to conform to the Hellenistic ideal of religious-ethical tolerance, instead claiming

---

[23]Millauer, *Leiden als Gnade*, 60.
[24]Leonhard Goppelt, *Der erste Petrusbrief* (ed. Ferdinand Hahn; MeyerK 12/1; Göttingen: Vandenhoeck & Ruprecht, 1978); ET, *A Commentary on I Peter* (ed. Ferdinand Hahn; trans. and aug. John E. Alsup; Grand Rapids: Eerdmans, 1993). Hereafter, page references are to the English translation. Although this commentary appeared in 1978, its overall perspective and main themes had already been suggested two years earlier in Goppelt's treatment of 1 Peter in his *Theologie des Neuen Testaments* (*Theology of the New Testament*, vol. 2, *The Variety and Unity of the Apostolic Witness to Christ* [ed. Jürgen Roloff; trans. John E. Alsup; Grand Rapids: Eerdmans, 1982; German original, Göttingen: Vandenhoeck & Ruprecht, 1976] 161-78).
[25]Goppelt, *I Peter*, 18-19.
[26]Goppelt, *I Peter*, 38.

exclusivity for their religion and awaiting an eschatological judgment of non-Christians. Hence, they incurred the abuse and ostracism of their neighbors. Furthermore, although no imperial persecution is in evidence, it does appear that the local authorities considered Christianity basically criminal, with the result that some had been arrested and even condemned to death for their faith (4:15-16).[27]

First Peter is a circular letter that responds to the situation of its addressees in three stages. First, the letter grounds their social alienation in the very nature of Christian life as the eschatological existence of the people of God. Christ's death and resurrection effect this new life, which manifests itself in hope, faith, and sibling love (1:1–2:10). Next, an apparent paradox is developed: Christians are obligated to participate responsibly in the institutions of society, as a witness to their faith, and then encouraged to overcome the resulting conflicts by means of their readiness to suffer (2:11–4:11). Here Christ's suffering is invoked both as atonement and as prototype for Christian suffering in society (2:21; 3:18). Finally, the author discloses that Christian suffering at the hands of society is not only unavoidable but, in fact, expresses concrete participation in the sufferings of Christ (4:12–5:14).[28]

The year after the publication of Goppelt's, another major commentary appeared: Norbert Brox's *Der erste Petrusbrief*.[29] Brox finds anachronistic Goppelt's statement of the theme of 1 Peter in terms of Christian responsibility within the institutions of society.[30] Rather, the theme, as stated in 3:15, is hope or, more specifically,

---

[27]Goppelt, *I Peter*, 20, 39-40.

[28]Goppelt, *I Peter*, 20-21, 114, 153, 201-6.

[29]Norbert Brox, *Der erste Petrusbrief* (EKKNT 21; Zurich: Benziger Verlag; Neukirchen-Vluyn: Neukirchener Verlag, 1979; 3d ed., 1989). Hereafter, page references are to the third edition, which, apart from an appended supplementary bibliography, is virtually identical to the first.

[30]Brox, *Petrusbrief*, 17. Goppelt's commentary had not yet appeared while Brox was writing; Brox is here responding to Goppelt's characterization of the theme of 1 Peter as "Christian responsibility in society" in Goppelt's *Theology of the New Testament* (vol. 2, *Variety and Unity*, 161-78). Although Goppelt gives a more nuanced statement of the theme in his commentary, the content of the exposition of 1 Peter in the earlier *Theology* is essentially the same as that in the commentary, where Goppelt treats 1 Pet 2:11–3:12 under the heading "Responsible Participation in the Institutions of Society" (*I Peter*, 155).

hope in salvation as the certain future for Christians. No comprehensive arrangement or continuous direction of thought can be discovered in the body of the letter. What ultimately gives the letter coherence is the leading idea stated in 5:12b: The author intends to show (1) how grace in the form of Christian existence amid discrimination and persecution is concretely possible and (2) that persecution is to be expected.[31]

The search for an exact identification of the historical situation addressed in 1 Peter is hopeless. The author knows neither the readers nor the founder of their communities; the letter speaks not of the concrete and unique but of the general conditions within which Christian faith must be lived.[32] First Peter is a circular letter addressing a situation that made hope difficult, a not-uncommon situation in early Christianity.[33] This situation was due not to the action of state or local officials but to the mistrust and hatred of and aggression toward Christians by their non-Christian neighbors, who were angered at the withdrawal of Christians from the common way of life. The Christians' voluntary withdrawal led to their isolation, which in turn resulted in discrimination and, ultimately, aggression.[34]

Using traditional parenetic and liturgical materials, the author fashions a document intended both to comfort its readers and to instruct them that Christian faith and hope are concretely realized where, in spite of suffering, the good is done.[35] Certain confessional traditions are invoked in order to place the declarations of faith over against current experience. Most important of these is the christological material, by which the author attempts to render intelligible and, therefore, bearable the suffering of the addressees. The one who suffers walks in the steps of Christ, who also experienced injustice and hostility; and the one who follows in Christ's footsteps will ultimately arrive at Christ's destination—glory.[36]

---

[31]Brox, *Petrusbrief*, 16.
[32]Brox, *Petrusbrief*, 29-32.
[33]Brox, *Petrusbrief*, 17, 23.
[34]Brox, *Petrusbrief*, 24, 29-30.
[35]Brox, *Petrusbrief*, 17, 22-23.
[36]Brox, *Petrusbrief*, 254, 257.

From Balch and Elliott to Martin and Feldmeier

In 1981 two important studies of 1 Peter were published: John H. Elliott's *A Home for the Homeless: A Sociological Exegesis of 1 Peter, Its Situation and Strategy*[37] and David L. Balch's *Let Wives Be Submissive: The Domestic Code in 1 Peter*.[38] Balch's work, a revision of his 1974 Yale University dissertation, seeks to "trace the origin and function of the code of household ethics found in 1 Peter."[39] The ultimate origin of the code, he argues, is Aristotle's topos "concerning household management," which outlined the domestic relationships necessary to the stability of the house and, ultimately, of the city. First Peter adopts the code of household ethics as a response to Greco-Roman slander directed at converts to Christianity. The author instructs slaves and wives to play the social roles assigned them by Aristotle in order to silence the criticisms of non-Christians. The code, thus, has an apologetic purpose, as is made explicit is 1 Pet 3:15, where the readers are enjoined to "be prepared to make a defense" before their detractors. Only the instruction to wives involves any missionary intent.[40] The main thrust of the household code is to "encourage Christians, as a new, Eastern religious community, to acculturate to Roman society."[41]

Elliott, in *A Home for the Homeless*, argues that historical criticism has tended to neglect the social forces and interactions that were an important part of the historical context of the biblical

---

[37] John H. Elliott, *A Home for the Homeless: A Sociological Exegesis of 1 Peter, Its Situation and Strategy* (Philadelphia: Fortress, 1981); paperback edition, *A Home for the Homeless: A Social-Scientific Criticism of 1 Peter, Its Situation and Strategy* (Minneapolis: Fortress, 1990). The 1981 edition is retained in its entirety in the 1990 paperback, and a new preface, introduction, and subtitle have been added. The only changes in pagination occur in the prefatory material. Whereas the original preface ended on p. xiv, several pages have been added to incorporate the new preface (on p. xiii [with the original preface moving to pp. xv-xvi] and introduction (on pp. xvii-xxxvi). Hence, Arabic numerals in my citations of *A Home for the Homeless* apply equally to both editions.

[38] David L. Balch, *Let Wives Be Submissive: The Domestic Code in 1 Peter* (SBLMS 26; Atlanta: Scholars Press, 1981).

[39] Balch, *Wives*, 2.

[40] Balch, *Wives*, 108-9, 121.

[41] Balch, *Wives*, 119.

documents. He therefore undertakes a "sociological exegesis" of 1 Peter in order to interpret the letter not just as a repository of theological ideas but as a "vehicle of socioreligious interaction."[42] The addressees, he insists, were *literally* "resident aliens" in Asia Minor and, as such, social outsiders. Upon their conversion, they became religious outsiders as well, and were therefore reviled by their neighbors.[43] This hostility from without threatened to erode their internal cohesion.[44] In response, 1 Peter affirms that these resident aliens have a home in the οἶκος τοῦ θεοῦ. Within this household, "alienation from society, zeal in doing the good, bearing the name of Christ, servitude and humility were transformed from Gentile-condemned 'vices' into the divinely rewarded 'virtues' of God's diaspora people."[45]

Elliott appeals especially to Bryan R. Wilson's analysis of sect development as a model for explicating the socioreligious strategy of 1 Peter.[46] The Petrine communities were "conversionist sects" whose conflicts with outsiders necessitated the creation of a characteristic ideology that would both interpret their experience and motivate sect-reinforcing behavior.[47] Virtually the total emphasis in Elliott's discussion of this ideology falls on the οἶκος motif. The few paragraphs that address 1 Peter's view of suffering interpret it largely in terms of the social conflict theories of Lewis Coser and Georg

---

[42]Elliott, *Home*, 8.
[43]Elliott, *Home*, 79. In his introduction to the paperback edition, Elliott seems to mitigate his position somewhat, now allowing that it is *possible* that these Christians were not literally resident aliens prior to their conversion, and characterizing his original thesis as a "possibility worthy of consideration" (xxx). Nevertheless, he clearly remains convinced of his original position and retains the argument unchanged in the paperback edition of *Home*.
[44]Elliott, *Home*, 83.
[45]Elliott, *Home*, 226.
[46]See especially Bryan R. Wilson, "An Analysis of Sect Development," *American Sociological Review* 24 (1959) 3-15; idem, *Magic and the Millennium: A Sociological Study of Religious Movements of Protest among Tribal and Third-World Peoples* (New York: Harper & Row, 1973); and idem, *Sects and Society: A Sociological Study of the Elim Tabernacle, Christian Science, and Christadelphians* (Berkeley: University of California Press, 1961).
[47]Elliott, *Home*, 102-6.

Simmel.[48] Suffering, Elliott argues, is seen by 1 Peter as a sign of the differentiation between the Christian communities and those outside and is therefore embraced.[49] In a society obsessed with the "love of prestige," 1 Peter invests Christian suffering with its own honor bestowed by God;[50] suffering, therefore, functions both to clarify the boundaries between the Petrine sects and outsiders and to increase cohesion within the sects. The intended result, according to Elliott, is the winning over of the sects' detractors through the consistent good conduct of the members of the communities comprising the household of God.[51]

Balch argues that 1 Peter utilizes the household code in order to promote acculturation; in sharp contrast, Elliott insists that the author's purpose is twofold: to prevent social conformity and to win over opponents. In a subsequent essay, Balch criticizes Elliott's "overemphasis on conflict theory and . . . rigid application of Bryan Wilson's early sociological theories," and he appeals to Wilson's statement that "in the matter of moral values . . . sectarian teaching is by no means always fundamentally different in kind from the traditional moral orientations."[52] Just as diaspora Jews tended to acculturate as much as possible within the constraints of their religious tradition, so does the author of 1 Peter encourage assimilation to the values of Greco-Roman society.[53] Furthermore, Elliott's emphasis on the οἶκος motif is inconsistent with a sociological exegesis of the letter. It is not the οἶκος motif, Balch insists, but christology that provides the identity symbol and ethical basis for the Petrine communities—not a mental idea or *ethos* but a *mythos*, the story of Christ.[54]

---

[48]Lewis Coser, *The Functions of Social Conflict* (New York: Free Press, 1956); Georg Simmel, *Conflict* (trans. Kurt H. Wolff; Glencoe: Free Press, 1955).

[49]Elliott, *Home*, 113-16.

[50]Elliott, *Home*, 122.

[51]Elliott, *Home*, 148-49.

[52]David L. Balch, "Hellenization/Acculturation in 1 Peter," *Perspectives on First Peter* (ed. Charles H. Talbert; NABPRSSS 9; Macon: Mercer University Press, 1986) 84, 93.

[53]Balch, "Hellenization/Acculturation," 90.

[54]Balch, "Hellenization/Acculturation," 100.

In response, Elliott acknowledges that there are some behaviors that the letter values in common with the society at large (such as doing good and avoiding evil); "where there is no conflict of interest between conformity to God's will and subordination to human authorities established by God (2:13), submission is recommended 'on account of the Lord.'"[55] Balch, however, focuses exclusively on the issue of social linkage, neglecting entirely the question of boundary maintenance. Maintaining open channels of communication with outsiders is quite different from assimilating, Elliott insists; 1 Peter views contacts with non-Christians not as the impetus for assimilation but as occasions for recruitment and for testifying to the works of God. The purpose of the letter is not to promote acculturation but to strengthen communal identity and solidarity so that the addressees could both resist external pressure to assimilate and make effective witness to outsiders.[56] Finally, Elliott wants to refute Balch's charge that he separates *ethos* from christological *mythos*. The Christ story functions in 1 Peter to affirm the identity of believers, to provide a rationale for their endurance of suffering, and to establish a basis for hope; but it is the household motif, with its familial metaphors (e.g., οἶκος, rebirth, sibling love), that relates the christological kerygma to the community of believers.[57]

Earl Richard, in a 1986 essay, examines precisely this question of how the christology of the letter responds to the social situation of its recipients.[58] Richard agrees with the majority today that the suffering with which 1 Peter is concerned is due not to imperial persecution but to "hostility, harassment, and social, unofficial ostracism on the part of the general populace."[59] To address this situation, 1 Peter highlights two aspects of the death of Jesus in succession. In the first part of the letter, the soteriological function

---

[55]John H. Elliott, "1 Peter, Its Situation and Strategy: A Discussion with David Balch," *Perspectives on First Peter* (ed. Charles H. Talbert; NABPRSSS 9; Macon: Mercer University Press, 1986) 73.

[56]Elliott, "1 Peter, Its Situation and Strategy," 72, 78.

[57]Elliott, "1 Peter, Its Situation and Strategy," 76-77.

[58]Earl Richard, "The Functional Christology of First Peter," *Perspectives on First Peter* (ed. Charles H. Talbert; NABPRSSS 9; Macon: Mercer University Press, 1986) 121-39.

[59]Richard, "Functional Christology," 127.

of the death of Jesus as atonement, which 1 Peter takes over from the early church, is explicated as the basis for the life of the community.[60] First Peter then proceeds to its "major thesis: Jesus as the Christian's model of suffering and glory."[61]

The author prefers the term "suffering" to "death" when referring to the demise of Jesus because the former fits the situation of the suffering community and, therefore, the author's own rhetorical strategy. Similarly, it is the portion of the domestic code dealing with slaves that provides the author the occasion to present Jesus, the servant who suffered unjustly and was consequently glorified by God, as the model for Christian behavior in the midst of a hostile pagan world. Christ's passage through time, therefore, is the pattern for the Christian disciple; by reference to Christ's experience, the letter assures the Christian sufferer of future participation in Christ's glory.[62] God has in fact called Christians to the goal of glory (5:10), which now awaits them as their inheritance kept in heaven (1:4); it is in this light that the πάροικος terminology is to be understood.

In his 1987 study *Suffering and Hope: The Biblical Vision and the Human Predicament*, J. Christiaan Beker argues that, to Christians marginalized and disenfranchised by their society, 1 Peter offers a tightly knit support group in the house-church. Within the house-church, believers find the social and spiritual cohesion denied them by the larger society. Their apocalyptic perspective assures them that the final reality is not suffering but God's glory; moreover, they already experience together the Spirit, both as the foretaste of ultimate glory and as the power to imitate Christ in his sufferings. Hence, they can experience joy amid suffering. Furthermore, proper conduct in the midst of suffering should convert antagonists or, at the very least, gain their respect.[63]

Paul J. Achtemeier engages the issues raised in the Balch-Elliott debate in his 1989 article "Newborn Babes and Living Stones:

---

[60]Richard, "Functional Christology," 134.
[61]Richard, "Functional Christology," 136.
[62]Richard, "Functional Christology," 136-37.
[63]J. Christiaan Beker, *Suffering and Hope: The Biblical Vision and the Human Predicament* (2d ed.; Grand Rapids: Eerdmans, 1994) 63-68.

Literal and Figurative in 1 Peter."⁶⁴ As the subtitle implies, Achtemeier argues, against Elliott, that the terms πάροικοι and παρεπίδημοι are used metaphorically in 1 Peter rather than literally. The author of 1 Peter does not consider the addressees to be literal resident aliens but characterizes them in terms of the alien residence of God's chosen people, Israel, in the diaspora. This figurative use of terminology that originally applied to OT Israel is but one component of the letter's "controlling metaphor" of "the Christian community as the new people of God constituted by the Christ who suffered (and rose)."⁶⁵ By his suffering, Christ both constituted this new people of God and provides its members with their model of Christian suffering. Achtemeier agrees with the emerging consensus that the suffering in view in 1 Peter is the result of sporadic pressure at the local level from those who viewed Christians as "nonconformists who threatened the religious, and hence the sociopolitical, status quo."⁶⁶ Against Balch, Achtemeier repeatedly asserts that 1 Peter, far from counseling assimilation to Greco-Roman culture in order to reduce suffering, calls Christians to break completely with their past and adopt a lifestyle commensurate with their new identity and in conformity to the model of Christ's suffering. Only then will they be assured of the glory that will be theirs when Christ returns.

In 1992, two lengthy monographs on 1 Peter were published: Troy W. Martin's *Metaphor and Composition in 1 Peter* and Reinhard Feldmeier's *Die Christen als Fremde: Die Metapher der Fremde in der antiken Welt, im Urchristentum und im 1. Petrusbrief.*⁶⁷ In the former, Martin attempts to resolve the perennial

---

⁶⁴Paul J. Achtemeier, "Newborn Babes and Living Stones: Literal and Figurative in 1 Peter," *To Touch the Text: Biblical and Related Studies in Honor of Joseph A. Fitzmyer, S.J.* (ed. Maurya P. Horgan and Paul J. Kobelski; New York: Crossroad, 1989) 207-36. See also Paul J. Achtemeier, *1 Peter: A Commentary on 1 Peter* (Hermeneia; Minneapolis: Fortress, 1996), a work that appeared too late to be considered in the present monograph.
⁶⁵Achtemeier, "Newborn Babes," 224 (italics deleted).
⁶⁶Achtemeier, "Newborn Babes," 211.
⁶⁷Troy W. Martin, *Metaphor and Composition in 1 Peter* (SBLDS 131; Atlanta: Scholars Press, 1992); Reinhard Feldmeier, *Die Christen als Fremde: Die Metapher der Fremde in der antiken Welt, im Urchristentum und im 1. Petrusbrief* (WUNT 64;

questions of the genre and compositional structure of 1 Peter, and along the way, he makes a number of comments about the content of the letter that are not without interest for my study. After analyzing the letter formulas in 1 Peter and examining the various letter genres in antiquity, Martin concludes that 1 Peter's genre is that of the parenetic letter.[68] Like all parenesis, 1 Peter's primary function is to prescribe certain kinds of behaviors or, in terms of the sociology of knowledge, to socialize its readers. To Christians undergoing persecution, 1 Peter offers encouragement based on both their past experience of entering into the Christian communities and their hope for the future. Whereas proper conduct in Greco-Roman society was supposed to result in δόξα, these Christians had experienced only grief since their conversion. In response to their nonrealization of δόξα, the author of 1 Peter adopts the apocalyptic scheme summarized in 5:10 and appeals to Jesus as the paradigm of the sufferer who is subsequently vindicated.[69] The author structures the hortatory and parenetic material by means of a series of metaphor clusters arranged under the controlling metaphor of the diaspora.[70] Like the Jews of the diaspora, Martin argues, the Petrine Christians were on a journey through a hostile land. The metaphor clusters together "contribute to the author's primary objectives of exposing conduct appropriate for his readers on their eschatological journey and of dissuading them from defection while persuading them to steadfast allegiance to the faith."[71]

Feldmeier's study is of greater interest to my investigation; although Feldmeier deals only briefly with 1 Peter's references to Christ, he provides the most detailed study yet of the concept of the stranger (*Fremde*) in antiquity, focusing particular attention on the words πάροικος and, to a lesser extent, παρεπίδημος and διασπορά. In the case of the παροικ- group, he finds a broad range of uses. In its literal sense, πάροικος could designate a neighbor, an entire colony or settlement, a resident alien, a stranger, or, more

---

Tübingen: Mohr-Siebeck, 1992).
[68]T. Martin, *Metaphor and Composition*, 81-134.
[69]T. Martin, *Metaphor and Composition*, 107-18.
[70]T. Martin, *Metaphor and Composition*, 144-60.
[71]T. Martin, *Metaphor and Composition*, 266.

technically, a noncitizen.⁷² When denoting an alien, a stranger, or a noncitizen, πάροικος bore a decidedly negative connotation; the stranger, whether called πάροικος or παρεπίδημος, was, from the standpoint of society, a second-class person.⁷³ The idea of the stranger was employed throughout the antique world, both in the literal and in metaphorical senses. In pagan Greek literature, the figurative notion of strangerhood turned on the opposition between the transitory body and the true self. In the OT, however, the concept was fundamentally relational: The stranger was constituted as such by his or her relation to God. In this connection, the originally negative concept became a positive self-designation: The strangers of the OT no longer depended for their identity on possession of the land or on an independent state; rather, they depended solely on the transcendent God.⁷⁴ In Philo and at Qumran, the concept was developed further: Although the two literatures have their differences, they hold in common that strangerhood is the reverse side of the life of the people of God, a life superior to that of the gentiles; strangerhood thus signifies belonging to the people of God and as such is an honorific self-designation.⁷⁵

First Peter's use of the concept is dependent, Feldmeier continues, not on the pagan or even the Philonic or Qumranic traditions but on the OT references to the dispersed people of God. In the social *Nichtidentität* of the OT people of God in the diaspora, 1 Peter finds the possibility of a positive identification that can provide contemporary Christians with their own identity.⁷⁶ Against Elliott, Feldmeier argues that the words οἶκος and πάροικος are neither central to 1 Peter nor correlates of one another. Πάροικος does not designate the legal standing of the addressees; nor does οἶκος provide the answer to their dilemma.⁷⁷ Rather, the letter's answer to its readers' dilemma lies in the Christian self-designation as strangers. The letter's stranger terminology does not refer

---

⁷²Feldmeier, *Christen als Fremde*, 12.
⁷³Feldmeier, *Christen als Fremde*, 21.
⁷⁴Feldmeier, *Christen als Fremde*, 53.
⁷⁵Feldmeier, *Christen als Fremde*, 72-74.
⁷⁶Feldmeier, *Christen als Fremde*, 95-96.
⁷⁷Feldmeier, *Christen als Fremde*, 204-10.

Christians to a heavenly commonwealth (although Elliott goes too far in his disavowal of the transcendent dimensions of the letter, e.g., in 1:3-5)[78] but to an earthly community of those whose strangerhood is the expression of both their divine election and their responsibility in the world.[79] The designation "strangers," thus, expresses the honorific distinction of the new people of God and, therefore, both comforts them amid their alienation from their neighbors and demands of them a new lifestyle corresponding to their election.[80]

The obligation attending their election is to testify to their election by means of a changed lifestyle within the hostile world. Rather than encouraging hatred of the world, 1 Peter calls for a lifestyle that aims to win over the world; rather than hoping for retribution, 1 Peter hopes for the world's reconciliation (2:12; 3:1-2, 15-20). First Peter neither calls for a sectarian identity (Elliott) nor encourages assimilation (Balch). Rather, the letter demands that its readers live "soberly and awake" and tread a middle path between the danger of assimilation on the one hand and the equal danger of isolation on the other. This astonishing (considering the circumstances) openness to the world is made possible by the letter's conscious, theological inclusion—through the notions of God's election and of Christ's suffering—of Christian suffering in the Christian stranger identity. These strangers live out of God's future now opened to them by the death and resurrection of Christ; they can, therefore, be full of joy and hope even amid their suffering.[81]

Conclusions

This survey of the literature has documented several important moments and trends in the history of the interpretation of 1 Peter, thereby setting the context for the present effort. (1) In the first place, two basically different ways of viewing 1 Peter are evident. The first, which was quite popular early in this century, sees 1 Peter as fundamentally a catechetical text—whether a baptismal sermon or

---

[78]Feldmeier, *Christen als Fremde*, 209.
[79]Feldmeier, *Christen als Fremde*, 103-4.
[80]Feldmeier, *Christen als Fremde*, 177.
[81]Feldmeier, *Christen als Fremde*, 185-91.

A History of Research   19

an entire baptismal liturgy—with an appended epistolary framework. The second views the document as an occasional letter composed with the help of diverse traditions in order to encourage suffering Christians to persevere in their faith and lifestyle. The latter is the majority view at present, and with good reason. The arguments of Lohse, Hill, Goppelt, and others decisively refute the earlier position in the eyes of most interpreters, the present writer included.[82] This study, therefore, will proceed from the working hypothesis that 1 Peter, whatever its sources, is a literary unity—a letter composed to meet certain needs of specific communities.

(2) A second issue is the social situation of these communities and the nature of their suffering. Virtually all scholars today agree that the suffering with which 1 Peter is concerned is not due to an Empire-wide persecution of Christians instigated by the emperor; and most describe the situation in terms of social ostracism on the local level, which the letter's addressees were experiencing at the hands of their non-Christian neighbors.[83] Most also argue that the recipients were already undergoing physical persecution, although no consensus exists on the intensity of this persecution or the degree to which it was formally initiated or sanctioned by local officials. Nor are scholars agreed upon the extent to which the social factors at work were known by the author of 1 Peter or can be known by present-day interpreters of the letter. Millauer and Brox, for example, are skeptical about contemporary efforts to reconstruct in detail the social situation of the addressees, whereas Goppelt, Balch, and Elliott are more optimistic about their prospects for uncovering at least the

---

[82]Along with the studies cited above, see also John H. Elliott, "Peter, First Epistle of," *ABD* 5. 270-71; Werner Georg Kümmel, *Introduction to the New Testament* (trans. Howard Clark Kee; 17th ed.; Nashville: Abingdon, 1973) 420; and J. Ramsey Michaels, *1 Peter* (WBC 49; Waco: Word, 1988) xxxvii-xxxix.

[83]E.g., Balch, *Wives*, 109, 119; Elliott, *Home*, 62-63; Goppelt, *I Peter*, 38-39; Millauer, *Leiden als Gnade*, 190; Richard, "Functional Christology," 121-39, Selwyn, *Epistle of St. Peter*, 10. For a list of scholars opposed to an official-persecution hypothesis, see William L. Schutter, *Hermeneutic and Composition in I Peter* (WUNT 2/30; Tübingen: Mohr-Siebeck, 1989) 13 n. 56. Cf. Kümmel, who agrees that the persecution is not instituted by Rome, but argues that the widespread persecution of which 1 Peter speaks refers to the beginning stages of civil persecution in which believers were tried simply for being Christians (4:16) (*Introduction*, 418-19, 424).

essentials of the social situation. In any case, contemporary scholarship *has* succeeded in demonstrating the link between the addressees' suffering and their social location.

Hence, if the explication of 1 Peter offered in the following pages is to be convincing, it must deal, as adequately as the sources allow, with the social realities that gave rise to that suffering. To that end, I shall look to the social sciences for assistance (beginning in chapter 2). In particular, I shall argue (in chapter 3) that recent anthropological work on honor and shame in the Mediterranean world throws light on the fundamental problem faced by the recipients of 1 Peter: the pervasive threat to their honor inherent in their daily social intercourse with the larger society. First Peter attempts to provide a means for these believers both to remain in the church and to retain their honor despite the disapproval of their non-Christian contemporaries.

(3) Moreover, the social realities that engendered suffering also provided the conditions within which 1 Peter could be understood by its readers as a response to their suffering. A third issue that emerges for my study of 1 Peter, therefore, concerns the nature of the letter's message vis-à-vis the sociohistorical situation to which it was addressed. The debate between Balch and Elliott is especially instructive at this point, for it brings to light two aspects of the letter's message that call for further investigation.

(a) The first may be stated in the form of a question: Is the overall thrust of the letter toward acculturation and assimilation to Greco-Roman society (Balch) or toward resisting assimilation in order to strengthen community solidarity and promote mission (Elliott)?[84] The Balch-Elliott debate itself suggests that 1 Peter provides data susceptible to both interpretations. Feldmeier offers a third alternative, but, as I shall argue in chapter 4, his notion of Christian *Nichtidentität* lacks sociopolitical specificity vis-à-vis the social realities of late-first-century Asia Minor; furthermore, in the

---

[84]Achtemeier sides with Elliott against Balch's view that 1 Peter urges assimilation; he also mentions Elliott's opinion that cohesion and evangelism are goals of the letter, and, although he does not really engage Elliott at this point, prefers to state the letter's objective in terms of encouragement to proper conduct lest believers forfeit the coming glory ("Newborn Babes," 219-20, 232 [esp. n. 99], 235-36).

effort to distinguish his proposal from Elliott's, he misconstrues the latter in terms of a sectarian flight from the world, and, to distance his position from Balch's, he grossly overstates 1 Peter's view of the evangelistic responsibility of its intended readers.

In this study, I shall suggest another option, one that accounts for both the data invoked by Elliott and those invoked by Balch, without relegating either set of data to a position of secondary importance. Drawing on the work of the anthropologist Victor Turner, I shall propose (in chapter 4) that 1 Peter offers its readers a vision of their existence as a "liminal" one: Both temporally and socially, they exist neither here nor there, but "in between." Temporally, they find themselves to be participants in both the old aeon and the new simultaneously yet not completely engaged in either; socially, they no longer participate fully in the institutions and lifestyle that defined their lives prior to conversion, yet they have not withdrawn entirely from relations with their non-Christian neighbors. It is precisely the ambiguity of their social location, in fact, that gives rise to the problem that occasioned the letter. First Peter, I contend, assays to fashion a vision of Christian liminality that would legitimate such an existence. Of first importance in the articulation of this vision is the precedent and model of Christ's experience, which brings us to the next point.

(b) The second aspect of the letter's message that calls for further investigation is its christology. That christology provides the ultimate rationale for parenesis in 1 Peter is underscored or implied by Lohse, Goppelt, Balch, Richard, and Achtemeier, among others. Furthermore, as the debate between Balch and Elliott shows, the christology of 1 Peter cannot be neatly separated out from the letter's parenesis, from its statements about the situation of the addressees, or from its response to the problem of social ostracism. Indeed, the references to Christ are integral components of the letter's overall response to the plight of its recipients. A crucial task for this study, therefore, is to disclose (in chapter 5) the function of 1 Peter's references to Christ within the letter itself and within the social world of its addressees. I shall argue that Christ's experience of suffering followed by glorification provides the paradigm for Christian liminal existence that is, by virtue of its fidelity to its model, invested with honor now at the same time as it anticipates future glorification.

CHAPTER 2

METHODOLOGY

The survey in the previous chapter demonstrates the widespread agreement among contemporary scholars that the problem 1 Peter addressed was a profoundly social one. First Peter is, of course, not unique at this point. Every document in the NT was composed within, and addressed to, a particular social situation. People wrote these pieces for the instruction, encouragement, and nurturing of other people. Moreover, we can usually detect—if not at the surface of a given text then just beneath it—still other people whose ideas and behaviors were being combatted.

In the case of 1 Peter, however, the social dimension of the text is especially prominent. Repeatedly, the letter alludes to or directly addresses the conflict between its Christian readers and their non-Christian neighbors (e.g., 2:12, 15; 3:13-18). A good portion of the letter, moreover, is devoted to internal relations within the communities (e.g., the household code). What is even more telling is the nearly complete lack of evidence of a theological or doctrinal conflict at the heart of the readers' dilemma. Missing is the kind of explicit theological argumentation that characterizes so many of the NT letters—especially those of Paul—as well as the more subtle kind of theological message conveyed by the Gospels and Acts. This is not to suggest that a qualitative difference exists between 1 Peter and the rest of the NT or that theology and sociology are to be pitted against each other as mutually exclusive categories. Clearly, either claim would be naive and specious. My point, rather, is that even a cursory reading of 1 Peter discloses the letter's preoccupation with the problematic character of the social situation of its addressees. In order to facilitate access to and analysis of the letter's social dimension, therefore, I shall utilize the work of a number of social scientists.

A lengthy discussion of the methods and results of the social sciences would be far beyond the scope of this monograph. Nor is it necessary to survey and to critique the efforts of biblical scholars to employ the social sciences in their work on the OT and the NT, a task that has been carried out nicely in a number of recent books and articles.[1] What I shall undertake in this chapter is a description of the task and the method of the present study.

Social Sciences, Exegesis, and the Present Task

In this monograph I shall attempt to answer the question How were 1 Peter's references to Christ's suffering and glory intended to function in response to the suffering of the communities addressed? Posing the question in terms of the letter's *function* acknowledges the social dimension of both the problem and its solution. It has become a common criticism of traditional biblical scholarship that it has tended to treat the documents of the NT primarily as repositories of historical data and theological ideas.[2] To whatever extent scholars have recognized that the problems and concerns of the communities addressed were socially determined, they have often thought of the answers offered by the biblical writings primarily in theological,

---

[1] See, e.g., R. E. Clements, *The World of Ancient Israel: Sociological, Anthropological and Political Perspectives* (New York: Cambridge University Press, 1989); John H. Elliott, *What Is Social-Scientific Criticism?* (GBS; Minneapolis: Fortress, 1993); Susan R. Garrett, "Sociology of Early Christianity," *ABD* 6. 89-99; Bengt Holmberg, *Sociology and the New Testament: An Appraisal* (Minneapolis: Fortress, 1990); Gerd Theissen, "Sociological Research into the New Testament: Some Ideas Offered by the Sociology of Knowledge for a New Exegetical Approach," *Social Reality and the Early Christians: Theology, Ethics, and the World of the New Testament* (trans. Margaret Kohl; Minneapolis: Fortress, 1992) 1-29; Robert R. Wilson, *Sociological Approaches to the Old Testament* (GBS; Philadelphia: Fortress, 1984).

[2] See, e.g., Holmberg, *Sociology*, 2; Wayne A. Meeks, *The First Urban Christians: The Social World of the Apostle Paul* (New Haven/London: Yale University Press, 1983) 1-2; Robin Scroggs, "The Sociological Interpretation of the New Testament: The Present State of Research," *The Text and the Times: New Testament Essays for Today* (Minneapolis: Fortress, 1993) 49.

ideational terms (though thankfully this situation has changed a great deal in recent years). To inquire into the function of 1 Peter's references to Christ is to inquire into the manner in which the christological statements were intended to interact not only with the rest of the letter but also with the social world in which the addressees live. My position is thus similar to the "moderate functionalism" adopted by Wayne A. Meeks in *The First Urban Christians: The Social World of the Apostle Paul*: "The comprehensive question concerning the texts that are our primary sources is not merely what each one says, but what it does."[3]

Speaking of the *intended* function of the letter, however, raises the methodological question of what is meant by "intended." To begin, what is *not* meant is the author's intention as construed by romanticist hermeneutics. Ludwig Wittgenstein has demonstrated the impossibility of entering into the mind of an author to relive the authorial experience of writing. For Wittgenstein, there is no mental state or process that the philosopher can identify unequivocally as "intending."[4] Wittgenstein does not, however, jettison altogether the notion of intention. "Describing an intention means describing what went on from a particular point of view, with a particular purpose. I paint a particular portrait of what went on."[5] Although "intending" is not some determinate mental process, there are numerous combinations of actions and states of mind that, in a given set of circumstances, we may refer to as "intending."[6] What Wittgenstein is cautioning against is the attempt to provide a psychological profile of an actor or author; in actuality, ascribing "intention" is but a way of describing human behavior within a given "language game." Similarly, Hans Georg Gadamer locates the meaning of a text in the text itself and not in the mental life of its author. In place of the intention and meaning of an author, Gadamer writes of the intention

---

[3] Meeks, *Urban Christians*, 7. See also Elliott, *Home*, 267.

[4] Ludwig Wittgenstein, *Zettel* (ed. G. E. M. Anscombe and G. H. von Wright; trans. G. E. M. Anscombe; Berkeley: University of California Press, 1967) § 45.

[5] Wittgenstein, *Zettel*, § 23.

[6] Ludwig Wittgenstein, *The Blue Book, The Blue and Brown Books* (2d ed.; Oxford: Blackwell, 1969) 32.

and meaning of the text.⁷ Having taken on a life of its own due to the "will to permanence" of the written word, "a text is not to be understood as an expression of life but with respect to what it says."⁸ The text, not the author who produced it, is the object of interpretation.

By referring to the *intended* function of the text of 1 Peter, therefore, I am focusing on the letter itself as an aspect of the socio-religious life of the communities in which the letter was read. In Wittgenstein's words, the point of view from which I am describing what went on is that of the historical critic. As a historical critic, I can interpret 1 Peter in terms of how it might have functioned within the context of the first-century Mediterranean world, but I cannot say whether it ever actually functioned in that way in the experience of any particular community. To put it another way, this monograph will unfold 1 Peter's answer to its readers' problem, but it cannot say whether any of the original readers actually accepted the proffered answer. "Intention" in this work, then, simply denotes that what 1 Peter appears to be trying to do—its function—may or may not have been accomplished.⁹

---

⁷Hans Georg Gadamer, *Truth and Method* (2d ed.; trans. and rev. Joel Weinsheimer and Donald G. Marshall; New York: Crossroad, 1989) 337-39, 394.

⁸Gadamer, *Truth and Method*, 391-92. Of course Gadamer insists, quite rightly in my view, that the act of writing cuts a text loose not only from its author but also from its original audience. At this point Gadamer and Paul Ricoeur are in agreement (see Paul Ricoeur, *Interpretation Theory: Discourse and the Surplus of Meaning* [Fort Worth: Texas Christian University Press, 1976]). Gadamer and Ricoeur, however, are explicating the nature and process of *interpretation*, while my treatment of 1 Peter aims at something else: historical-critical explanation. That is to say, if Gadamer is correct (as I think he is) that theological and legal interpretation are paradigmatic for hermeneutics as a whole, then the kind of historical-critical investigation that follows is but a moment in the interpretive process. Indeed, Ricoeur seems to say as much when he states that distanciation and appropriation are both necessary to interpretation, and that it is only when this last stage—appropriation—is reached that interpretation is complete (*Interpretation Theory*, 91-92). Rather than conceiving of this study as but one stage in a larger project, however, it would be better to conceive of this monograph as offering one kind of reading of a sacred text—a historical-critical reading—that has its own integrity and needs not aspire to fuse horizons in the manner of Gadamerian-Ricoeurian interpretation.

⁹Elliott also speaks of the intended function of a document but in a manner that puts too much emphasis on the notion of authorial intention. I share his concern to "explore the manner in which the 'comprehensive patterns of cognitive and moral

Methodology

With John H. Elliott, I view 1 Peter as a "vehicle of socio-religious interaction."[10] The image of the text as vehicle should not, however, be pressed too far, as if the text were only the conduit through which the author's meaning flowed to the readers. Such a model approaches that of romanticist hermeneutics, in which the object of investigation was the mind of the author, and the text was merely the means by which the author's subjectivity could be accessed by the critic. Alongside the methodological problems with this model that have already been mentioned, another quite concrete problem arises in the case of 1 Peter: Its Petrine authorship is disputed.[11] Regardless of the identity of its author, however, the text may be said to function as vehicle in a dual sense: It presents itself as a participant in the interaction of reading, and it provides the catalyst for interaction within the community of readers/hearers. As Meeks points out:

> Texts do not carry their meanings within themselves, but "mean" insofar as they function intelligibly within specific cultures or subcultures.... What a given text meant... was the resultant of the dialectic between text and the cultural-linguistic world inhabited by its hearers.[12]

It is meaning in this sense—that which emerges in the dialectic between text and cultural-linguistic world—that is the object of the following investigation.

Another similarity between this study and Elliott's work on 1 Peter lies in his conception of social-scientific criticism as a

---

beliefs about man, society and the universe in relation to man and society' contained and advanced in a given document are intended to *function* in the social order, the collective needs and interests they represent, and the way they exemplify the intersection of ideas, ideals, and social action" (*Home*, 267). I do not share his desire "to advance toward an understanding of the interests which motivated the composition of 1 Peter" (*Home*, 272).

[10]Elliott, *Home*, 8.

[11]See below, pp. 43-47.

[12]Wayne A. Meeks, "A Hermeneutics of Social Embodiment," *Christians among Jews and Gentiles: Essays in Honor of Krister Stendahl on His Sixty-fifth Birthday* (ed. George W. E. Nickelsburg with George W. MacRae; Philadelphia: Fortress, 1986) 183-84.

subdiscipline of exegesis and, therefore, an expansion rather than a replacement of conventional historical criticism.[13]

> Social-scientific criticism ... expands the historical-critical method by adding to its repertoire of foci and operations the perspectives, theory, models, and research of the social sciences in order to enable the reader of the Bible to understand and interpret more adequately the biblical texts and their contexts.[14]

It is no exaggeration to say that the recent turn by biblical scholars to the social sciences was mandated by the historical-critical method itself. The historical process is not determined solely—or even primarily—by ideas, whether theological or other. Ideas are themselves radically conditioned by the social contexts in which they emerge and of which they are linguistic expressions. If, therefore, the task of historical-critical exegesis is to be carried out, both the social dimension of the historical process and the interaction between ideas and social reality must be taken seriously.[15]

The social sciences may offer exegesis an avenue toward a more comprehensive understanding of the alien cultures in which the NT documents are historically embedded than historical criticism has achieved alone. Not infrequently, when exegetes use such terms as class, status, community, kinship, and even society and culture, they do so in a naive, uncritical way. The social sciences provide models, theories, and types by means of which such concepts can be sharply defined and, therefore, usefully exploited. "Models bring hitherto unconscious levels of thought into awareness. They also enlarge our conscious control over the ways in which we handle data."[16] It is precisely the generalizing tendency inherent in model building, furthermore, that proves helpful to the historian interested in *particular* places, people, and events. As Michael Mann explains,

---

[13]Elliott, *Home*, xix; idem, *What Is Social-Scientific Criticism?* 7.
[14]Elliott, *What Is Social-Scientific Criticism?* 15.
[15]Cf. Holmberg, *Sociology*, 1-3.
[16]T. F. Carney, *The Shape of the Past: Models and Antiquity* (Lawrence, KS: Coronado, 1975) 6. Cf. Geoffrey Barraclough, *Main Trends in History* (Main Trends in the Social and Human Sciences; New York/London: Holmes & Meier, 1979) 54-59.

> If historians eschew theory of how societies operate, they imprison themselves in the commonsense notions of their own society.... A strong sense of theory enables us to decide what might be the key facts, what might be central and what marginal to an understanding of how a particular society works.[17]

Social-scientific paradigms are heuristic devices; they suggest lines of inquiry about social phenomena and relationships that ultimately disclose not only what is typical about historical phenomena but also what is unique.[18]

This interest in the unique, which the historian and the social scientist have in common, brings us back to the purpose of this study: to uncover the intended function of 1 Peter's christological material within the social world of its addressees. My goal is not merely to describe the individual christological statements of 1 Peter or even to construct a "christology" of the letter but to understand and interpret the letter's christological references in terms of their socioreligious function. In the tradition of Weberian *Verstehen*, my objective is hermeneutical. Clifford Geertz's characterization of his cultural-anthropological work applies equally well to my own exegetical task:

> Believing, with Max Weber, that man is an animal suspended in webs of significance he himself has spun, I take culture to be those webs, and the analysis of it to be therefore not an experimental science in search of law but an interpretive one in search of meaning.[19]

Richard K. Fenn's statement of the goal of his sociological work in terms of "explanation" is similar:

> By explanation I do not mean some reference to "supposedly universal laws of social behavior." Instead, I mean by "explanation" something very close to what used to pass for *Verstehen*: an understanding of the

---

[17]Michael Mann, *The Sources of Social Power*, vol. 1, *A History of Power from the Beginning to A.D. 1760* (Cambridge/New York/New Rochelle/Melbourne/Sidney: Cambridge University Press, 1986) vii; quoted by Bruce J. Malina, review of *The Origins of Christian Morality: The First Two Centuries*, by Wayne A. Meeks, *TToday* 52 (July 1995) 270.

[18]Cf. Barraclough, *Main Trends in History*, 52-54.

[19]Clifford Geertz, *The Interpretation of Cultures* (New York: Basic, 1973) 5.

sense in which things "hang together." Social phenomena that hang together are reflections, results, responses, or sources of one another. Explanation senses a system-at-work.[20]

Whether couched in terms of explanation, *Verstehen*, interpretation, or understanding, what this monograph endeavors to do—by means of historical-critical exegesis informed by the social sciences—is to explicate the meaning and function, within the socioreligious world of the letter's addressees, of 1 Peter's references to Christ's suffering and glory.[21]

Sociology of Knowledge

The unifying perspective for this study is provided by the sociology of knowledge as articulated by Peter L. Berger and Thomas Luckmann.[22] As the name suggests, the sociology of knowledge is concerned with the way in which reality comes to be "known" by individuals in a society. Berger and Luckmann are interested not only in the variety of "realities" that are known by people in particular societies but, even more, in the processes by which *any* body of knowledge comes to be accepted as reality within a given society. That is to say, they seek to articulate a theory that

---

[20]Richard K. Fenn, "Sociology and Social History: A Preface to a Sociology of the New Testament," *JSP* 1 (1987) 107. See also his *The Death of Herod: An Essay in the Sociology of Religion* (Cambridge: Cambridge University Press, 1992), 2, 21.

[21]It would be impossible to demonstrate a priori that the work of the sociologists and anthropologists invoked below is appropriate to or sufficient for the task of explicating 1 Peter. Rather, the utility of these materials can only become evident as they are applied in the interpretive process. In a sense, then, this study is an experiment in interpretation. The ultimate rationale for my use of the social-scientific literature cited in this study is that it has proven to have heuristic and explanatory power in my exegesis of 1 Peter.

[22]Peter L. Berger and Thomas Luckmann, *The Social Construction of Reality: A Treatise in the Sociology of Knowledge* (New York: Doubleday, 1966; Anchor, 1967). While this work provides the classic formulation of the theory, I also take into account in the following discussion Berger's *The Sacred Canopy: Elements of a Sociological Theory of Religion* (New York: Doubleday, 1967; Anchor, 1969). On the history of the sociology of knowledge, see Berger and Luckmann, *Social Construction*, 4-13.

accounts for the way reality is socially constructed.[23] What follows is a brief description of the main lines of their theory with emphasis on those aspects that are especially relevant to this investigation.[24]

I begin with some definitions. *Culture* designates the totality of humankind's products, both material and nonmaterial, including everything from tools to language to society. *Society* is nothing more than that aspect of nonmaterial culture—including institutions, roles, and values—that structures human beings' relations with each other.[25] *Knowledge* is "the certainty that phenomena are real and that they possess specific characteristics"; *reality* is that "quality appertaining to phenomena that we recognize as having a being independent of our own volition" (that is to say, such phenomena cannot be "wished away").[26] Culture and society are such phenomena; both are apprehended by the individual as realities already objectified prior to his or her arrival on the scene, and yet they are obviously human creations. "Institutions, roles, and identities exist as objectively real phenomena in the social world, though they and this world are at the same time nothing but human productions."[27]

The human construction of reality is due to the interaction of three processes: externalization, objectivation, and internalization. *Externalization* refers to the physical and mental activity by which human beings, as it were, pour themselves into their environment.[28] *Objectivation* is the process by which such human activity is first habituated and then institutionalized.[29] Finally, *internalization* is the process by which the humanly constructed world of social institutions is reappropriated by individuals, as when children learn how their world works and what their role in it is. Here objectivated reality becomes subjective reality in human consciousness. Hence

---

[23]Berger and Luckmann, *Social Construction*, 3.

[24]Perhaps the best summary of the theory is provided by Berger himself in the first two chapters of *The Sacred Canopy*, in which he brings the argument of *The Social Construction of Reality* to bear on the special case of religion.

[25]Berger, *Sacred Canopy*, 6-7.

[26]Berger and Luckmann, *Social Construction*, 1.

[27]Berger, *Sacred Canopy*, 13.

[28]Berger and Luckmann, *Social Construction*, 47-52; Berger, *Sacred Canopy*, 4.

[29]Berger and Luckmann, *Social Construction*, 60.

the dialectical relationship between human beings and their world: Society is the product of human activity (externalization) that confronts human beings as an objective reality (objectivation) and shapes their existence in society (internalization). Society is a human product and human beings are social products.[30]

Once constructed, the social order is taken for granted as long as everyday life goes smoothly for its inhabitants. When a situation arises that calls the social order into question, however, reflection upon it becomes necessary.[31] The quintessential such occasion is when the social world is transmitted to the next generation. At this point, the institutional order must be justified and explained if it is to appear viable as an inhabitable world to those for whom the originating events of its various institutions are not a matter of personal memory. What is needed, according to Berger and Luckmann, is *legitimation*, that is, a second-order objectivation of meaning that legitimates the world that emerged from the first-order objectivation, institutionalization.[32] Legitimations are both cognitive and normative; they explain *why* things are as they are and *how* the individual should, therefore, behave.[33]

For analytical purposes, legitimation may be said to occur at several levels, although empirically these categories overlap. First is the pretheoretical level of *incipient legitimation*, which includes traditional statements to the effect that "this is how it is done." Second are *rudimentary theoretical propositions* in the form of proverbs, maxims, legends, folk tales, myths, and the like. At a third level are explicit *theories*, which are usually developed by experts using specialized bodies of knowledge. Fourth are *symbolic universes*.[34] It is this fourth level that is of greatest relevance to my

---

[30]Berger and Luckmann, *Social Construction*, 61; Berger, *Sacred Canopy*, 4.

[31]Berger and Luckmann, *Social Construction*, 24, 44, 104-5; Berger, *Sacred Canopy*, 30-31.

[32]Berger and Luckmann, *Social Construction*, 61, 92-93.

[33]Berger and Luckmann, *Social Construction*, 94; Berger, *Sacred Canopy*, 29-30.

[34]Berger and Luckmann, *Social Construction*, 94-95; Berger, *Sacred Canopy*, 31-32.

investigation. Prior to defining a symbolic universe, however, a preliminary word on symbols is in order.

A symbol, for Berger and Luckmann, is any signification that spans spheres of reality.[35] Symbols, whether linguistic or other, transcend the reality of everyday life to refer to another sphere of reality—another province of meaning—thereby bringing that reality to bear on everyday life. Paradigmatic of the reality-spanning function of symbols are religion, philosophy, art, and science, which have historically been the most important symbol systems.[36]

To return to symbolic universes, "These are bodies of theoretical tradition that integrate different provinces of meaning and encompass the institutional order in a symbolic totality."[37] At this level of legitimation, everyday reality is transcended by means of symbols that refer to other spheres of reality in order to justify the institutional order. Moreover, not just some aspects of society but the *entire* institutional order is encompassed by the symbolic universe. "The symbolic universe is conceived of as the matrix of *all* socially objectivated and subjectively real meanings; the entire historic society and the entire biography of the individual are seen as events taking place *within* this universe."[38] By far the most frequently occurring type of symbolic universe throughout history, and the kind with which 1 Peter is concerned, is the religious one, the "sacred cosmos."[39] Geertz's definition of a religion is apropos:

> (1) a system of symbols which acts to (2) establish powerful, pervasive, and long-lasting moods and motivations in men by (3) formulating conceptions of a general order of existence and (4) clothing these conceptions with such an aura of factuality that (5) the moods and motivations seem uniquely realistic.[40]

Once a symbolic universe is produced as a first product of theoretical thought, it is generally taken for granted by the individu-

---

[35]Berger and Luckmann, *Social Construction*, 40, 95.
[36]Berger and Luckmann, *Social Construction*, 25, 40, 95.
[37]Berger and Luckmann, *Social Construction*, 95.
[38]Berger and Luckmann, *Social Construction*, 96.
[39]Berger, *Sacred Canopy*, 25, 32.
[40]Geertz, *Interpretation of Cultures*, 90 (italics deleted).

als in a society until such time as it becomes problematic, as for example, when the threat of deviance or—in the case of a religious symbolic universe—heresy arises from another society or from a subsociety within the larger collective. At that point, the symbolic universe itself becomes the object of legitimating theoretical reflection, just as the social world had earlier, when it became problematic. If the symbolic universe emerged as a result of a first-order legitimation of the social world, then symbolic-universe maintenance may be called a second-order legitimation.[41] Moreover, in the course of legitimating a symbolic universe, inevitably the symbolic universe itself undergoes alteration. When the "official" christology of the early church was challenged, for example, the doctrine of the Trinity emerged in response; the "heretics" failed to win the day, and the official christology was itself altered in the course of its defense.[42]

Berger and Luckmann list four conspicuous types of universe-maintenance machineries—mythology, theology, philosophy, and science—as well as two additional types—therapy and nihilation or negative legitimation—that may operate within the context of any of the previous four. Since the universe of 1 Peter is clearly religious, only mythology and theology need concern us here. For Berger and Luckmann, the difference between the two lies in the greater degree of theoretical systematization that characterizes theology. Whereas mythology conceives of all reality as cut from a single cloth and, so, has no trouble positing "an ongoing penetration of the world of everyday experience by sacred forces," theology acknowledges that the tie between the human and the divine has become tenuous and, therefore, attempts to provide a theoretically integrated mediation between the two realities.[43] For our purposes, the question of whether a given project of religious-universe maintenance is strictly mythological or theological may remain open, since the dividing line between the two is blurry at best and subject to individual judgments about what constitutes sufficient "theoretical systematization" to warrant the label "theology."

---

[41]Berger and Luckmann, *Social Construction*, 104-5.
[42]Berger and Luckmann, *Social Construction*, 106-7.
[43]Berger and Luckmann, *Social Construction*, 110-16.

Most of the foregoing survey has concentrated on the first two processes in the social construction of reality—externalization and objectivation. These processes, however, represent only half of the story. Society is not only objective reality but also subjective reality. Internalization, as noted earlier, is the "reabsorption into consciousness of the objectivated world in such a way that the structures of this world come to determine the subjective structures of consciousness itself."[44] Although all three moments in the social construction of reality are present at all times in a given society, in the case of individuals, there is a temporal sequence. The social world exists prior to the individual who would become a member of it. Such a person must internalize that world; he or she must be socialized into it. *Socialization* is the process of internalization as it applies to the particular individual.[45] Berger and Luckmann distinguish three kinds of socialization.

Primary socialization is the first socialization an individual undergoes in childhood (usually under the tutelage of parents); it is the means by which an individual becomes a member of the society within which he or she is born.[46] *Secondary socialization* refers to any subsequent process by which an already-socialized individual is inducted into a specific sector of the society with its own body of specialized knowledge.[47] The aspiring medical doctor, for example, undergoes a protracted process of secondary socialization under the guidance of innumerable specialists en route to becoming a licensed physician. There is still a third type of socialization, however, and it is this type that most applies to the case of 1 Peter. *Resocialization* is the process by which one "switches worlds" or undergoes "alternation," as in the case of religious conversion. In such cases, the individual must be resocialized; he or she must experience a dismantling of the subjective reality achieved during primary socialization and must internalize the new social world, which is transmitted via significant others in much the same way the primary socializers (usually parents) conveyed the original world to the

---

[44] Berger, *Sacred Canopy*, 15.
[45] Berger and Luckmann, *Social Construction*, 129-30.
[46] Berger and Luckmann, *Social Construction*, 129-35.
[47] Berger and Luckmann, *Social Construction*, 138-39.

individual. Whereas secondary socialization builds on the foundation laid by primary socialization, resocialization attempts to obliterate this foundation and to replace it with a new reality.[48]

Socialization is successful to the extent that a symmetry is established between the external and internal worlds, so that the individual experiences a fit between the social order and his or her own subjective reality. Significant others enable socialization to occur by mediating the *plausibility structure* of the social world to the individual. The plausibility structure is the foundation upon which a social world rests, including social definitions of reality, social relations that take these definitions for granted, and the legitimations (including the symbolic universe) supporting these definitions and relationships.[49] In short, the plausibility structure is that which makes a world plausible. As such it undergirds both the world itself (objective reality) and the individual's participation in it (subjective reality).

Socialization is never really completed. Just as the world itself must be constantly maintained via legitimations, so must the individual's subjective reality be continually maintained through the ongoing mediation of the plausibility structure. In the case of religion: "To have a conversion experience is nothing much. The real thing is to be able to keep on taking it seriously; to retain a sense of its plausibility."[50] If the converted are to remain converted, they must locate themselves within the religious community, which will displace their old reality with its reality and confirm their new identity. The religious community provides the indispensable plausibility structure for the new reality.

For Berger and Luckmann, therefore, knowledge lies at the very heart of the fundamental dialectic of society. Every society has a socially objectivated body of knowledge about reality that, once internalized, guides the individual's everyday life and conduct and orders his or her world. "Knowledge about society is thus a *realiza-*

---

[48]Berger and Luckmann, *Social Construction*, 156-63.

[49]Peter L. Berger, *A Rumor of Angels: Modern Society and the Rediscovery of the Supernatural* (expanded ed.; New York: Doubleday, Anchor, 1990) 39-40; Berger, *Sacred Canopy*, 45; Berger and Luckmann, *Social Construction*, 157-58.

[50]Berger and Luckmann, *Social Construction*, 158.

tion in the double sense of the word, in the sense of apprehending the objectivated social reality, and in the sense of ongoingly producing this reality."[51] Such knowledge is not, therefore, simply an aggregate of ideas, in the sense of theoretical thought. Ideas are part of a society's reality, but they cannot be abstracted from the processes by which society creates and maintains itself. "It is precisely this 'knowledge' that constitutes the fabric of meanings without which no society could exist."[52]

Furthermore, as has already been implied above, *language* is of the utmost importance in the construction and maintenance of human worlds. Of all human objectivations, the most important is *signification*, that is, the production of signs intended to point to their user's subjective meanings;[53] and language is by far the most important sign system.[54] As Murray Edelman states, "Language does not mirror an objective 'reality,' but rather creates it by organizing meaningful perceptions abstracted from a complex, bewildering world."[55] It is primarily through language that worlds are constituted and legitimated, and it is primarily through language that individuals are socialized and sustained within these worlds.

> Language objectifies the world, transforming the *panta rhei* of experience into a cohesive order. In the establishment of this order language *realizes* a world, in the double sense of apprehending and producing it. Conversation is the actualizing of this realizing efficacy of language in the face-to-face situations of individual existence.[56]

---

[51] Berger and Luckmann, *Social Construction*, 66.

[52] Berger and Luckmann, *Social Construction*, 15. Cf. Geertz's definition of culture, which embraces Berger and Luckmann's "culture" and "society": "It denotes an historically transmitted pattern of meanings embodied in symbols, a system of inherited conceptions expressed in symbolic forms by means of which men communicate, perpetuate, and develop their knowledge about and attitudes toward life" (*Interpretation of Cultures*, 89).

[53] Berger and Luckmann, *Social Construction*, 35-36.

[54] Berger and Luckmann, *Social Construction*, 37.

[55] Murray Edelman, *Politics as Symbolic Action: Mass Arousal and Quiescence* (Institute for Research on Poverty Monograph Series; Chicago: Markham, 1971) 66.

[56] Berger and Luckmann, *Social Construction*, 153.

And, we might add, conversation need not be face-to-face but can also take place across great distances via the written word, as in the case of 1 Peter.

Turning now to 1 Peter, I have noted above that the letter appears to be confronting *primarily* social problems rather than doctrinal or theological ones. In terms of the sociology of knowledge, the letter deals not with a direct threat to the religious symbolic universe of its addressees but with a threat to their status within the social order. Since this threat emerged as a result of their religious commitment, it is the religious symbolic universe as much as their social status that is in need of legitimation. As a kind of mythological-theological legitimation, 1 Peter discloses *certain elements* of a religious symbolic universe, though certainly not anything like a symbolic universe in its entirety. And although the letter offers these elements of a symbolic universe to its readers, we do not have direct access to their symbolic universe. An exhaustive description of either symbolic universe—that of the letter or that of its audience—would therefore be impossible. In any case, my interest lies in the more specific question of the means by which the letter attempts to redress the problematic aspects of its addressees' social experience.

Berger and Luckmann provide a theory with which to analyze the relationship between the linguistic-symbolic phenomena of 1 Peter and the social world the letter addresses. My task is to inquire into this relationship and to ask how the Christ symbolism of the letter functions as one aspect of a legitimation that sanctions the sacred symbolic universe of these suffering Christians. Geertz incisively states that, "As a religious problem, the problem of suffering is, paradoxically, not how to avoid suffering but how to suffer."[57] Geertz's characterization of the role of religious symbolism in addressing the problem of suffering in general might have been written of 1 Peter in particular:

> For those able to embrace them, and for so long as they are able to embrace them, religious symbols provide a cosmic guarantee not only for their ability to comprehend the world, but also, comprehending it,

---

[57]Geertz, *Interpretation of Cultures*, 104.

to give a precision to their feeling, a definition to their emotions which enables them . . . to endure it.[58]

In what follows, I shall endeavor to show how embracing 1 Peter's Christ symbolism might have affected a Petrine believer's knowledge of reality and, consequently, his or her ability to endure suffering. Or, to return to an earlier formulation, I shall seek to answer the question of how 1 Peter's christological statements were intended to function as part of the letter's total response to its recipients' experience of suffering.

The Design of the Study

The remainder of this study consists of three chapters. In the first, I shall set the context for exegesis, not only by placing the letter in its chronological and geographical setting but, more important, by uncovering the socioreligious dimension of the suffering of the communities addressed. Here the social-scientific literature on honor and shame will be examined and brought to bear on the specific situation of 1 Peter, a document rife with honor-and-shame terminology. The essential problem, I shall argue, is that, in a society preoccupied with accumulation and loss of honor, the honor of the Petrine addressees is constantly at risk in their interactions with outsiders—interactions whose effects on the intended readers are characterized by the letter as "suffering."

Then, in chapter 4, I shall begin to explicate 1 Peter's response to this problem of suffering. Here I shall focus on the letter's vision of the nature of Christian communal life within a hostile society, appealing for assistance to the anthropologist Victor Turner's notion of liminality. Turner's concept of liminality will be discussed, and the points of correspondence and of contrast between Turner's liminality and 1 Peter's characterization of Christian life within the

---

[58]Geertz, *Interpretation of Cultures*, 104. Geertz is here speaking not of suffering as a result of one's religious faith, but of a religious symbol system that deals with the kinds of suffering endemic to life itself, e.g., illness and mourning (see Geertz, *Interpretation of Cultures*, 103). His remarks on the function of religious symbol systems in dealing with the problem of suffering, however, are equally applicable in both cases.

larger society will be explored. I hope to show that the letter offers its readers a legitimation of an alternative symbolic universe within which their ambiguous relationship with the society at large need not be feared but may be embraced as the liminal place of the people of God. In this liminal existence, honor and shame are determined not by outsiders to the community but by God.

Finally, chapter 5 will present exegeses of the passages in 1 Peter in which Christ is explicitly invoked in response to the suffering of the letter's addressees. Here I shall bring together the results of the previous two chapters and demonstrate the function of the christological passages within the total project of the letter. I shall argue that the image of the Christ who suffered and was subsequently glorified provides the pivotal symbol around which the letter's symbolic universe is oriented and by which this universe—along with the existence of all who are willing to inhabit it—is ultimately legitimized. Within this symbolic universe, suffering at the hands of non-Christians does not compromise one's honor and social status but underscores one's legitimate place in the community of those who are following Christ's footsteps through suffering to honor.

CHAPTER 3

THE PROBLEM: SUFFERING AND DISGRACE

If we are to explicate 1 Peter's response to the plight of its addressees, we must first situate the letter and its intended readers within their sociohistorical contexts in order to describe the problem addressed as precisely as possible. Only then can we hope to discover how the letter might have functioned as an intelligible response to the dilemma of the addressees. Because this study focuses on the dynamics of the reception of the letter rather than on the processes of its composition, two elements traditionally associated with introductory matters—authorship and provenance—are of concern here only insofar as they shed light on the historical context.[1] The date of the letter is of greater moment, again, not as a datum in itself but only insofar as it helps to illuminate the social and political milieu of the recipients. Authorship, date, and provenance are, therefore, treated only briefly in the pages below. The bulk of this chapter is devoted to answering the twofold question of the identity of the communities addressed and the nature of their suffering.

---

[1] In accordance with the methodology outlined in chap. 2, I am here distancing my approach from that of Elliott, who seeks to uncover the "interests which motivated the composition of 1 Peter" (*Home*, 272), and, even more so, from that of William Joseph Dalton, who argues that "much of the interpretation of the text of 1 Peter . . . depends on presuppositions about the background of 1 Peter, its sources, its date and its author" (*Christ's Proclamation to the Spirits: A Study of 1 Peter 3:18–4:6* [AnBib 23; 2d ed.; Rome: Pontifical Biblical Institute, 1989] 77). My study seeks to discover how the text of 1 Peter might have functioned within the communities to which the letter was addressed, not the theology, ideology, strategy, motivations, psychological state, or religious pedigree of its author.

Authorship, Date, and Provenance

The authorship, date, and provenance of 1 Peter are notoriously controversial; perhaps no other NT document has given rise to as much disagreement over these matters.[2] Furthermore, how one deals with any one of these issues is utterly dependent upon how the other two are treated. If, for example, one is convinced that the apostle Peter wrote the letter, then a date after the time of Nero is precluded, since Peter almost certainly died during Nero's reign (ca. 64-68).[3] Nor can these matters be adjudicated apart from one's determination of the nature of the suffering addressed in the letter. To use another example, if one sees the Trajanic persecution lying behind 4:12-17, then a date early in the second century, well after Peter's death, is indicated. Before turning attention to the question of the identity and

---

[2] In this respect the situation has changed little since Stephen Neill's declaration more than thirty years ago that "It may be that definite solutions of this Petrine problem will for ever evade us" (*The Interpretation of the New Testament, 1861-1961: The Firth Lectures, 1962* [corrected ed.; Oxford/New York: Oxford University Press, 1966] 344). Compare the statement in Tom Wright's 1988 revision of Neill's book: "We are still a long way from anything like scholarly consensus on . . . any of the basic, if apparently undramatic, issues such as authorship, date, and place of composition" (*The Interpretation of the New Testament, 1861-1986* [2d ed.; Oxford/ New York: Oxford University Press, 1988] 367). Elliott, on the other hand, thinks he detects an emerging consensus on date (the latter third of the first century), pseudonymity, and Roman provenance (*Home*, xxviii). Although the majority does agree on Roman provenance, however, vigorous debates continue over date and authorship.

[3] A few scholars argue that Peter lived beyond the Neronian period (e.g., William M. Ramsay, *The Church in the Roman Empire* [London: Hodder & Stoughton, 1893] 283; Michaels, *1 Peter*, lvii-lxi), but the evidence is decisively against them. See Richard J. Bauckham, "The Martyrdom of Peter in Early Christian Literature," *ANRW* 2/26/1. 539-95; Oscar Cullmann, *Peter—Disciple, Apostle, Martyr: A Historical and Theological Study* (trans. Floyd V. Filson; Library of History and Doctrine; 2d. ed.; Philadelphia: Westminster, 1962) 71-157; Goppelt, *1 Peter*, 9-14; Daniel Wm. O'Connor, *Peter in Rome: The Literary, Liturgical, and Archeological Evidence* (New York/London: Columbia University Press, 1969) 61-89; Pheme Perkins, *Peter: Apostle for the Whole Church* (Studies on Personalities of the New Testament; Columbia: University of South Carolina Press, 1994) 146; Carsten Peter Thiede, *Simon Peter: From Galilee to Rome* (Grand Rapids: Zondervan, Academie, 1988) 190-91. Michaels's caution against tying the questions of authorship and date too closely together (*1 Peter*, lxi) loses its force when the traditional date of Peter's death is accepted. If Peter wrote this letter, it must be dated in the early sixties; conversely, if the letter originated after 70, it is not the work of Peter.

suffering of the addressees, however, a few preliminary comments on authorship, date, and provenance are in order.

Authorship

Beginning with 2 Peter (see 2 Pet 3:1), early-Christian tradition was unanimous in assigning the authorship of 1 Peter to the apostle Peter.[4] Since the rise of critical scholarship, however, numerous arguments against the letter's authenticity have been raised, the most important of which follow: (1) The use of "Babylon" as a cipher for Rome (1 Pet 5:13) only developed after the fall of Jerusalem in 70, several years after Peter's death. (2) First Peter is too Pauline to have come from Peter; particularly conspicuous is the pervasive influence of Romans and Ephesians. (3) The Greek of 1 Peter is more elegant and the rhetorical skill more refined than could be expected of a Galilean fisherman. (4) Similarly, the command of the LXX is beyond the ken of the apostle Peter. (5) Peter would probably have used Σίμων instead of the honorific Πέτρος in referring to himself. (6) It is questionable whether Peter would have written to communities that were unknown to himself and in the area of the Pauline mission, but if so, he would certainly have mentioned Paul. (7) The letter lacks autobiographical allusions and (8) eyewitness reminiscences about Jesus, whose suffering occupies so much of its space.[5]

These arguments have not gone unchallenged: (1) Although "Babylon" as a cipher for Rome is only attested in post-70 Jewish literature, the author of 1 Peter could have used the metaphor earlier

---

[4]For a discussion of the evidence of the first three centuries, see Michaels, *1 Peter*, xxxii-xxxiv.

[5]It is rare to find all these arguments invoked by any one author; most of them are listed by Schutter, who cautiously accepts the pseudepigraphy of 1 Peter as a working hypothesis (*Hermeneutic*, 5-6), and by Feldmeier, who also concludes that the letter is a pseudepigraphon (*Christen als Fremde*, 193-98). For greater detail, see the following, all of whom think the letter is pseudepigraphic: Beare, *Epistle of Peter*, 43-50; Best, *1 Peter*, 49-51; Brox, *Petrusbrief*, 43-51; Goppelt, *1 Peter*, 48-50; Kümmel, *Introduction*, 423-24; Wolfgang Schrage, "Der erste Petrusbrief," *Die "katholischen" Briefe: Die Briefe des Jakobus, Petrus, Johannes und Judas* (by Horst Balz and Wolfgang Schrage; NTD 10; 12th ed; Göttingen: Vandenhoeck & Ruprecht, 1980) 64-65.

(as had Daniel with reference to the Seleucid Empire).⁶ (2) The affinities to Pauline and deutero-Pauline letters could be due to a common early-Christian tradition and to a similar time and orientation to the church(es) in Rome; furthermore, Paul penned Romans in the mid-fifties, early enough for Peter to have read it or for its message to have permeated the tradition in Rome.⁷ (3) Peter's leadership in the Christian communities in Antioch and Rome suggests that he had considerable facility with the Greek language;⁸

---

⁶Charles Bigg, *A Critical and Exegetical Commentary on the Epistles of St. Peter and St. Jude* (ICC; New York: Scribner's, 1901) 76; Goppelt, *1 Peter*, 374; Selwyn, *Epistle of St. Peter*, 303-4; I. Howard Marshall, *1 Peter* (IVPNTCS; Downers Grove/Leicester, England: InterVarsity, 1991) 23. Schutter suggests the analogy of Qumran's equation of the "Kittim" with the "Chaldeans"; if Jewish groups could have been thinking in such terms prior to 70, there is no reason why Christians could not have been doing so (*Hermeneutic*, 5 n. 8). Also relevant here is Carsten Peter Thiede, "Babylon, der andere Ort: Anmerkungen zu 1 Petr 5,13 und Apg 12,17," in *Das Petrusbild in der neueren Forschung* (ed. Carsten Peter Thiede; Wuppertal: Brockhaus, 1987) 221-29, esp. 222-24. Thiede fails in his endeavor to demonstrate that "Babylon" was widely recognized as a metaphor for Rome in both Jewish and non-Jewish circles by the early sixties CE. He does, however, show that "Babylonian" was used metaphorically by the Roman dramatist Terence (ca. 160 BCE) and by the Roman satirist Petronius (ca. 61 CE). In the case of Petronius, the connection with Rome is particularly close, as Rome is said to have become wealthy and decadent, like a caged peacock enveloped by Babylonian plumage of gold. These data, however, hardly constitute convincing evidence that the word "Babylon" was commonly recognized as a metaphor for Rome and imperial life. Michaels, who thinks that Peter outlived Nero, argues that the letter *was* written after the events of 70, by Peter (*1 Peter*, lx-lxvi, esp. lxvi). Given the strong evidence for Peter's death during Nero's reign, however, Michaels's position fails to commend itself (see above, p. 42 n. 3).

⁷See Boismard, "Pierre," 1449; Dalton, *Christ's Proclamation*, 87; Peter H. Davids, *The First Epistle of Peter* (NICNT; Grand Rapids: Eerdmans, 1990) 5-6; Elliott, "Peter, First Epistle of," 276; Goppelt, *1 Peter*, 49; Donald Guthrie, *New Testament Introduction* (3d ed; Downers Grove: InterVarsity, 1970) 785-86; Michaels, *1 Peter*, xliv-xlv; John A. T. Robinson, *Redating the New Testament* (Philadelphia: Westminster, 1976) 166; Lauri Thurén, *The Rhetorical Strategy of 1 Peter, with Special Regard to Ambiguous Expressions* (Åbo, Finland: Åbo Academy Press, 1990) 33.

⁸Guthrie, *Introduction*, 778; Robinson, *Redating*, 167; Ceslas Spicq, *Les épîtres de Saint Pierre* (SB; Paris: Gabalda, 1966) 21-23; cf. Wayne A. Grudem, *The First Epistle of Peter: An Introduction and Commentary* (Tyndale New Testament Commentaries; Leicester, England: InterVarsity; Grand Rapids: Eerdmans, 1988) 26-30. Cf. J. N. D. Kelly, who argues both that Peter's Greek could not have been quite as bad as some have claimed and that the Greek of the letter is not as elegant as some

moreover, Peter probably had an amanuensis who did the actual writing.[9] (4) It would be quite natural for Peter to use the LXX—the standard Greek translation of the scriptures—when writing to a Greek-speaking, largely gentile audience.[10] (5) If Peter was called "Peter," which he probably was in the Greek-speaking church, he would likely have used this name of himself.[11] (6) The members of the communities addressed, if they were within the orb of Paul's mission activity, which is doubtful, would not necessarily have known Paul personally; and in any case, there is no reason why Peter, probably writing after Paul's demise, should have mentioned him.[12] (7 and 8) That an intimate of Jesus would have had to make explicit references to certain events of Jesus' life is a remarkably subjective determination; in any case, numerous veiled allusions do occur (e.g.,

---

would have it, but nevertheless concludes that the language of the letter is too literary to have come from Peter without an amanuensis (*The Epistles of Peter and of Jude* [BNTC; Peabody: Hendrickson, 1969] 31-32); cf. also Dalton, *Christ's Proclamation*, 87.

[9] Virtually all who argue for Petrine authorship also argue that Peter had an amanuensis. (One conspicuous exception is Grudem, *Epistle of Peter*, 24, 32-33.) Beare rightly rejects the use of the Silvanus-as-amanuensis theory as a blanket response to doubts about Peter's authorship of this letter (*Epistle of Peter*, 212-26). Although he does think that the letter claims that Silvanus was the amanuensis (*Epistle of Peter*, 209), Beare doubts that Silvanus was any more immersed in the thought and language of Hellenistic culture than was Peter (*Epistle of Peter*, 212-213; contra Selwyn, *Epistle of St. Peter*, 9-17). Goppelt rightly points out, however, that Silvanus, though a product of the Palestinian church, was a diaspora Jew and worked closely with Paul in the Greek-speaking mission, which would make him a more likely candidate than Peter to have penned the kind of Greek found in 1 Peter (*I Peter*, 50). Robinson, following F. H. Chase ("Peter, First Epistle of," *A Dictionary of the Bible, Dealing with Its Language, Literature, and Contents Including the Biblical Theology* [ed. James Hastings; Edinburgh: Clark, 1898; reprint, Peabody: Hendrickson, 1988] 3. 790), argues that διὰ Σιλουανοῦ ὑμῖν . . . ἔγραψα (1 Pet 5:12) indicates that Silvanus was not the secretary at all but the bearer of the letter; for parallels, see Acts 15:23; Ign. *Rom.* 10:1; Ign. *Phld.* 11:2; Ign. *Smyrn.* 12:1; Pol. *Phil.* 14 (*Redating*, 167-69; cf. Elliott, "Peter, First Epistle of," 277; Kümmel, 424; against this view see Goppelt, *I Peter*, 369-71). I am convinced by the arguments of Chase and Robinson, but their reading of 5:12 as indicating that Silvanus was the bearer of the letter does not preclude his being its amanuensis as well. As with so many other questions concerning 1 Peter, this one must be left open.

[10] Guthrie, *Introduction*, 778; Robinson, *Redating*, 166.

[11] Thurén, *Rhetorical Strategy*, 34; cf. Selwyn, *Epistle of St. Peter*, 117.

[12] Guthrie, *Introduction*, 784; Marshall, *I Peter*, 23.

1:8; 2:23; 5:1).[13] Finally, it is alleged, no evidence has been uncovered that is sufficient to overturn the testimony of the longstanding tradition of 1 Peter's authenticity.

Although space limitations preclude a detailed analysis of these arguments, on the whole I find the case against Petrine authorship more persuasive than the argument in its favor. No single piece of evidence is in itself persuasive, but several data *taken together* do undermine the claim of authenticity. In the first place, the literary style of the letter does appear to be beyond the capacity of the disciple Peter, even if, as is likely, he was bilingual. Especially telling here is the radical form of the amanuensis theory to which most adherents of Petrine authorship must resort: The gist of their argument is that the letter was written (1) at Peter's request and (2) during his lifetime, and that (3) he did not object to the finished product. To argue along these lines, however, is to redefine the concept of authorship, thereby rendering the claim of authenticity virtually unfalsifiable—unless one could prove that the letter could not have originated during Peter's lifetime.[14] Second, the use of "Babylon" for Rome, not in the context of a full-blown narrative or myth (as found in Revelation, *2 Baruch*, *4 Ezra*, or *Sibylline Oracle 5*) but in an abrupt, apparently self-explanatory way, suggests a time period after 70, when such narratives and myths were emerging in Jewish and Christian circles. Finally, the similarities between 1 Peter and *1 Clement* (which was written in Rome in the mid-nineties)[15] and

---

[13]Dalton, *Christ's Proclamation*, 87; Michaels, *1 Peter*, lxvi; Robinson, *Redating*, 164-65; Selwyn, *Epistle of St. Peter*, 27-33; A. M. Stibbs and A. F. Walls, *The First Epistle General of Peter: An Introduction and Commentary* (Tyndale New Testament Commentaries; London: Tyndale; Grand Rapids: Eerdmans, 1959) 33-35.

[14]Peter H. Davids, however, allows that the letter may have been written after Peter's death but still rejects the designation "pseudepigraphical" since, in his view, Silvanus penned the letter at Peter's direction using Peter's thoughts—whether during or after Peter's lifetime (*Epistle of Peter*, 10, 198).

[15]For the parallels with *1 Clement*, see Donald Alfred Hagner, *The Use of the Old and New Testaments in Clement of Rome* (NovTSup 34; Leiden: Brill, 1973) 239-46. I accept the critical consensus on a date of 95-96 for *1 Clement*, despite Robinson's argument for a date in early 70 (*Redating*, 327-35; following George Edmundson, *The Church in Rome in the First Century: An Examination of Various Controverted Questions Relating to Its History, Chronology, Literature and Traditions* [London/New York: Longmans Green, 1913] 188-202).

Suffering and Disgrace 47

between 1 Peter and Ephesians (which I take to be post-Pauline),[16] although not sufficient to prove literary dependence, are extensive enough to indicate similar dates and perhaps, in the case of *1 Clement*, a common provenance.[17] Nevertheless, although I find the case for pseudepigraphy more convincing than that for authenticity, the evidence is hardly overwhelming. Nor, to anticipate the findings of the remainder of this chapter, does the kind of suffering presupposed in the letter decisively shift the weight of evidence in either direction. We may, therefore, leave the question open.[18]

---

[16] For a convenient listing of the passages containing similarities with Romans and Ephesians, see Goppelt, *1 Peter*, 28; supplemented by the slightly different list in C. L. Mitton, "The Relationship between 1 Peter and Ephesians," *JTS* n.s. 1 (1950) 67-73.

[17] Mitton has argued on the basis of a comparison of passages in 1 Peter that are similar both to sections of Colossians and to sections of Ephesians, that the line of dependence runs from Colossians to Ephesians to 1 Peter. Although he fails to *prove* that the author of 1 Peter knew Ephesians, he has shown it to be likely; at the very least, his study indicates a post-Petrine date for 1 Peter, either after or roughly contemporaneous with Ephesians ("Relationship," 67-73). Following Mitton are Beare (*Epistle of Peter*, 219) and Best (*1 Peter*, 35-36); scholars who reject literary dependence in favor of a shared tradition include Goppelt (*1 Peter*, 28-29), Kelly (*Epistles of Peter*, 14), Kümmel (*Introduction*, 243), Michaels (*1 Peter*, xliv), and Selwyn (*Epistle of St. Peter*, 19). As for the relationship between 1 Peter and *1 Clement*, I think it probable that the author of the latter knew 1 Peter (with Hagner, *Use*, 246), or at least that 1 Peter contributed to the tradition on which *1 Clement* drew (Elliott, "Peter, First Epistle of," 276). Best (*1 Peter*, 36), Goppelt (*1 Peter*, 32), and Kelly (*Epistles of Peter*, 12) reject literary dependence but agree that the affinities point to a common traditional milieu; of these, only Best suggests that these affinities also point to a similar date.

[18] Cf. C. E. B. Cranfield, *I & II Peter and Jude: Introduction and Commentary* (Torch Bible Commentaries; London: SCM, 1960) 16; Kelly, *Epistles of Peter*, 30-33; Karl Hermann Schelkle, *Die Petrusbriefe; Der Judasbrief* (HTKNT 13/2; Freiburg/Basel/Vienna: Herder, 1961) 15; Thurén, *Rhetorical Strategy*, 32-38. The wide diversity of contemporary scholarly positions testifies to the difficulty of the problem. On the two extremes are those who think the evidence clearly indicates authenticity (e.g., Dalton, *Christ's Proclamation*, 77-91; Grudem, *Epistle of Peter*, 21-35; Selwyn, *Epistle of St. Peter*, 7-38; Spicq, *Les épîtres*, 17-26) and those who think the evidence points unambiguously to pseudepigraphy (e.g., Beare, *Epistle of Peter*, 43-50; Best, *1 Peter*, 49-63; Brox, *Petrusbrief*, 44-47). The scholars situated between the extremes, however, are particularly instructive. Consider, e.g., the contrasting approaches and results of Schutter and Michaels. Schutter, having concluded that the matter of authorship is far from resolved, adopts as his working hypothesis "the dominant scholarly opinion"—that 1 Peter is a pseudepigraphon (*Hermeneutic*, 7). Michaels, on the other

Date

Two of the three reasons cited above for doubting 1 Peter's authenticity—the use of "Babylon" for Rome and the similarities to Ephesians and *1 Clement*—are in the first place evidence for a particular *date* of the letter, one after 70 and, therefore, after Peter's death. Neither of these, it has been noted, is anything like conclusive; and much the same must be said of the remaining evidence for dating the letter.

First Peter's terminus ad quem is determined by its use in Polycarp's *Letter to the Philippians*, written sometime around 110-115.[19] The terminus a quo is more difficult to establish;[20] but since

---

hand, having found no conclusive evidence *against the traditional view*, assumes the letter's authenticity (*1 Peter*, lxvi-lxvii). Finally, to cite yet a third scholar, Davids accepts the traditional view in the face of what he admits are formidable critical objections based on content and style, but can only do so on the basis of what must be judged to be an extreme form of the amanuensis theory: "How much Peter personally had to do with the letter is unknown.... But the letter was written, written in the style in which Silvanus was accustomed to writing, that is, Paul's, written with whatever he knew of Peter's teaching and ideas, and attributed to Peter as it should have been" (*Epistle of Peter*, 6-7; cf. also Reicke, *Epistles of James, Peter*, 69-71).

[19]P. N. Harrison, expanding on an early thesis of Adolf von Harnack—which Harnack later rejected—dates Polycarp's *Letter to the Philippians* around 135 (P. N. Harrison, *Polycarp's Two Epistles to the Philippians* [Cambridge: Cambridge University Press, 1936] 15-16, 183-206, 267-68; Adolf von Harnack "Bishop Lightfoot on the Genuineness and Date of the Ignatian Epistles," *The Expositor* 3d ser., no. 15 [March 1886] 185-89; agreeing with Harrison is Helmut Koester, *Synoptische Überlieferung bei den Apostolischen Vätern* [TU 65; Berlin: Akademie-Verlag, 1957] 122-23; cf. idem, *Introduction to the New Testament* [2 vols.; FFNT; Philadelphia: Fortress; Berlin/New York: de Gruyter, 1982] 2. 306-7). Harrison's thesis is not supported by the evidence, however, and the majority of scholars correctly holds to the traditional dating ca. 110-115. See William R. Schoedel, *Polycarp, Martyrdom of Polycarp, Fragments of Papias* (The Apostolic Fathers: A New Translation and Commentary 5; London/Camden/Toronto: Nelson & Sons, 1967) 4, 23-26; idem, "Polycarp, Epistle of," *ABD* 5. 390; Michael W. Holmes, in *The Apostolic Fathers: Greek Texts and English Translations of Their Writings* (trans. and ed. J. B. Lightfoot and J. R. Harmer; ed. and rev. Michael W. Holmes; 2d ed.; Grand Rapids: Baker, 1992) 203-4.

[20]Certainly, a situation of hostility between Christians and the larger society is presupposed, but attempts to locate a terminus a quo for this situation must resort to speculation. Selwyn, for example, sets the death of James in 62 as the terminus a quo, because, in his view, it was James's death that signalled the kind of alienation between

1 Peter is rarely (if ever) dated prior to 62, we may take that year—about two years before Peter's death—as a sort of consensual terminus a quo.²¹ These considerations leave a range of approximately half a century within which to locate 1 Peter. We must ask, therefore, whether the letter affords any clues to a more precise dating; and here it is necessary to turn attention to the letter's characterization of the plight of its addressees.²²

In chapter 1, I documented the trend in recent scholarship away from identifying the suffering addressed in 1 Peter with any organized, imperial persecution of Christians. Since scholarship of the past several decades has by no means been unanimous on this point, some additional comment is in order. Although some scholars identify the suffering of the Petrine communities with the persecution of Christians during the reign of Domitian²³ or during Trajan's

---

Christians and their environment that 1 Peter portrays with the terms παρεπίδημοι and πάροικοι (*Epistle of St. Peter*, 56-57). Although the death of James certainly manifested a growing hostility between Jews and Christians within Jerusalem, however, it is not at all clear why James's death should be underscored in particular nor how definitive this Jewish-Christian conflict within Jerusalem was for the situation in Asia Minor in the early sixties. Or, to take up another issue, Goppelt states that the dissemination of Christianity throughout Asia Minor that is presupposed in the opening of 1 Peter may have occurred as early as 65 (*I Peter*, 46), while Thurén says that it could not have occurred earlier than 60 (*Rhetorical Strategy*, 31). Why not, we may ask, push this date back to 58 or even 55? Nor are the criteria of church organization—a mixture of both charismatic worship (4:10-11) and primitive presbyterian order (5:1-5) (Goppelt, *I Peter*, 46-47; Kelly, *Epistles of Peter*, 30; Selwyn, *Epistle of St. Peter*, 56)—and theology—e.g., primitive eschatology, servant christology (Cross, *I. Peter*, 43; Kelly, *Epistles of Peter*, 30) terribly helpful.

²¹Among scholars who argue for 1 Peter's authenticity, Bigg opts for a date sometime between 58 and 64 (*Commentary*, 87), and Robinson for April 65 (*Redating*, 169), but most date the letter sometime in the period 62-64 (e.g., Grudem, *Epistle of Peter*, 63-64; Guthrie, *New Testament Introduction*, 796; Selwyn, *Epistle of St. Peter*, 62; Spicq, *Les épîtres*, 26, esp. n. 4). The peculiar cases of Ramsay and Michaels, who date Peter's authorship of the letter and his martyrdom after 70, have already been discussed above (see p. 42 n. 3).

²²This material will be treated in greater depth later in this chapter, where I describe the social situation of the intended audience (pp. 94-104); here I am interested only in clarifying the letter's chronological setting.

²³Kümmel, *Introduction*, 425.

time,[24] the one passage in the letter in which the emperor is explicitly mentioned—2:13-17—tells against imperial persecution. Here the letter enjoins fear of God and honor of the emperor in a single breath and commands subjection to the emperor in recognition of his status as ὑπερέχων. Nor does 1 Peter elsewhere exhibit the kind of hostility to, or at least wariness of, Rome to be expected in a document dealing with imperial persecution (cf. Revelation).[25]

Those who hold to a Neronian date of 1 Peter argue that the letter was written immediately prior to Nero's initiative against Christians in Rome. Once Petrine authorship is accepted, 1 Pet 2:13-17 can then be invoked as evidence that Nero had not yet launched his attack on Christians at the time of Peter's writing.[26] Indeed, if a Neronian date is established on other grounds, 2:13-17 would appear to indicate a time prior to Nero's initiative against Christians. Several scholars who hold this view, however, go one step further to argue that the injunctions in 2:13-17 could not have been written *anytime* after Nero's persecution—even after his death.[27] This argument is refuted, however, by the presence of a similar disposition toward the Empire in at least two documents that postdate Nero by a considerable margin, *1 Clement* (see 60:4–61:2) and 1 Timothy (see 2:1-2).[28] Although 1 Pet 2:13-17 would appear to preclude a date during or immediately after a period of imperial persecution of Christians, therefore, these verses certainly cannot be taken as evidence against a post-Neronian date.

One piece of evidence that deserves special attention here comes not so much from 1 Peter as from a comparison of 1 Peter with Pliny's correspondence with Trajan. Writing in approximately 111, Pliny, Trajan's imperial legate to Bithynia-Pontus, informs the emperor that many people in Bithynia-Pontus are being brought to

---

[24]Beare, *Epistle of Peter*, 32-34; John Knox, "Pliny and I Peter: A Note on I Pet 4:14-16 and 3:15," *JBL* 72 (1953) 187-89; Koester, *Introduction*, 2. 194; Leaney, *Letters of Peter*, 8-10.

[25]Cf. Michaels, *1 Peter*, lxiii; Schelkle, *Petrusbriefe*, 12.

[26]Grudem, *Epistle of Peter*, 35-36; Guthrie, *Introduction*, 796; Selwyn, *Epistle of St. Peter*, 59-60.

[27]Dalton, *Christ's Proclamation*; Robinson, *Redating*, 157.

[28]Goppelt, *I Peter*, 22, 43 n. 15.

Suffering and Disgrace 51

trial on the charge of being Christian, and that he has already passed the death sentence on a number of the accused when they refused to renounce their faith, even after being warned three times of the impending consequences. Only those who denied that they were Christians, repeated Pliny's invocation of the gods, made offerings to Trajan's image, and cursed the name of Christ were exonerated. Since the charges are becoming more widespread, Pliny explains, he thought it best to postpone adjudication of any more cases until consulting Trajan. Among the questions Pliny puts to Trajan is whether mere confession of being a Christian is grounds for punishment or whether the Christians must be convicted of "crimes associated with the name" (*flagitia cohaerentia nomini*) (Pliny *Ep.* 10.96.2).[29] In reply, Trajan commends Pliny's course of action. Although he does not directly address Pliny's question of whether being a Christian is itself punishable apart from specific criminal acts, Trajan implies as much by affirming that those accused of being Christians must be tried and, if convicted, punished (Pliny *Ep.* 10.97). Trajan does not, however, say anything about the severity of the punishment.

The exchange between Pliny and Trajan appears to reflect a later stage in the hostile relations between Christians and their neighbors in Asia Minor than that presupposed in 1 Peter. In particular, the issue of worshiping at the image of the emperor is never raised in 1 Peter.[30] Nor does 1 Peter give any clear indications that trials of people charged solely with being Christians are a principal concern. Although 1 Pet 3:15 raises the possibility that some judicial proceedings may have been in view, the lone occurrence of the word ἀπολογία here is hardly compelling evidence for a situation corresponding to that depicted by Pliny. Nor, finally, does 1 Peter display any awareness of widespread executions of Christians in Asia Minor.[31] Hence, the evidence does not support a correlation of the situation depicted in the Pliny-Trajan correspon-

---

[29]Trans. Betty Radice (LCL).
[30]Goppelt, *1 Peter*, 43; Michaels, *1 Peter*, lxvi; cf. Balch, *Wives*, 86.
[31]On the questions of whether formal trials are in view in 1 Peter and whether the letter presupposes the condemnation and execution of Christians in Asia Minor, see below, pp. 87-94.

dence with that presupposed in 1 Peter. In light of Pliny's statement that the number of cases being brought against Christians was increasing at the time of his writing, however, it would appear reasonable to conclude that 1 Peter was addressing an earlier moment in the history of the increasingly hostile relations between Christians and their neighbors in Asia Minor, although how much earlier must remain a matter of conjecture.[32] At the very least, this evidence pushes back 1 Peter's terminus ad quem to a few years prior to Pliny's correspondence with Trajan, or approximately 105.

In conclusion, these considerations, along with the suspicion stated above that 1 Peter postdates the apostle's death, incline me to date the letter during the period 75-105. The evidence, however, is not unequivocal. Setting the terminus ad quem at 105 represents a fairly conservative judgment based on the evidence of Polycarp's *Letter to the Philippians* and of Pliny's correspondence with Trajan. But the terminus a quo of 75 presupposes a post-Petrine date of the letter, which, as we have seen, cannot be demonstrated with certainty. Thus, although we have narrowed slightly the half-century range identified above within which the letter may have originated, we are, once again, left with an open question.

Provenance

In 5:13, the letter refers to its place of origin as "Babylon," which, as we have seen, is almost certainly a cryptogram for Rome;[33] and most commentators accept Rome as the actual place of origin.[34] Brox, however, argues that the reference to Babylon—like the names Peter, Mark, and Silvanus—is part of the letter's pseudepigraphic framework and that nothing regarding provenance should be inferred

---

[32]Cf. Michaels, *1 Peter*, lxvi.

[33]Kümmel, although not altogether convinced, thinks it likely that Babylon is a cipher for Rome (*Introduction*, 422, 425). Boismard doubted the equation in his 1957 article ("Une liturgie," pt. 2, p. 181 n. 2), but seems to accept it in his commentary of 1966 ("Pierre," 1448).

[34]E.g., Best, *1 Peter*, 64-65; Elliott, *Home*, 270-80; Goppelt, *1 Peter*, 48; Kelly, *Epistles of Peter*, 33-34; Michaels, *1 Peter*, xlvii, lxiii-lxvi; Robinson, *Redating*, 150-51; Spicq, *Les épîtres*, 26.

from this fiction.³⁵ Several scholars who agree that "Babylon" is a pseudepigraphic device think the letter was actually written in the East, close to the communities addressed.³⁶ The absence of 1 Peter from the Muratorian canon (thought to be of Roman origin) and the early attestation of the letter in the East (by Papias and Polycarp)³⁷ are sometimes cited as evidence for an Eastern provenance.³⁸ These data, however, are far from compelling. Early attestation in the East is to be expected of a document *addressed to* the East.³⁹ And the letter's absence from the Muratorian canon proves nothing about its origin, especially now that the old scholarly consensus on a late-second-century, Roman provenance of the canon appears to be collapsing, as a number of scholars argue that it is an Eastern, fourth-century list.⁴⁰ Moreover, the affinities between 1 Peter and other

---

³⁵Brox, *Petrusbrief*, 42-43; idem, "Zur pseudepigraphischen Rahmung des ersten Petrusbriefes," *BZ* n.s. 19 (1976) 84-96. Cf. Karl Heussi, *Die römische Petrustradition in kritischer Sicht* (Tübingen: Mohr, 1955) 39-40.

³⁶Those who think the letter emanated from Asia Minor include Beare (*Epistle of Peter*, 50, 209), Conzelmann and Lindemann (*Arbeitsbuch*, 354-55), Claus-Hunno Hunzinger ("Babylon als Deckname für Rom und die Datierung des 1. Petrusbriefes," *Gottes Wort und Gottes Land: Hans-Wilhelm Hertzberg zum 70. Geburtstag am 16. Januar 1965 dargebracht von Kollegen, Freunden und Schülern* [ed. Henning Graf Reventlow; Göttingen: Vandenhoeck & Ruprecht, 1965] 77), and Schutter (*Hermeneutic*, 7). Streeter pinpoints the location as Smyrna (and the author as Aristion, a bishop of Smyrna!) (*Primitive Church*, 130-33). Boismard looks further east to Antioch ("Pierre" 1453; "Une liturgie," pt. 2, p. 183 n. 1).

³⁷For Papias, see Eusebius *Hist. eccl.* 3.39.17; for Polycarp, see Pol. *Phil.* 1:3; 8:1; 10:2.

³⁸On the Eastern citation, see Streeter, *Primitive Church*, 126. On the absence from the Muratorian canon, see Beare, *Epistle of Peter*, 50 (but cf. also p. 226); cf. Kelly, *Epistles of Peter*, 33; Schutter, *Hermeneutic*, 7.

³⁹Goppelt, *I Peter*, 48; cf. Kümmel, *Introduction*, 425.

⁴⁰Even if the canon were of Roman origin, 1 Peter's absence would prove nothing about its provenance (Kümmel, *Introduction*, 425). For a cogent argument in favor of a fourth-century date and Eastern provenance of the Muratorian fragment, see Albert C. Sundberg, Jr., "Canon Muratori: A Fourth-Century List," *HTR* 66 (1973) 1-41; and, following Sundberg, Geoffrey Mark Hahneman, *The Muratorian Fragment and the Development of the Canon* (Oxford Theological Monographs; Oxford: Clarendon, 1992). For criticism of Sundberg's thesis, see Everett Ferguson, "Canon Muratori: Date and Provenance," *Studia Patristica* 18 (1982) 677-83. Although I find the case for a later, Eastern origin convincing, the debate itself shows how little importance should be attached to 1 Peter's absence from the Muratorian fragment.

early-Christian documents associated with Rome—especially Romans and *1 Clement*—suggest a Roman provenance.[41]

I concur, therefore, with the majority of scholars that Rome was in all likelihood the place of 1 Peter's composition, although here, as above in the case of authorship, the evidence is less than compelling. Interestingly, a Roman provenance fits nicely with either position on authenticity: Since tradition places Peter in Rome during his final years, a letter from his hand toward the end of his life would have been composed in Rome; on the other hand, Rome would also have been the most likely place for a Petrine circle to have gathered, out of which a document like 1 Peter could well have issued in Peter's name after his death.[42] The authorship of the letter remains, therefore, an open question.

The Social Location of the Addressees

Methodological Prolegomenon

As we turn from questions about the letter's origin to questions about its destination, a few methodological statements are in order. We begin by recalling the skepticism with which Millauer and Brox approach the question of uncovering the historical situation to which the letter is addressed.[43] Aside from 1 Peter, the sources are virtually nonexistent. Furthermore, 1 Peter itself is a dubious source. In the first place, one cannot know how much the letter's author actually knew about the communities addressed. Moreover, even if we were to assume an intimate knowledge of the situation on the part of the author, we still could not assume that even the most direct statements in the letter reflect the actual historical conditions of the addressees. In Goppelt's terms, the letter's perspective on and language about its

---

[41]Best, *1 Peter*, 32-36, 65; Elliott, *Home*, 290 n. 15; Goppelt, *1 Peter*, 48; Kelly, *Epistles of Peter*, 11-12, 33.

[42]The question of the existence of a "Petrine circle" or "school" in Rome need not be discussed here, except to say that if the letter is pseudepigraphic (as I think), then it is reasonable to suspect that it originated among some devotees of the apostle and/or his teachings. See Elliott, *Home*, 270-82; Marion L. Soards, "1 Peter, 2 Peter, and Jude as Evidence for a Petrine School," *ANRW* 2/25/5. 3827-49.

[43]See above, pp. 6-9.

addressees is thoroughly kerygmatic.⁴⁴ That is to say, what 1 Peter gives us is not the historical situation and a response to that situation—both of which could be easily read off the surface of the letter—but only the response. The letter's characterization of its readers is, in fact, part of its response.

The debate between Lloyd F. Bitzer and Richard E. Vatz concerning the relationship between situation and rhetoric is instructive. Bitzer defines rhetorical situation as "a natural context of persons, events, objects, relations, and an exigence which strongly invites utterance." A particular discourse, in his view, is created as a result of a specific condition or situation that invites it.⁴⁵ Vatz responds that it is not the situation that creates the discourse but the discourse that creates the situation. That is to say, meaning does not naturally and necessarily reside in events; it is only when rhetoric endows them with meaning that events gain salience and become rhetorical situations. In a given discourse, according to Vatz, "Statements may ostensibly describe situations, but they actually only inform us as to the phenomenological perspective of the speaker."⁴⁶ From the standpoint of the sociology of knowledge, the latter statement is certainly true, and Vatz on the whole presents a more persuasive account of the relationship between rhetoric and historical events.⁴⁷

---

⁴⁴Goppelt, *I Peter*, 38.

⁴⁵Lloyd F. Bitzer, "The Rhetorical Situation," *Philosophy and Rhetoric* 1 (1968) 4-5, quotation from p. 5.

⁴⁶Richard E. Vatz, "The Myth of the Rhetorical Situation," *Philosophy and Rhetoric* 6 (1973) 154. Although George A. Kennedy, in his widely read *New Testament Interpretation through Rhetorical Criticism* (Studies in Religion; Chapel Hill/London: University of North Carolina Press, 1985), invokes Bitzer's concept of rhetorical situation as "a useful tool of practical criticism" (34), his examples indicate his own similar modification of Bitzer's definition: "The reports which reached Paul of the situation in Corinth *seemed to him to require a response*; . . . an evangelist *felt an exigence* to proclaim the gospel, and . . . *felt an exigence* to include certain of the doings or sayings of Jesus" (35 [emphasis mine]). It is not the events themselves, therefore, but their interpretation by Paul and the evangelists that constitutes the events as rhetorical situations.

⁴⁷For a much more nuanced discussion of what they occasionally refer to as "argumentative situation," see Chaïm Perelman and L. Olbrechts-Tyteca, *The New Rhetoric: A Treatise on Argumentation* (trans. John Wilkinson and Purcell Weaver;

Nevertheless, Vatz claims a bit too much for his position over against Bitzer's. While it is true that events do not naturally bear meaning within themselves, it is also true that events do not occur outside of some preexisting context within which most observers at least recognize the importance of the events, even if they do not agree on their meaning. Vatz is correct, for example, that Winston Churchill did not discover crisis situations, as Bitzer claims, as much as his discourse created them.[48] On the other hand, it would be ludicrous to suggest that many of Churchill's "crises" were not already perceived by most Britons as important events worthy of their prime minister's attention and response—indeed as crises. The symbolic universe and social world of most mid-twentieth-century Britons provided the webs of significance (in Geertz's words) within which such events gained salience even before Churchill's pronouncements about them.

So it is, in a sense, with 1 Peter. If, as I assume, 1 Peter is an actual letter, then we can also assume that it must have exhibited enough points of contact with the social world and symbolic universe of its addressees to ensure that it was at least intelligible—if not necessarily persuasive—to them, that is, that it had a chance to fulfill its mission as a letter. If this starting point be granted, then, although we cannot simply read the letter as a window into the actual historical situation of its addressees, we can critically evaluate the various passages characterizing its addressees in light of both this particular letter as a whole and what we know about the socio-religious milieu of first-century Asia Minor in general.[49]

Nevertheless, in this study I am primarily interested in the rhetorical situation rather than in attempting to probe behind the

---

Notre Dame: University of Notre Dame Press, 1969) 1-26.

[48]Vatz, "Myth," 159.

[49]Cf. Perelman and Olbrechts-Tyteca's remarks on the relationship between audience and orator: "Every social circle or milieu is distinguishable in terms of its dominant opinions and unquestioned beliefs, of the premises that it takes for granted without hesitation: these views form an integral part of its culture, and an orator wishing to persuade a particular audience must of necessity adapt himself to it. Thus the particular culture of a given audience shows so strongly through the speeches addressed to it that we feel we can rely on them to a considerable extent for our knowledge of the character of past civilizations" (*New Rhetoric*, 21).

rhetorical situation to the actual situation of specific persons in Asia Minor. In the remainder of this monograph, therefore, when I refer to 1 Peter's addressees or intended readers/audience (and their antagonists), I have in mind not actual, historical individuals but the situation constructed by 1 Peter. This is not to say that a sharp distinction must be drawn between actual readers and the rhetorically constructed intended readers. Rather, it is to recognize that we must not assume a one-to-one correspondence between the situation depicted by the letter and any actual, historical persons and states of affairs in late-first-century Asia Minor. Just as I earlier employed the term "intended function" to refer to a description of what the letter appears to be trying to accomplish without making any claim about the intentions of the actual author of 1 Peter or about the effects of the letter upon any actual first-century readers, so the terms "intended readers/audience" and "addressees" will refer to the situation presupposed and addressed by the letter without making any claim about the correspondence between this situation and actual, historical circumstances in Asia Minor of the late first century.[50]

Geographical Area

First Peter is addressed to persons living in Pontus, Galatia, Cappadocia, Asia, and Bithynia (1:1). In light of (1) the preceding methodological reflections and (2) my earlier remarks concerning the figurative use of "Babylon" and the likelihood that "Peter" is a pseudonym, it would appear necessary to ask whether these place names are to be read literally or figuratively. To my knowledge, however, nobody has suggested that the names should not to be taken

---

[50]Cf. Thurén's three-part definition of the rhetorical situation: "The rhetorical situation consists of the picture of the audience which the author seems to presuppose, of the audiences's premises and expectations, and as a result thereof, of the intended effects of the text" (*Rhetorical Strategy*, 70-71). In this study, I take only the first two components of Thurén's definition as constitutive of the rhetorical situation. To the extent that the 1 Peter's characterization of its intended readers is already part of the answer to the problems the letter addresses, the third part of Thurén's definition is also presupposed in mine. For analytical purposes, however, I prefer to separate the letter's intended effects from the presupposed situation to which it addresses itself. The latter I call the rhetorical situation.

literally.⁵¹ The reason for the scholarly unanimity on this point is simple: It is difficult to conceive of a motive for addressing the letter to any groups other than its actual, intended readers—whether they are concretely known to the letter (or its writer) or not. As I shall argue below, the three-word phrase immediately preceding the place names—ἐκλεκτοῖς παρεπιδήμοις διασπορᾶς—is rife with metaphorical significance and serves both to characterize the intended readers' situation and to suggest a rationale for it in terms of the experience of the people of God in the LXX. The five place names, on the other hand, simply designate the regions in which these "diaspora" people reside.⁵²

Virtually all scholars today agree that these names designate Roman provinces rather than the older ethnic territories that gave the provinces their names.⁵³ These contiguous provinces (actually four in number, Pontus and Bithynia having been united as a single province in ca. 63 BCE) comprised an area of some 128,889 square miles, bordered on the north by the Black Sea, on the west by the Aegean Sea, and on the south and east by the Taurus mountains.⁵⁴ This portion of the Empire was characterized by tremendous diversity in almost every respect; there were forests and mountains, fertile plains and valleys, and virtually barren steppes; and regions differed widely as to their temperature ranges, annual rainfalls, and

---

⁵¹Elliott does rhetorically wonder why those scholars who take "diaspora" figuratively do not follow the logic of their position and take the five place names figuratively too (*Home*, 56-57 n. 81). What Elliott is objecting to here is not a figurative reading of "diaspora"—which he also adopts—but a particular kind of figurative reading—a spiritualizing reading in which the Petrine believers are viewed as scattered across the earth far from their true home in heaven.

⁵²Even Brox, who thinks that all the other names in the prescript and the closing—Peter, Silvanus, Mark, and Babylon—are part of the pseudepigraphical framework of the letter, does not read the place names of the adscript figuratively. He does think that 1 Peter's intended readers probably extended beyond the area covered by the named regions, but he does not argue that the five geographical names figuratively designate some other place (Brox, *Petrusbrief*, 26, 56; idem, *Rahmung*, 78-96).

⁵³One exception is Guthrie, *Introduction*, 792-93.

⁵⁴See Elliott, *Home*, 60; for the estimation of the total area of the provinces, Elliott cites T. R. S. Broughton, "Roman Asia Minor," *An Economic Survey of Ancient Rome* (ed. Tenney Frank; Baltimore: Johns Hopkins Press, 1938) 4. 812-16, esp. 815.

Suffering and Disgrace 59

seasonal changes. The diversity of the land, moreover, was matched by the diversity of its people;[55] many mountainous and heavily forested areas had few or no inhabitants, while the villages of the vast arable countryside were home to farmers and herders of numerous species of animals, and the cities, which were mainly on the western coast, were occupied by people of various social standings and professions, including artisans, business people, laborers, government officials, and slaves.[56]

Scores of religions claimed adherents in this part of Asia Minor, including several cults that originated here (among them Cybele, Sabazius, and Men), as well as Christianity and Judaism.[57] Jews had begun to arrive in Asia Minor in the third century BCE, and by the first century CE there were sizable Jewish communities throughout the area.[58] The clearest evidence for a considerable

---

[55] T. R. S. Broughton estimates the population of early-first-century Asia Minor at ca. 8,500,000 (Broughton, "Roman Asia Minor," 812-16; cited by Elliott, *Home*, 60). While Broughton thinks his estimate probably errs by being too low ("Roman Asia Minor," 815), Bo Reicke's estimate of 4,000,000 is less than Broughton's by one-half (Bo Reicke, *The New Testament Era: The World of the Bible from 500 B.C. to A.D. 100* [trans. David E. Green; Philadelphia: Fortress, 1968] 303; cited by Elliott, *Home*, 91 n. 14). Broughton acknowledges that the evidence is so scant that any general estimate "will have a very large margin of error, and perhaps is foolish to attempt" ("Roman Asia Minor," 814). Indeed, all such estimates must be taken with a grain of salt.

[56] For an extensive treatment of the social and economic life of the area, see Broughton, "Roman Asia Minor," 607-902. Cicero's characterization of the richness and diversity of the province of Asia in the middle of the first century BCE would have applied as well to the larger area of 1 Peter's address a century later: "Asia is so rich and fertile as easily to surpass all other countries in the productiveness of her soil, the variety of her crops, the extent of her pastures and the volume of her exports" (*De Imp. Cn. Pomp.* 14 [trans. H Grose Hodge (LCL)]; cited by David Magie, *Roman Rule in Asia Minor to the End of the Third Century after Christ* [2 vols.; Princeton: Princeton University Press, 1950] 1. 34).

[57] Schutter, *Hermeneutic*, 9, esp. n. 36. Illustrative of the religious diversity is the Bithynian city of Nicomedia, whose excavated coins testify to the worship of more than forty deities (Ramsay MacMullen, *Paganism in the Roman Empire* [New Haven/London: Yale University Press, 1981] 1).

[58] For the literary, inscriptional, and archaeological evidence, see Emil Schürer, *The History of the Jewish People in the Age of Jesus Christ (175 B.C.- A.D. 135)* (rev. ed.; rev. and ed. Geza Vermes, et al.; 3 vols.; Edinburgh: Clark, 1973-87) 3/1. 17-36; M. Stern, "The Jewish Diaspora," *The Jewish People in the First Century: Historical*

Christian presence in Asia Minor is provided by Pliny, in the case of the province of Bithynia-Pontus.[59] In his letter to Trajan (ca. 111), Pliny states that some of the individuals accused before him of being Christians insisted, under examination, that they had forsaken Christianity twenty years earlier (*Ep.* 10.96.7). Pliny's letter thus attests to a thriving Christian population whose origins must have predated his correspondence with Trajan by some two to three decades at least.[60] The book of Revelation and the letters of Ignatius also testify to the presence of Christian communities in Asia by the nineties.[61] As for the origins of these Christian communities, we know that Paul had evangelized parts of Asia and Galatia by the fifties and that Pauline believers, perhaps from Ephesus, had undertaken to evangelize the cities of Hierapolis, Laodicea, and Colossae in the Lycus valley, probably as early as the fifties. Whether other areas were missionized by Pauline Christians and/or

---

Geography, Political History, Social, Cultural and Religious Life and Institutions (ed. S. Safrai and M. Stern; CRINT; Philadelphia: Fortress, 1974) 1. 143-55. See also the less detailed sketches in E. Mary Smallwood, *The Jews under Roman Rule, from Pompey to Diocletian: A Study in Political Relations* (SJLA 20; 2d ed.; Leiden: Brill, 1981) 121-22; and Victor Tcherikover, *Hellenistic Civilization and the Jews* (trans. S. Applebaum; Philadelphia: Jewish Publication Society; Jerusalem: Magnes Press, Hebrew University, 1959) 287-89. Although Elliott estimates the Jewish population of Asia Minor at one million (Elliott, "Peter, First Epistle of," 273), it would be preferable to heed Stern's advice: "Undoubtedly the numerical strength of the Jews in the Roman Empire was considerable, but it is impossible to arrive at an actual estimate nor is there any firm basis for assessing their share in the total population of the Roman Empire" (Stern, "Jewish Diaspora," 122, see also 122 n. 4).

[59]Elliott cites Reicke's estimates of ca. 5,000 Christians in Asia Minor prior to 67 CE and ca. 80,000 by the turn of the century (Elliott, *Home*, 45, 63, 91 n. 14; citing Reicke, *New Testament Era*, 302-5). Placing the total population of Asia Minor at a constant 4 million, and extrapolating the growth and effects of Christianity from Pliny's remarks in his correspondence with Trajan, Reicke says of the end of the first century: "If the local pagans considered the Christians so ominous a factor, they can hardly have numbered less than a fiftieth of the total population of Asia Minor," i.e., ca. 80,000 (Reicke, *New Testament Era*, 303). Reicke's rationale for his figures is imaginative but highly suspect. Stern's caveat quoted above (p. 60 n. 58) applies, mutatis mutandis, here as well.

[60]So Michaels, *1 Peter*, lxvi.

[61]Goppelt, *1 Peter*, 6.

by others, however, is unknown.[62] What we do know is that this section of Asia Minor was home not only to gentiles of numerous religious beliefs but also to large numbers of Jews and Christians.

Ethnic Composition

For most of Christian history, scholars have debated whether the ἐκλεκτοῖς παρεπιδήμοις διασπορᾶς to whom the letter is addressed were of Jewish or gentile origin.[63] Those who held that the communities addressed were predominantly Jewish pointed to the abundance of LXX quotations and allusions in the letter, and took the word "diaspora" literally. The letter's explicit references to the recipients' pre-Christian lives, however, indicate that gentiles rather than Jews are envisioned (1:14-18; 4:3-4).[64] First Peter's immersion in the imagery and terminology of the LXX is best explained, therefore, not by recourse to a Jewish readership but by the influence of the LXX on early-Christian catechetical instruction, of which the readers would have had an intimate knowledge.[65] In addition, some

---

[62] Goppelt thinks that Christianity may well have spread as quickly from Galatia as it had up the Lycus valley from Ephesus, so that Bithynia, Cappadocia, and Pontus could have been reached by the sixties (Goppelt, *I Peter*, 5). Selwyn and Elliott may be correct in suggesting that Jews from Pontus and Cappadocia, who were converted to Christianity in Jerusalem at the church's first Pentecost (Acts 2:9-36), may have initiated Christian missions when they returned home (Elliott, *Home*, 64; Selwyn, *Epistle of St. Peter*, 46). These suggestions, while quite plausible, remain speculation.

[63] For a list of significant scholars throughout history who held that the addressees were exclusively Jewish and of those who thought that they were exclusively gentile see Wilhelm Steiger, *Exposition of the First Epistle of Peter* (trans. Patrick Fairbairn; Edinburgh: Clark, 1836) 19-20; German original, 1832; cited by T. Martin, *Metaphor and Composition*, 45. Already by 1832, Steiger could point to a number of scholars who held that the congregations addressed were *mixed*, and to at least one scholar—Guerike—who held that among these mixed congregations the majority was gentile.

[64] Steiger incisively states that the one passage in 1 Peter that "clearly designates the reader as having once been a heathen" is 4:3 (*Exposition*, 20-21; cited by T. Martin, *Metaphor and Composition*, 45 n. 15). 1:14 may also be cited in light of 1:18 and 4:3-4. See, e.g., Kelly, *Epistles of Peter*, 4; Michaels, *1 Peter*, xlvi. I am reticent to join Kelly in including in this list 2:9-10 and 3:5-6, passages which seem to me to have more to do with the letter's proposal than the recipients' situation.

[65] See Selwyn, *Epistle of St. Peter*, 43.

scholars suggest the presence of former proselytes to Judaism and/or God-fearers, whose attachment to the synagogues had familiarized them with the Jewish scriptures.[66] In recent years, therefore, most critics have championed the view that the communities were comprised predominantly of gentile believers—including former God-fearers—with a small minority of Jewish Christians as well.[67]

In my view, the presence of Jewish Christians and gentile God-fearers among 1 Peter's intended audience cannot be deduced from the letter itself (unless one mistakes the LXX citations and imagery as evidence for a Jewish audience) but must be inferred from (1) the Jewish diaspora of Asia Minor and (2) the pervasive contact between Judaism and Christianity as depicted, for example, in Acts.[68] That is to say, a distinction must be made between the actual, historical communities, which almost certainly did include some Jewish Christians and former God-fearers, and the addressees of the letter, who are gentiles. Furthermore, militating against the possibility that God-fearers numbered among these gentiles, 1 Pet 1:14-19 and 4:3-4 attribute the behavioral changes that engendered the addressees' suffering not to any pre-Christian adoption of Jewish worship and lifestyle but to their conversion to Christianity. In 1:18, 1 Peter designates its readers' previous way of life as ἀναστροφὴ

---

[66]Elliott, *Home*, 66; Kelly, *Epistles of Peter*, 5. Since I am interested in ethnic identity here, scholars who assume the presence of proselytes to Judaism and those who assume the presence of gentile God-fearers can be grouped together. The debate among these scholars is whether the terms φοβούμενοι τὸν θεόν (Acts 10:2, 22, 35; 13:16, 26) and σεβόμενοι (τὸν θεόν) (Acts 13:50; 16:14; 17:4, 17; 18:7; Josephus *Ant.* 14 § 110) refer to proselytes or to some other category of people who worshiped the God of Israel. On the phenomenon of God-fearers who were not full proselytes but attended Jewish synagogal worship and observed many of the Jewish laws, see Paula Fredriksen, "Judaism, the Circumcision of Gentiles, and Apocalyptic Hope: Another Look at Galatians 1 and 2," *JTS* n.s. 42 (1991) 540-48; Schürer, *History*, 3/1. 161-71.

[67]E.g., Elliott, Home, 65; Goppelt, *1 Peter*, 6; Michaels, *1 Peter*, xlvi; Kelly, *Epistles of Peter*, 4; Schelkle, *Petrusbriefe*, 2; Schutter, *Hermeneutic*, 9-10; Selwyn, *Epistle of St. Peter*, 44; Spicq, *Les épîtres*, 13.

[68]Contra Elliott, who appeals to the large Jewish diaspora of Asia Minor; to the rapid spread of Christianity, which he attributes to early gains among diaspora Jews; to LXX allusions; and to terms common to Christian and Jewish missionary propaganda in support of his contention that people of Jewish extraction were abundantly represented in the letter's audience (*Home*, 45-46, 55-56 n. 77, 66).

πατροπαράδοτος. The adjective πατροπαράδοτος derives from Hellenistic Greek rhetoric, where it was used positively to indicate that which was traditional and, as such, venerable and trustworthy. First Peter, however, evaluates traditional gentile behavior quite negatively as μάταια (1:18), in stark contrast to the new behavior appropriate to Christian faith (1:15, 17; 2:12; 3:1-2, 16).[69] The words μάταια (in 1:18) and ἄγνοια (in 1:14), used to characterize the former way of life of the intended readers and their forebears, reflect the typical Jewish condemnation of gentile idolatry found in the LXX (e.g., Wis 14:22; Hos 5:11; Isa 2:20; Jer 10:25) and later adapted for Christian missionary propaganda (see Acts 14:15; 17:30; Eph 4:18; 1 Thess 4:5).[70] Indeed, idolatry is one of the gentile vices proscribed in 4:4. Despite the address to Christians scattered throughout most of Asia Minor, therefore, the body of the letter shows that gentile Christians alone are the intended audience.[71] This is not to say that 1 Peter's orientation to gentiles represents a rhetorical strategy designed to exclude Jewish Christians from the letter's readership but only that 1 Peter depicts the origin of the problem addressed as an *intragentile* conflict: It is nonbelieving gentiles who are reviling believing gentiles because the latter have adopted a strange, new religion along with its antisocial lifestyle.

---

[69]W. C. van Unnik, "The Critique of Paganism in 1 Peter 1:18," *Neotestamentica et Semitica: Studies in Honour of Matthew Black* (ed. E. Earle Ellis and Max Wilcox; Edinburgh: Clark, 1969) 129-34, 140.

[70]Schutter, *Hermeneutic*, 10, esp. n. 41; cf. Horst Balz, "μάταιος," *Exegetical Dictionary of the New Testament*, vol. 2 (ed. Horst Balz and Gerhard Schneider; Grand Rapids: Eerdmans, 1991) 396; Goppelt, *I Peter*, 109-10; Selwyn, *Epistle of St. Peter*, 145.

[71]Cf. Best, *I Peter*, 19-20; Schutter, *Hermeneutic*, 9-10. Michaels's position is not entirely consistent: He argues that the letter was written to Christians who were "not Jewish by either birth, circumcision, or full legal observance" (*1 Peter*, liii), but he stops short of urging that the intended audience was exclusively non-Jewish, saying that "1 Peter was written primarily to Gentile Christians" (*1 Peter*, xlvi). Similarly, Feldmeier says that 1:18 and 4:3 cannot refer to a Jewish past and yet he too allows for some Jews among the intended readers (*Christen als Fremde*, 199). Beare, on the other hand, does not equivocate: "It is clear that First Peter is addressed to people who had been converted to Christianity from paganism" (*Epistle of Peter*, 74). Given the plurality of religions and of ethnic groups in first-century Asia Minor, it would be an exercise in futility to try to identify the religious backgrounds or to specify the ethnic origins of these gentiles.

The contradiction between the inclusive adscript of 1:1 and the orientation to gentiles elsewhere must have threatened to undermine the letter whenever it was read in a mixed congregation. In rhetorical-critical terms, the audience constructed by the letter was inadequate to the actual audience.[72] It would appear that at least three possibilities were open to Jewish Christian readers of 1 Peter. (1) They might have found the letter unintelligible. This reaction was probably not widespread since the gentile-specific passages are too few to obscure the message of the bulk of the letter. (2) They might have identified themselves with gentile Christians, figuratively becoming gentiles by taking such passages as 1:14-19 and 4:3-4 as applicable to their own history as well as to the history of their gentile fellow believers. This option would appear to be no more likely for the majority of Jewish Christian readers than the first. Given the disputes among Jews, Jewish Christians, and gentile Christians over who represented the authentic legacy of God's people Israel in the first century CE (as reflected in Matthew, Luke-Acts, John, Galatians, and Romans), it is unlikely that the Jewish Christians of Asia Minor would have readily consigned their religious heritage to the same judgment leveled at gentile idolatry. (3) A more likely response would have been to steer a middle course, finding points of contact in such images as the elect aliens of the diaspora (1:1) and the holy priesthood (2:5), while reading 1:14-19 and 4:3-4 as applicable only to gentile Christians.

Social Stratum

In *A Home for the Homeless*, John H. Elliott subjected 1 Peter to a thorough examination in light of the social, economic, and political world of first-century Asia Minor as reconstructed from archaeological and literary evidence as well as secondary sources. Elliott thereby set the terms for the subsequent debate, and *A Home for the Homeless* remains the preeminent treatment of the subject.[73]

---

[72]See Perelman and Olbrechts-Tyteca, *New Rhetoric*, 19-20.

[73]In addition to Elliott, the most important work is: Armand Puig Tàrrech, "Le milieu de la premiére épître de Pierre," *Revista Catalana de Teologia* 5 (1980) 95-129, 331-402. Tàrrech's essay is dated a year earlier than Elliott's *Home*, but was originally

I shall begin my analysis of the social standing of 1 Peter's addressees, therefore, with an extended critique of Elliott's work.

The starting point of Elliott's study is his correlation of the terms πάροικος and οἶκος (τοῦ θεοῦ).[74] Given the book's title—*A Home for the Homeless*—it almost goes without saying that Elliott views the οἶκος motif as the primary vehicle for the letter's message to its addressees. He sees the πάροικος motif with its related terminology (especially παρεπίδημος), on the other hand, as reflecting the actual, legal social standing of the addressees.[75] Elliott devotes virtually all of his first chapter (covering thirty-eight pages) to the significance of 1 Peter's application of the words πάροικοι and παροικία to its readers, arguing that the addressees were literally resident aliens (πάροικοι) and visiting strangers (παρεπίδημοι) in Asia Minor.[76]

Chapter 2, building on the foundation laid in chapter 1, provides a social profile of the addressees. Most of the evidence

---

written for a course Elliott taught in the spring of 1978—shortly after the first draft of *Home* was already completed—and was revised in light of Elliott's criticisms; moreover, Elliott only mentions Tàrrech's work in the introduction to the 1990 paperback edition of *Home*. I shall, therefore, treat Tàrrech's essay as chronologically later than Elliott's *Home*. Two full-length monographs whose titles seem to indicate a greater interest in this subject than the volumes actually exhibit are: Friedrich Schröger, *Gemeinde im 1. Petrusbrief: Untersuchungen zum Selbstverständnis einer christlichen Gemeinde an der Wende vom 1. zum 2. Jahrhundert* (Schriften der Universität Passau, Reihe katholische Theologie 1; Passau: Passavia Universitätsverlag, 1981); and Marie-Louise Lamau, *Des chrétiens dans le monde: Communautés pétriniennes au Ier siècle* (LD 134; Paris: Cerf, 1988). Schröger's *Gemeinde*, which appeared the same year as Elliott's *Home*, deals with "community" in 1 Peter almost exclusively from the perspective of theological ideas. Schröger devotes only a few pages to the setting of the Petrine addressees, where he inquires into the origin and nature of their suffering in light of what is known from other sources about Christian suffering in the first two centuries (*Gemeinde*, 157-59); see Elliott's review in *CBQ* 45 (1983) 705-6. Lamau's 1988 work also deals only briefly with the sociohistorical situation addressed. Lamau thinks Elliott is wrong to insist that such terms as διασπορά and παροικία are used by 1 Peter as technical, socioeconomic terms (81), but her position is otherwise similar to Elliott's: the addressees were rurally situated, relatively poor people, probably tenant farmers and slaves (97-99). Unlike Elliott, she does not provide much argumentation in support of her construction of the addressees.

[74]Elliott, *Home*, 23.
[75]Elliott, *Home*, 23, 48-49, 231-32.
[76]Elliott, *Home*, 48.

cited here for the legal, economic, and social status of the addressees derives not from the text of 1 Peter but from external literary and archaeological sources concerning Asia Minor in general and πάροικοι in particular, as Elliott himself acknowledges:

> Such is a description of the legal, economic and social condition of the addressees based on their identification as *paroikoi*.... The *occupations* of the addressees may be surmised from those of the *paroikoi* of Asia Minor in general and from what is known of the land's natural resources and related industries.... Information from 1 Peter on the economic condition of the addressees is, at best, inferential.[77]

The text of 1 Peter can only supply "further correlative detail" to the portrait of the addressees that Elliott sketches based on his identification of them as literal resident aliens and visiting strangers.[78] The passages he cites from 1 Peter, however, although providing some correlation, do not offer much corroboration.

First, Elliott points to the contrast between the letter's exhortation to social distinctiveness (e.g., 1:3, 14-16, 18-19; 2:11; 4:2-4) and its call for civic responsibility (2:12, 13-17; 3:15-16; 4:15-16) as evidence of the addressees' "in-between" status legally and socially.[79] The question, however, is not whether the addressees were in a precarious "in-between" position socially; that much is understood by all interpreters of the letter. The question is whether the addressees were *literally and legally* παρεπίδημοι and πάροικοι. Elliott begs the question here, taking the letter's religiously motivated exhortations to certain kinds of public behavior as evidence for a particular legal social position of the addressees.

Second, Elliott asks whether the addressees were located in rural or urban settings. The predominantly rural character of the provinces addressed and the rural metaphors used in the letter suggest to Elliott a mostly rural population. In a similar fashion, Armand Puig Tàrrech, a former student of Elliott, points to 1 Peter's

---

[77]Elliott, *Home*, 69-70.
[78]Elliott, *Home*, 69.
[79]Elliott, *Home*, 69.

rural metaphors and to the largely rural location of Asia Minor's *peregrini* as evidence that 1 Peter's addressees were rurally situated.[80] The mostly rural location of the *peregrini*, of course, is only significant if one grants that the addressees were actually from the social stratum of *peregrini*. In any case, neither the mostly rural location of *peregrini* nor the predominantly rural nature of the provinces addressed is a correlative detail from the letter; both are drawn from external sources concerning Asia Minor. As for the alleged rural character of 1 Peter's metaphors, Frederick W. Danker points out that "agrarian metaphors are stock-in-trade for the most urbanized Roman authors and their urbanized auditors"; Paul's letters to Corinth and to Rome are cases in point (see, e.g., Romans 11; 1 Cor 3:8-9; 9:7-11; 15:23, 37-39, 42-44; 2 Cor 9:6-10).[81] Moreover, 1 Peter is not particularly rich in "rural metaphors." In chap. 1, for example, the metaphors of the diaspora (1:1), rebirth (1:3, 23), the purification of gold by fire (1:7), childlike obedience (1:14), ransom (1:18), the impermanence of silver and gold (1:18), and the sacrificial lamb (1:19) are hardly "rural metaphors."[82] Nor is the image of the lion stalking its prey (5:8) an "obviously rural metaphor";[83] to quote Danker again, "lions were more likely to be seen in First Peter's time in the arenas located in large urban centers. Moreover, Greek writers of comedy and tragedy mention lions and other voracious animals in their dramas, which are designed for urban constituencies."[84]

---

[80]Tàrrech, "Le milieu," 97, 106-7, 395-6, esp. 107 n. 28.

[81]Frederick W. Danker, review of *A Home for the Homeless: A Sociological Exegesis of 1 Peter, Its Situation and Strategy*, by John H. Elliott, *Int* 37 (1983) 87.

[82]Tàrrech argues that the word σπορά in 1:23 and the quotation in 1:24-25 of Isa 40:6-8 combine to form "une image agricole *globale*," an "analogie fort connue et compréhensible" to the rural addressees ("Le milieu," 336). The extended metaphor of which σπορά forms an integral part, however, is not agricultural but reproductive; it begins in 1:3, continues in 1:23, and concludes in 2:2-3. Isa 40:6-8 is invoked only to demonstrate the permanence and vitality of the word of God, which is the means by which their rebirth ἐκ σπορᾶς . . . ἀφθάρτου was accomplished. Not only is the σπορά metaphor not primarily agricultural, but even the agricultural aspect of 1:23-25 does not necessarily presuppose a rural background for intelligibility, since it comes directly from the Isaiah 40.

[83]Elliott, *Home*, 63; similarly, Tàrrech, "Le milieu," 343-44.

[84]Danker, review of *Home*, 87.

Elliott then cites the reference to οἰκέται in 2:18-20 as evidence for at least some urban members, only to negate this assertion two sentences later where he points out that household servants were also to be found on country estates. He concludes that the explicit appeal to household servants and the paradigmatic function this appeal plays in the letter indicate that, whether rural or urban, "the communities addressed were those of households."[85] In other words, the address to οἰκέται provides no help in determining whether the addressees were rustics or urbanites but only indicates that they were members of households—which is not saying much, since virtually everyone in the Mediterranean world of late antiquity was a member of an οἰκία, however small. In short, the letter offers virtually no clues as to whether its intended recipients were located in the country, in the cities, or both.

Third, Elliott correctly notes that little can be deduced about the social, economic, and political status from the specific recipients addressed in 2:16 (ἐλεύθεροι), 3:1-6 (wives of unbelievers), 3:7 (husbands), 5:1-4 (πρεσβύτεροι), and 5:5 (νεώτεροι). He does make two suggestions: (1) "A modicum of wealth" may be indicated in 3:3; but (2) the absence of any word to slave owners in 2:19-20 appears to point to "a generally inferior economic position of the addressees as was characteristic of *paroikoi* on the whole."[86] First Peter 3:3 and 2:19-20, however, are susceptible to other interpretations as well. Elliott might have strengthened his case by noting that the stereotypical nature of the exhortation in 3:3 to women should caution against taking it too literally;[87] moreover, Marie-Louise Lamau points out that in traditional societies, "la coiffure et les vêtements féminins peuvent relever de coutumes locales et faire appel plus à l'ingéniosité et à l'entraide entre femmes qu'à la

---

[85]Elliott, *Home*, 69.

[86]Elliott, *Home*, 70.

[87]See Balch, *Wives*, 101-3. Achtemeier points out the similarity between the language of 1 Pet 3:1-4 and Isa 3:18 but fails to demonstrate that "the source of the material addressed to the wives is anything but Hellenistic" ("Newborn Babes," 221). Whether the source is Isaiah or Greco-Roman social theory, however, the injunction in 1 Pet 3:3 is stereotypical and so should not be used as evidence for the economic status of the women addressed.

richesse."[88] The absence of any exhortation to slave owners is probably the strongest "correlative detail" Elliott cites in chapter 2. This argument from silence, however, can only function as a correlative detail for a thesis well established on other grounds. A scarcity of slave owners does not necessarily indicate that a given community was comprised of poor, rural πάροικοι and παρεπίδημοι. Furthermore, the absence of any mention of slave owners could be attributed to the letter's rhetorical strategy of casting the Christian addressees in the role of slaves badly treated by their non-Christian owners.[89] Neither 3:3 nor 2:19-20, therefore, provides much help in constructing a social profile of the addressees.

Finally, Elliott sees depicted in 4:3 the kind of behavior characteristic of industrial guilds and traders' associations. In light of the predominance of "the working proletariat" among the πάροικοι of Asia Minor, Elliott sees 4:3 as evidence that the addressees were part of this labor class.[90] The language of 4:3, however, reflects the stereotyped vice lists of Jewish, Christian, and Hellenistic moral exhortation[91] and so should not be taken as evidence—even as correlative evidence—for former involvement in guilds and associations.[92]

---

[88]Lamau, "Des chrétiens," 99.

[89]Lamau, "Des chrétiens," 98; cf. Danker, review of *Home*, 88. Schutter suggests that the absence of a directive to slave owners may be attributed to the superior social position slave owners enjoyed, which would have precluded their suffering the hardships endured by the poorer members of the communities (*Hermeneutic*, 11 n. 48). Schutter's suggestion is plausible, but we simply do not have sufficient data either to confirm or to refute it. I want to argue, however, that the failure to mention slave owners means that they are not part of the audience constructed by the letter (whether or not slave owners were among the actual communities who received the letter). Just as there probably were Jews among the actual readers, so there may have been slave owners among them as well.

[90]Elliott, *Home*, 70.

[91]Goppelt, *I Peter*, 284-85, esp. n. 34; Michaels, *1 Peter*, 231-32; Selwyn, *Epistle of St. Peter*, 211-12.

[92]Danker cites several inscriptions that seem to indicate a more subdued style of celebration among the associations (review of *Home*, 86). Nevertheless, there is ample evidence that some—if not most—labor and professional guilds engaged in quite rowdy behavior, not unlike that decried in 1 Pet 4:3. See Ramsay MacMullen, *Enemies of the Roman Order: Treason, Unrest, and Alienation in the Empire* (Cambridge: Harvard University Press, 1966) 173-78, 341-44 nn. 14-17.

What all of this means is that Elliott's description, in chapter 2 of *A Home for the Homeless*, of the social, economic, and political status of 1 Peter's addressees is almost entirely dependent on his prior identification of them as παρεπίδημοι and πάροικοι in the technical, legal sense, in chapter 1. It remains, therefore, to take a close look at the argument of that chapter.

Elliott begins by stating that the term πάροικος was used in two senses in late antiquity. In its general sense, πάροικος denoted "strangers, foreigners, aliens, people who are not at home, or who lack native roots, in the language, customs, culture, or political, social, and religious allegiances of the people among whom they dwell." The πάροικοι were the displaced and dislocated.[93] (Elliott fails to note that πάροικος was also used in a still more general sense to designate a resident of a given locale, a neighbor, or even a settlement or colony.)[94] Much more frequently, says Elliott, πάροικοι was used in a specific, political-legal sense. When he assays to define this political-legal sense, however, Elliott actually offers two different definitions and then vacillates between them for the remainder of the book, sometimes referring to one or the other and sometimes conflating the two.

Elliott's first definition of the technical, legal sense of the term comes from Karl Ludwig Schmidt and Martin Anton Schmidt, who say that παροικία denotes "the state, position or fate of a resident alien, 'dwelling abroad' without civil or native rights."[95] This definition identifies the technical, legal use of πάροικοι in terms of geographical displacement. A few lines later in the same paragraph, however, Elliott offers another definition, this one based on Hans Schaefer's summary of the literary and inscriptional evidence: "*Paroikoi* . . . constituted a politically recognized institution of the state and a registered stratum of the population which was distinguished legally and socially from the superior full citizens, on the

---

[93]Elliott, *Home*, 24.
[94]Feldmeier, *Christen als Fremde*, 12.
[95]Elliott, *Home*, 25; quoting Karl Ludwig Schmidt and Martin Anton Schmidt, "πάροικος, παροικία, παροικέω," *TDNT* 5. 842.

Suffering and Disgrace

one hand, and the inferior transient strangers, on the other."[96] Here πάροικοι is defined in terms of noncitizenship rather than geographic displacement. The πάροικοι, in Schaefer's definition, were those noncitizens who were of higher social standing than transients. For the most part, Elliott treats these two definitions of the legal sense of πάροικοι as synonymous.[97] When he does note the distinction between the two, he takes the notion of displacement as primary: "Since impermanent residence also affected political status, the Greek *paroikos* and its Latin equivalent *peregrinus* were the conventional terms used to designate the rank and class of the noncitizen."[98] As the following discussion will show, however, geographic dislocation was not the essence of the legal sense of πάροικοι in late antiquity. Whatever the origin of the legal use of the terms, in the first century CE πάροικοι and *peregrini*, as technical terms, had to do first of all with citizenship.

The problem stems from Elliott's adoption of K. L. and M. A. Schmidt's definition of *the LXX use* of παροικία as the starting point for his discussion of the technical, *legal use* of πάροικος current in the first century CE.[99] Although Schmidt and Schmidt recognize that πάροικος as a first-century technical term basically meant noncitizen, they assume that the πάροικοι referred to in secular literature and inscriptions were always nonnatives as well as noncitizens.[100] In the LXX the word does refer to nonnatives, that is,

---

[96]Elliott, *Home*, 25; citing Hans Schaefer, "Paroikoi," PW 18/4. 1698. See also Elliott, *Home*, 68.

[97]E.g., Elliott quotes a section from Michael Rostovtzeff's *The Social and Economic History of the Roman Empire* ([2d ed.; revised by P. M. Fraser; 2 vols.; Oxford: Clarendon, 1957] 1. 255-57) in which Rostovtzeff explicitly says that the πάροικοι or κάτοικοι under discussion are "natives" (*Home*, 26), and in the very next paragraph characterizes the evidence for πάροικοι in terms of "the situation and the political, legal, and social and religious conditions of living abroad as resident aliens" (*Home*, 27). Here the Schmidt-and-Schmidt definition of the LXX usage controls Elliott's reading of Rostovtzeff's definition.

[98]Elliott, *Home*, 36.

[99]It is no wonder, therefore, that, when he turns to the LXX, Elliott finds the meaning of πάροικοι to be consistent with its use in the secular sources, designating "the situation and the political, legal, and social and religious conditions of living abroad as resident aliens" (*Home*, 27).

[100]K. L. Schmidt and M. A.Schmidt, "πάροικος," 842.

resident aliens—whether literally or figuratively—but such is not necessarily the case in Hellenistic Greek literature and inscriptions. What was decisive in those contexts was not whether one was native to an area or not but whether one was a citizen. The words πάροικοι, κάτοικοι, and *peregrini* could all be used more or less synonymously in this technical, legal sense to denote noncitizens.[101] The πάροικοι were "eine Bevölkerungsschicht, die nicht dem Vollbürgertum zugerechnet wird, aber auch nicht zu den Fremden gehört, sondern zwischen diesen beiden Gegensätzen in der Mitte steht."[102] The κάτοικοι were "die Bewohner von unselbständigen Ortschaften ohne Stadtrecht . . . in hellenistischer Zeit."[103] The *peregrinus* "ist der Freie, der nicht römischer Bürger ist. . . . Der Gegensatz zu *p[eregrinus]* ist *civis.*"[104] These three words were not always used synonymously; nor did they always bear this technical meaning. The important point here is that when either πάροικος or *peregrinus* was used in a *technical* sense in antiquity, what it denoted was *noncitizenship.*[105]

Many—probably most—first-century-CE πάροικοι/*peregrini*, in this technical sense, were native to the regions in which they lived; they were πάροικοι/*peregrini* not as a result of physical relocation but due to their relationship to the political powers of the day. Prior

---

[101]Elliott correctly notes that πάροικοι eventually displaced μέτοικοι in Asia Minor in the Hellenistic period, and that *peregrini* often functioned, in effect, as the Latin equivalent of πάροικοι (*Home*, 25, 36); see H. Hommel, "Metoikoi," PW 15/2. 1420; Schaefer, "Paroikoi," 1695-6, 1706-7. The older term μέτοικοι, however, appears have conveyed the idea of foreignness more frequently than do the words πάροικοι, κάτοικοι, and *peregrini*. On the limited interchangeability of these terms, see Rostovtzeff, *History* 1. 249-50, 255-56, 346-47; and Tcherikover, *Hellenistic Civilization*, 26-27. For a well-articulated caveat against assuming that πάροικοι and μέτοικοι were always interchangeable, see Philippe Gauthier, "Métèques, périèques et *paroikoi*: Bilan et points d'interrogation." *l'Etranger dans le monde grec* (ed. Raoul Lonis; Nancy: Presses Universitaries de Nancy, 1988) 23-46; and, following Gauthier, Feldmeier, *Christen als Fremde*, 13-14.

[102]Schaefer, "Paroikoi," 1698.

[103]F. Oertel, "Katoikoi," PW 11/1. 2.

[104]B. Kübler, "Peregrinus," PW 19/1. 639. Cf. G. Humbert, "Peregrinus," *Dictionnaire des antiquités grecques et romaines* (ed. Ch. Daremberg and Edmond Saglio; Paris: Librairie Hachette, n.d.) 14/1. 389.

[105]Cf. Feldmeier, *Christen als Fremde*, 15.

Suffering and Disgrace

to Roman rule, those who lived outside the Greek cities of Asia Minor and elsewhere had no part in the administrative affairs of the cities and were considered not to be municipal citizens; they were not mere strangers (ξένοι), nor were they visitors (παρεπιδημοῦντες ξένοι or παρεπίδημοι), but neither were they citizens (πολῖται).[106] Subsequently, most of those in the Roman provinces of Asia Minor who had been considered noncitizens from the Greek perspective remained noncitizens—*peregrini*—from the Roman point of view.[107] Of course, πάροικοι as a technical term could also refer to nonnative residents of a locale, just as it did, in less technical fashion, in the LXX; Schaefer, in fact, explains that a long-term nonnative resident could be transferred from ξένος to πάροικος status, just as the state could grant πάροικος status to slaves, freed persons, and other lower-class individuals.[108] The important point here is that the terms πάροικοι and *peregrini*—as technical terms—were not simply legal designations for resident aliens but denoted a recognized social stratum *that included both native and nonnative residents* who were not full citizens and so did not possess the rights of citizenship.[109]

---

[106]See, e.g., *OGIS* 339.28-30 (differentiating between οἱ πολῖται, οἱ ἄλλοι οἱ κατοικοῦντες τὴν πόλιν, and οἱ παρεπιδημοῦντες ξένοι); cf. *OGIS* 268.9; 329.28. Of course the participial form of παροικέω could also be used to modify ξένος (as in Diodorus Siculus *Bib. hist.* 13.47.4 [differentiating between πολῖται and παροικοῦντες ξένοι]). For a number of different combinations, see the inscriptions quoted in Schaefer, "Paroikoi," 1695-98, 1702, 1706. The flexibility of the various terms prevents one from drawing too rigid a distinction between them in the abstract. Each individual case must be examined on its own, with special attention to the distinctions made within each document or inscription.

[107]See Broughton, "Roman Asia Minor," 632-40; Rostovtzeff, *History*, 1. 249-50, 255-56.

[108]Schaefer, "Paroikoi," 1698. For more on Roman citizenship in the early Principate, provincial *peregrini*, and the processes by which individual *peregrini* and peregrine communities could become Roman citizens, see Adrian N. Sherwin-White, *The Roman Citizenship* (2d ed.; Oxford: Clarendon, 1973) 221-74, 337-59; and idem, "The Roman Citizenship: A Survey of Its Development into a World Franchise," *ANRW* I/2. 23-58, esp. 40-55; see also A. H. M. Jones, *Studies in Roman Government and Law* (Oxford: Blackwell, 1960) 129-49.

[109]Feldmeier correctly says of Elliott that "die von ihm einseitig favorisierte Bedeutung von πάροικος als schichtenspezifischer Terminus im römischen Reich für diese Zeit gerade nicht (mehr) nachgewiesen werden kann" (*Christen als Fremde*, 206-7). Feldmeier would not, however, exclude the possibility that the παροικ- word

Elliott's contention that 1 Peter's addressees were nonnative residents and visiting strangers in Asia Minor, therefore, is not warranted by the evidence for the first-century-CE technical use of the words πάροικοι, παρεπίδημοι, and *peregrini*. In this regard, Tàrrech, beginning from the same point of departure as Elliott's, argues a stronger case. Like Elliott, Tàrrech contends that the addressees were literally *peregrini*. Tàrrech, however, acknowledges that a *peregrinus*, while not necessarily a literal pilgrim, was certainly a noncitizen.[110] Interestingly, had Elliott recognized that the primary technical use of πάροικοι had to do with noncitizenship rather than foreignness, his thesis would have been strengthened in one respect: He would not have had to argue the highly implausible position that the addressees were literally displaced persons in order to demonstrate that, as πάροικοι and παρεπίδημοι, they lacked the social position and legal rights of citizens. Nevertheless, even the thesis that the addressees were literally πάροικοι/*peregrini*, on which Elliott and Tàrrech both insist, is not supported by the evidence, as I shall now demonstrate.

(1) In the first place, the addressees are explicitly called παρεπίδημοι in 1:1. Elliott devotes several pages to the significance of 1 Peter's use of the words πάροικοι and παροικία, but only a few lines to the adscript of 1:1. If the παροικ- word group is

---

group *could* have been used in a technical sense in the first century CE. He argues that such a usage (a *rechtlichen Terminus* [12]) is found earlier in Diodorus Siculus *Bib. hist.* 13.47.4 (ca. 305 BCE) (see above, p. 73 n. 106) and may be reflected in Dio Chrysostom *Or.* 46.12 (13 n. 31). He rightly cautions, however, that, given the scant evidence, it is not clear to what extent the word group functioned in the first century as a legal term denoting a "stadtrechtlichen Kategorie im engeren Sinn" (14). He concludes that, during this time, πάροικος designated a noncitizen (15). In the preceding pages, I have granted that a technical use of the παροικ- family was current in the first century CE, a use analogous both to the technical sense of the word group in Diodorus Siculus and to the later use of the Latin *peregrinus*. I have argued neither that a legal, technical use of the παροικ- family was *widespread* in the first century CE nor that, when used in a technical sense, the παροικ- family denoted a specific, universally recognized, legally defined social stratum. What I have insisted is that, when the παροικ- family was used in a technical sense in the first century, it denoted not literal foreignness but noncitizenship. On this point Feldmeier's thesis and mine are in essential agreement.

[110]Tàrrech, "Le milieu," 101-7.

used in the technical, legal sense by 1 Peter, one might ask Elliott, how can the letter address its πάροικοι readers as παρεπίδημοι in 1:1? As Elliott acknowledges, the technical senses of the two words are not synonymous. Whereas πάροικοι were noncitizens (and possibly nonnatives), παρεπίδημοι were transients temporarily resident in a given locale.[111] Elliott takes the combination of πάροικοι and παρεπίδημοι in 2:11 literally: The readers are identified legally as "resident aliens with specified limited rights and status" (πάροικοι) and more generally as "temporary visitors, transients, immigrants or wanderers" (παρεπίδημοι).[112] That is to say, he recognizes two distinct groups in this combination in 2:11. Both groups, he would apparently have us believe, are addressed with the single term παρεπίδημοι in 1:1. By Elliott's own logic, however, this phenomenon suggests that παρεπίδημοι is being used in 1:1 not as a strictly delimited technical term but quite loosely— perhaps even metaphorically: It is not merely visiting strangers who are addressed in 1 Peter but people who can be designated either simply as παρεπίδημοι (as they are in 1:1) or as both πάροικοι and παρεπίδημοι (as in 2:11).[113]

(2) Other considerations, moreover, point to a figurative use not only of παρεπίδημοι in 1:1 but also of παροικία in 1:17 and of both παρεπίδημοι and πάροικοι in 2:11. The most obvious place to begin is with the other terms in the adscript. The addressees are not simply παρεπίδημοι but ἐκλεκτοὶ παρεπίδημοι διασπορᾶς. Taking the last word first, διασπορά is found only once outside of Jewish and Christian literature (i.e., in Plutarch),[114]

---

[111]See K. L. and M. A. Schmidt's distinction: "The πάροικος is not a παρεπίδημος, who lives in a place for only a short time, but a resident alien ("πάροικος," 842). Similarly, Walter Grundmann defines παρεπίδημος as "one who is (temporarily) resident in a place as an alien" (Walter Grundmann, "δῆμος, ἐκδημέω, ἐνδημέω," *TDNT* 2. 64). This is not to say that the words could not be used somewhat loosely as synonyms, but only that as technical terms they seem to denote two distinct social positions.

[112]Elliott, *Home*, 36.

[113]Cf. Bruce W. Winter, *Seek the Welfare of the City: Christians as Benefactors and Citizens* (Grand Rapids: Eerdmans; Carlisle, England: Paternoster, 1994) 16 n. 13.

[114]Plutarch characterizes Epicurus's dissolution of the soul as a "διασπορά into emptiness and atoms" (*Mor.* 1105A [trans. Benedict Einarson and Phillip H. De Lacy

which means that with this word we are clearly in the realm of early-Jewish terminology rather than the Greco-Roman legal language about citizenship. In eleven of the twelve occurrences of the term in the LXX—as well as in *Pss. Sol.* 8:28 and 9:2 and *T. Ash.* 7:2—διασπορά is a technical term referring to the dispersion of the Jews or to the Jews in the dispersion.[115] Already in Dan 12:2, furthermore, the technical term is appropriated as a metaphor; one of three post-resurrection conditions is here called διασπορὰ καὶ αἰσχύνη αἰώνιος (as opposed to ζωὴ αἰώνιος and ὀνειδισμός).[116]

Turning to the NT, John 7:35 uses διασπορά in the literal sense of the Jewish diaspora, while in Jas 1:1 and 1 Pet 1:1, the word is used metaphorically in reference to Christians, as virtually all modern commentators note and even Elliott admits, although not in so many words.[117] Elliott insists that the literal sense of διασπορά as a scattering of persons beyond the land of Palestine continues to apply in both Jas 1:1 and 1 Pet 1:1.[118] Strictly speaking, however, even this sense is metaphorical, since διασπορά as a technical term refers to the *Jewish* dispersion. Elliott, moreover, is forced to acknowledge that, alongside this alleged literal sense of the word, διασπορά in 1 Pet 1:1 conveys a "further historical and religious aspect" of the addressees' situation and indicates "their religious identity and roots as well as their social condition of displacement." He is loath to acknowledge that διασπορά is here used metaphorically or figuratively, but he implicitly admits as much when he says

---

(LCL)]). Karl Ludwig Schmidt, "διασπορά," *TDNT* 2. 98.

[115]Cf. K. L. Schmidt, "διασπορά," 99. The references are: Deut 28:25; 30:4; 2 Esdr 11:9; Jdt 5:19; Pss 138:1 (A); 146:2; Isa 49:6; Jer 13:14 (ℵ); 15:7; 41:17; 2 Macc 1:27.

[116]Cf. Philo *Praem.* 115, in which Philo refers to διασπορὰ ψυχική. Although this usage has affinities with Plutarch's earlier (in *Mor.* 1105A [see above, p. 75 n. 114]) and with that of Clement of Alexandria later (*Protr.* 9.88.3), it probably reflects a figurative appropriation of the early-Jewish notion of διασπορά (see K. L. Schmidt, "διασπορά," 101).

[117]Whether or not they actually use the adjectives "figurative" or "metaphorical," the clear consensus among commentators is that διασπορά is used metaphorically in 1 Pet 1:1. See, e.g., Brox, *Petrusbrief*, 57; Goppelt, *I Peter*, 64-66; Kelly, *Epistles of Peter*, 40-41; T. Martin, *Metaphor and Composition*, 45, 144; Michaels, *1 Peter*, 6, 8-9; cf. Selwyn, *Epistle of St. Peter*, 118-19.

[118]Elliott, *Home*, 38.

of the occurrences in Jas 1:1 and 1 Pet 1:1: "This novel usage reflects a stage in the Christian movement in which epithets once proper to Judaism alone ('diaspora,' 'the twelve tribes,' 'elect') are expropriated and now are used to designate the Christian community as coheirs or perhaps sole heirs of the legacy of Israel."[119]

(3) If the LXX technical term διασπορά is being used metaphorically in reference to Christians in 1 Pet 1:1, then the same is true also of ἐκλεκτοί.[120] The adjective ἐκλεκτός (-οί) occurs frequently in the literature of Hellenistic Judaism as a designation for the people of Israel as a whole or for those righteous, faithful ones who will be vindicated in the end.[121] In Christian circles, the word was applied to Christians as the eschatological people of God (e.g., Matt 22:14; Mark 13:20//Matt 24:22; Mark 13:22//Matt 24:24; Mark 13:27//Matt 24:31; Luke 18:7; Rom 8:33; Col 3:12).[122] Of course, Christians, like biblical Israel and early Judaism, understood themselves to be chosen by God in the most literal sense; and the personal agency of God in electing the Petrine addressees is made explicit in 1 Pet 1:2.[123] In 1:1, however, the readers are addressed not with the single word ἐκλεκτοῖς but with the phrase ἐκλεκτοῖς παρεπιδήμοις διασπορᾶς. Like διασπορά, ἐκλεκτοί is an epithet "once proper to Judaism alone"[124] but now applied to the gentile Christian addressees of 1 Peter. By calling the addressees ἐκλεκτοί, the letter is not merely characterizing their election as analogous to and continuous with Israel's election (although it is

---

[119]Elliott, *Home*, 38.

[120]I am here bracketing the question of whether the notion of God's choosing is inherently metaphorical; for the sake of argument, I am granting the biblical position that God can literally choose people.

[121]E.g., 1 Chr 16:13; Esth 8:12t; Pss 88:4; 104:6, 43; 105:5; Wis 3:9; Sir 46:1; Isa 43:20; 65:9, 15, 23; *1 Enoch* 1:1, 8; 38:2-5; 39:6-7; 48:1; 58:1-4; cf. *As. Mos.* 4:2. Michaels, *1 Peter*, 7; Gottlob Schrenk, "ἐκλεκτός," *TDNT* 4. 183.

[122]See also, e.g., 2 Tim 2:10; Tit 1:1; Rev 17:14; *1 Clem.* 1:1; 2:4; 6:1; 46:3-4, 8; 49:5; 58:2; 59:2; *Herm. Vis.* 1.3.4; 2.1.3; 2.2.5; 2.4.2; 3.8.3; *Mart. Pol.* 16:1.

[123]The adjective ἐκλεκτοί does not stand alone in v. 1; the prepositional phrases of v. 2 show that their election is God's gracious act. Cf. Goppelt, *I Peter*, 70; Schrenk, "ἐκλεκτός," 190. Goppelt rightly connects the prepositional phrases of v. 2 with ἐκλεκτοί, in contradistinction to Selwyn, who connects them with the more remote word ἀπόστολος (Selwyn, *Epistle of St. Peter*, 119).

[124]Using Elliott's language (*Home*, 38).

doing this too); rather, 1 Peter is metaphorically transferring a predicate of the LXX people of God to its gentile addressees in Asia Minor.[125] This metaphorical transfer of Israel's election is even more explicit in 2:9, where the epithet "chosen race" (γένος ἐκλεκτόν), used of Israel in Isa 43:20 (τὸ γένος μου τὸ ἐκλεκτόν) and Esth 8:12t (τὸ ἐκλεκτὸν γένος), is now applied to 1 Peter's Christian addressees. The evidence, therefore, is all in favor of taking the two words on either side of παρεπιδήμοις—ἐκλεκτοῖς and διασπορᾶς—as metaphors drawn ultimately from the LXX.[126] In all likelihood, therefore, παρεπιδήμοις itself is also part of this metaphor complex. Before turning to the likely background of παρεπίδημος in the LXX, however, I shall make a few comments on the word παροικία.

(4) Given the significance that Elliott attaches to the παροικ- word group, it is important to note that words in this group appear only twice in the entire letter—πάροικοι in 2:11 and παροικία in 1:17. Furthermore, both occurrences have inextricable links to the LXX. The noun παροικία is never found in Hellenistic Greek literature outside the writings of Judaism and Christianity, although the (often synonymous) nouns παροικεσία and παροίκησις occur frequently, as do the verbal and adjectival forms of the word.[127] In the LXX, however, παροικία occurs some sixteen times. In the case of the technical use of the word in the LXX, the Schmidt-and-Schmidt definition quoted above (which Elliott wrongly applies more broadly to Hellenistic Greek usage in general) is entirely accurate: Παροικία denotes "the state, position or fate of a resident alien, 'dwelling abroad' without civil or native rights."[128] Almost always

---

[125]So Schrenk, "ἐκλεκτός," 190.

[126]Certainly this use of ἐκλεκτός was mediated to 1 Peter via early-Christian tradition. Whether the same should be said of διασπορά is an open question; 1 Peter may be innovating here. In any case, both metaphors ultimately derive from the LXX.

[127]See Achtemeier, "Newborn Babes," 217; K. L. Schmidt and M. A. Schmidt, "πάροικος," 844-50. Achtemeier lists the sixteen passages in which παροικία occurs in non-NT literature from the period 100 BCE to 200 CE, according to the Thesaurus Linguae Graecae Pilot CD-ROM ("Newborn Babes," 217 n. 41). Only one of these passages—Philo Conf. 80—predates 1 Peter.

[128]K. L. Schmidt and M. A. Schmidt, "πάροικος," 842. The LXX exceptions to this technical use, in which the word simply refers to place, are in Sir 16:8; 41:5;

Suffering and Disgrace

in early-Jewish literature, it is the Jews or their forebears whose παροικία is in view, so that "παροικία might simply be taken as an equivalent of διασπορά."[129] Furthermore, the Psalmist can use παροικία as a metaphor, thereby evoking the alienation from and animosity of one's neighbors that are implicit in the technical term (Pss 33:5; 118:54; 119:5; cf. 54:16). In the NT outside of 1 Peter, the παροικ- word group occurs six times, four of which quote or allude to the LXX concept of the patriarchal or Israelite πάροικος existence.[130] First Peter 2:11, furthermore, invokes the same LXX background by paraphrasing Gen 23:4, where Abraham refers to himself as πάροικος καὶ παρεπίδημος during his alien residence among the Hittites. In all likelihood, therefore, 1 Peter's use of παροικία in 1:17 is also to be understood within the context of early-Christian usage of the LXX. It would appear, then, that 1 Peter's use of παροικία stands in the tradition of early-Jewish usage of the word to denote the alien residence of Jews and their forebears outside Palestine or, by metaphorical extension, any condition of alienness and hostility in which God's people may find themselves.

44:6 (B). Cf. also Hab 3:16 and Lam 2:22, in which παροικία appears to refer to actual enemies surrounding the speakers; but here the hostility implied in the more technical use of the word is almost certainly invoked in this figurative usage. Another nontechnical use is found in *Ps. Sol.* 12:3 and 3 Macc 7:19, where παροικία simply denotes a visit. In the latter, παροικία is used in a temporal construction (ἐπὶ τὸν τῆς παροικίας αὐτῶν χρόνον) that is nearly identical to that found in 1 Pet 1:17 (τὸν τῆς παροικίας ὑμῶν χρόνον), although the παροικία time of 3 Macc 7:19 does not refer to a perilous diaspora residence but a joyous brief stopover of Jews en route to their homes after being released from captivity in Egypt.

[129]K. L. Schmidt and M. A. Schmidt, "παροικία," 842 n. 6. See 1 Esdr 5:7; 2 Esdr 8:35; Jdt 5:9; 3 Macc 6:36; 7:19; Wis 19:10; Sir Prologue 34; Lam 2:22; *Ps. Sol.* 17:17; *T. Levi* 11:2. See also Hab 3:16, where Israel's invading enemies are called λαὸς παροικίας μου. One notable exception is Philo, who allegorizes the patriarchs' sojourns in foreign lands, using both the verb and the noun to refer to human sojourning in bodies, on earth, while the true citizenship is in heaven (Philo *Cher.* 120-121; *Conf.* 77-82).

[130]Acts 7:6 (quoting Gen 15:13), 29 (quoting Exod 2:15, 22); 13:17 (referring to Israel's παροικία in Egypt; cf. Exod 6:1, 6; 18:3; Deut 23:8; Wis 19:10); Heb 11:9 (referring to the patriarchs as πάροικοι; cf. Gen 23:4; 26:3). Eph 2:19 also alludes to a LXX usage of πάροικος, this time in reference not to Israel but to gentile resident aliens within Israel's borders. Finally, Luke 24:18 uses the verb form in the general sense, meaning "to visit." Cf. K. L. Schmidt and M. A. Schmidt, "πάροικος," 851-53.

(5) Returning now to the word παρεπίδημοι in 1:1, we have seen above that (a) this word serves as one part of the metaphorical construct ἐκλεκτοῖς παρεπιδήμοις διασπορᾶς, and (b) the words on either side of παρεπιδήμοις derive from the terminology of early Judaism. In light of the other occurrence of παρεπίδημοι in the letter (2:11), we can now affirm that the background of 1 Peter's use of παρεπίδημοι is also to be found in the language of early Judaism, specifically, in the LXX. Outside the biblical literature, the substantive παρεπιδημία and the verb παρεπιδημέω, which do not occur at all in the LXX or the NT, are quite common, but παρεπίδημος is extremely rare.[131] In the LXX and the NT, however, παρεπίδημος is found five times—once each in Genesis, the Psalms, and Hebrews, and twice in 1 Peter. What is most striking about its LXX usage, from the point of view of this study, is that in both Gen 23:4 and Ps 38:13 παρεπίδημος occurs in conjunction with πάροικος, just as it does in 1 Pet 2:11. In Gen 23:4, Abraham says to the Hittites, πάροικος καὶ παρεπίδημος εἰμι μεθ' ὑμῶν. Here πάροικος and παρεπίδημος, although not necessarily synonymous, are used together to convey the single concept of Abraham's foreignness vis-à-vis the Hittites.[132] This combination, which expresses a literal state of affairs in Gen 23:4, is employed metaphorically in Ps 38:13—with explicit reference to the Psalmist's forebears, of whom Abraham is certainly to be numbered—to denote the writer's consciousness of his position before God: Πάροικος ἐγώ εἰμι παρὰ σοὶ καὶ παρεπίδημος καθὼς πάντες οἱ πατέρες μου. While Heb 11:13-16 allegorizes Abraham's παρεπίδημος status (using ξένοι καὶ παρεπίδημοι), 1 Pet 2:11 follows the tradition of Ps 38:13 in appropriating terms proper to the quintessential LXX resident alien, Abraham, now figuratively applying these terms to the socioreligious situation of the gentile Christians of Asia

---

[131] Grundmann, "δῆμος," 64. In Jewish literature of late antiquity it occurs only in Philo *Conf.* 79, where Philo quotes Gen 23:4. Feldmeier cites six occurrences in the literature, papyri, and inscriptions from the third century BCE to the second century CE (*Christen als Fremde*, 8 nn. 2-4).

[132] For a virtually identical construction, see Lev 25:23, in which the same Hebrew words as occur in Gen 23:4 are translated slightly differently but still together name a single concept: προσήλυτοι καὶ πάροικοι ὑμεῖς ἐστε ἐναντίον μου (cf. K. L. Schmidt and M. A. Schmidt, "πάροικος," 848).

Minor. A clearer background for 1 Peter's use of παρεπίδημοι in general and for its use in 2:11 in particular can scarcely be imagined.

All of the evidence, therefore, speaks against Elliott's and Tàrrech's assumption that πάροικοι and παροικία in 1 Peter are literal references to a legally recognized Greco-Roman social stratum to which the Petrine addressees belonged.[133] Several of the terms discussed in the previous pages, namely διασπορά, ἐκλεκτοί, and παροικία, clearly derive from early-Jewish traditions concerning the wandering and foreign sojourns of the patriarchs and presettlement Israel and the displacement of the Jewish diaspora; and only these traditions can provide the connection between these three terms and παρεπίδημοι and πάροικοι. These five words certainly do reflect the letter's perception of the situation of its intended readers; in this regard Elliott and Tàrrech are correct. But these terms are figures of speech, metaphors, by which a situation of social alienness is characterized, rather than literal designations of a legally recognized social stratum, whether of the intended audience or of the actual readers.[134] Precisely what role these metaphors play in the letter will be treated in chapter 4, in which I shall examine 1 Peter's response to the situation of its intended readers.

I earlier called into question most of the assumptions underlying Elliott's social profile of 1 Peter's addressees in chapter 2 of *A Home for the Homeless*. Now I have also rejected the thesis of his first chapter, that the addressees were literally resident aliens. What evidence, then, does the letter provide for identifying the social position of 1 Peter's intended readers? The answer, in short, is very little. It is one thing to sketch a picture of the social situation of the

---

[133] Paul J. Achtemeier's criticism that Elliott does not so much argue this point as he does assert it is even more apropos of Tàrrech's article (Paul J. Achtemeier, review of *A Home for the Homeless: A Sociological Exegesis of 1 Peter, Its Situation and Strategy*, by John H. Elliott, *JBL* 103 [1984] 132).

[134] Similarly, Achtemeier writes that the phrase πάροικοι καὶ παρεπίδημοι (2:11) "is drawn not from the political arena of the Greco-Roman world to describe the political status of the readers both before and after their conversion, as Elliott had argued, but rather is . . . chosen under the influence of the controlling metaphor, the chosen people, and applied to the Christians" ("Newborn Babes," 228). I would prefer not to call the chosen people of God "the controlling metaphor" of the letter, but I agree with Achtemeier that Elliott has fundamentally misread 1 Pet 1:1, 17; 2:11.

addressees based on what is known in general about the four provinces of Asia Minor to which the letter is directed; this is basically what both Elliott and Tàrrech do. It is another thing entirely to sketch a portrait of the intended audience based on the evidence of the letter itself.

As to the former, given the predominance of rural areas over cities in these provinces, it is *possible* that the majority of actual readers were rustics, perhaps *peregrini* in the technical sense (i.e., noncitizens of Rome), and members of the country peasantry or working class. On the other hand, several important pieces of external evidence—from Pliny's correspondence with Trajan—that neither Elliott nor Tàrrech cites in this connection may point in a different direction. Pliny clearly states that some of the Christians brought before him were Roman citizens (*cives Romani*); these he intended to send to Rome for trial (*Ep.* 10.96.4). He also says that the Christians being brought to trial came from every order (*ordinis*) (*Ep.* 10.96.9). Since the three elite orders were comprised solely (senatorial and equestrian) or mostly (decurion) of Roman citizens, with the remaining citizens belonging to the order of free persons (which also included noncitizens), these two statements of Pliny indicate that a significant number of the Christians brought before him were Roman citizens.[135] The rest of the accused, whom Pliny at first took it upon himself to try and to punish before deciding to postpone further cases until he could query Trajan about his policy, were apparently not Roman citizens but *peregrini*.[136] Pliny further

---

[135]On the Roman *ordo* system, see Peter Garnsey and Richard Saller, *The Roman Empire: Economy, Society and Culture* (Berkeley/Los Angeles: University of California Press, 1987) 112-18; Peter Garnsey, "Legal Privilege in the Roman Empire," *Studies in Ancient Society* (ed. M. I. Finley; Past and Present Series; London/Boston: Routledge & Kegan Paul, 1974) 159-65; Keith Hopkins, "Élite Mobility in the Roman Empire," *Studies in Ancient Society* (ed. M. I. Finley; Past and Present Series; London/Boston: Routledge & Kegan Paul, 1974) 103-20; and below, pp. 98-99.

[136]Although the word *peregrini* does not occur in this letter, the fact that Pliny executed some while intending to send Roman citizens to Rome implies that those executed were *peregrini*. See A. H. M. Jones, *The Criminal Courts of the Roman Republic and Principate* (Oxford: Blackwell, 1972) 102; Adrian N. Sherwin-White, *Roman Law and Roman Society in the New Testament* (Oxford: Oxford University Press, 1963; reprint, Grand Rapids: Baker, 1992) 13-23; and Robert L. Wilken, *The*

states that not only the cities (*civitates*) but also the villages and rural districts (*vicos etiam atque agros*) were being infiltrated by Christianity (*Ep.* 10.96.9).[137] These data show that, at the end of the first decade of the second century CE, Christians were to be found in both the cities and the countryside and among both the citizens and the noncitizens of the province of Bithynia-Pontus, and, although the harsher treatment by far was meted out by Pliny on the *peregrini*, both citizen and peregrine Christians alike were under attack for their faith. The actual readers of 1 Peter, therefore, could just as easily have been citizens as noncitizens.

To conclude, nothing in 1 Peter precludes an intended (or actual) urban readership; nor should we assume that the intended audience was composed exclusively, or even predominantly, of noncitizens, whether urban or rural. All that is clear from the letter itself is that the intended readers were gentile Christians in the four designated provinces of Asia Minor, and that they were undergoing some kind of suffering at the hands of their non-Christian neighbors.

The Suffering of the Addressees

The Origin of Their Suffering

The source of the conflict between 1 Peter's addressees and their neighbors is not difficult to locate; the passages that indicate that the letter's intended audience was gentile Christian rather than Jewish Christian—1 Pet 1:14-19 and 4:3-4—also disclose the origin of the hostility. Upon conversion, Christians ceased participating in certain social activities that they deemed inappropriate and, ulti-

---

Christians as the Romans Saw Them (New Haven/London: Yale University Press, 1984) 23. Wilken may be correct that "the majority of the group [brought before Pliny] came from humble backgrounds, freedmen and slaves, working people engaged in menial tasks, artisans" (*Christians*, 23), but this is not explicitly stated in Pliny's letter. And the fact that the greater part of Pliny's letter is concerned with the accused *peregrini* is attributable not necessarily to their greater numbers but to Pliny's uncertainty about how to handle their cases.

[137] Oddly, Elliott cites this statement in support of his contention that, among the Christians in Asia Minor by 100 CE, "it may be reasonably assumed that a rural population constituted the majority" (*Home*, 64).

mately, idolatrous. Given the close connection between Roman religious and civic life, it is not surprising that such "conspicuous non-participation" in the public life was viewed by the larger society as profoundly antisocial behavior.[138]

All three early-second-century Roman writers who mention Christianity—Pliny, Tacitus, and Suetonius—refer to it as a *superstitio*.[139] Although many religions were so labeled, few, if any, attracted the hostility that was directed toward Christianity.[140] Robert L. Wilken explains that Roman religious sensibility and practice had both theological and social dimensions, which were inextricably bound together; in Roman eyes, Christianity, unlike traditional religions, was an inferior upstart lacking an authentic, ancient heritage and any notion of the connection between religious observance and the integrity and well-being of society.[141] Furthermore, Christianity's claim to sole possession of the truth violated an important tenet of Roman society, what Goppelt calls "conforming

---

[138] The quoted phrase is Schutter's (*Hermeneutic*, 11). Martin Goodman nicely summarizes the situation of converts to Christianity in the late first century: "The biggest agent of transformation for the convert was negative: withdrawal from pagan worship. Withdrawal from cult immediately separated Christians from the surrounding society. Each day they marked their difference from their non-Christian neighbours simply by abstention, for pagan cult infringed upon every aspect of life. It was probably precisely the pressure of such separation from ordinary people that led Christians to stick together to form their alternative communities. The position of an isolated atheist (as pagans would have viewed solitary Christians) was well-nigh insupportable" (*Mission and Conversion: Proselytizing in the Religious History of the Roman Empire* [Oxford: Clarendon, 1994] 105).

[139] Wilken, *Christians*, 48-50. Pliny, whose investigation into Christian practices failed to turn up any specific criminal activity, calls Christianity "a degenerate sort of cult (*superstitionem*) carried to extravagant lengths"; he is concerned about the interruption of traditional religious worship in the towns, villages, and rural areas that "are infected through contact with this wretched cult (*superstitionis*)" (*Ep.* 10.96.8 [trans. Betty Radice (LCL)]; cf. 10.96.9). Tacitus only mentions Christianity in a single section of the *Annals*, where he calls it a "pernicious superstition" whose members were executed by Nero on the charge of "hatred of the human race" (*Ann.* 15.45 [trans. John Jackson (LCL)]). And Suetonius, who, like Tacitus, mentions Christianity only once and in connection with Nero, labels it a "new and mischievous superstition" (*Ner.* 16.2 [trans. J. C. Rolfe (LCL)]).

[140] See G. E. M. de Ste Croix, "Why Were the Early Christians Persecuted?—A Rejoinder," *Past and Present* 27 (April 1964) 32-33.

[141] Wilken, *Christians*, 63.

tolerance, i.e., reciprocal acceptance."[142] Consistent with a society that cherished "reciprocal acceptance," conversion—in the sense of abandonment of one religion in favor of exclusive devotion to another one—was rare, and conversion in response to active proselytizing was virtually unheard of.[143] In a society in which virtually any religion was tolerated as long as it did not violate Roman ethical sensibilities or display a tendency toward political

---

[142]Goppelt, *I Peter*, 40.

[143]Goodman refers to Christian proselytizing as "a shocking novelty in the ancient world" (*Mission and Conversion*, 105); see also Goodman, *Mission and Conversion*, 20-37; MacMullen, *Paganism*, 94-112; and Wilken, *Christians*, 64. In the case of conversion, a notable exception was conversion to Judaism. Inscriptional and literary evidence suggests that in the Roman period, substantial numbers of gentiles either attended synagogues and followed some precepts of Judaism or actually converted to Judaism, although the numbers of actual converts are very much in dispute (see Shaye J. D. Cohen, "Crossing the Boundary and Becoming a Jew," *HTR* 82 [1989] 13-33; idem, "Was Judaism in Antiquity a Missionary Religion?" *Jewish Assimilation, Acculturation and Accommodation: Past Traditions, Current Issues and Future Prospects* [ed. Menachem Mor; Lanham/New York/London: University Press of America, 1992] 14-23; and, for Asia Minor in particular, Paul R. Trebilco, *Jewish Communities in Asia Minor* [SNTSMS 69; Cambridge: Cambridge University Press, 1991] 145-85). Although largely protected by Roman law, furthermore, Judaism was frequently vilified by Romans (largely for its exclusivism) in much the same way that Christianity was (see, e.g., Cicero *Flac.* 28.66-69; Tacitus *Hist.* 5.1-13, esp. 5.4-5; Juvenal *Sat.* 14.96-106); on the other hand, Judaism could also command a respect that Christianity seems never to have achieved (see Cohen, "Crossing the Boundary," 14-20; John G. Gager, *The Origins of Anti-Semitism: Attitudes toward Judaism in Pagan and Christian Antiquity* [New York/Oxford: Oxford University Press, 1985] 67-88). What is unclear, however, is to what extent gentile synagogue attendance and proselytism to Judaism were due to intentional proselytizing activity on the part of Jewish communities and to what extent these phenomena were the result of everyday, informal contacts among Jews and their gentile neighbors; "receiving and encouraging converts is one thing; actively soliciting them is another" (Fredriksen, "Judaism," 538; see also Gager, *Origins*, 59-62). Jewish proselytizing activity was probably not widespread during the Roman period. For the debate on the question of the extent to which Jews actively engaged in proselytizing missions during the Hellenistic period, see Cohen, "Missionary Religion?" 14-23; Louis H. Feldman, "Was Judaism a Missionary Religion in Ancient Times?" *Jewish Assimilation, Acculturation and Accommodation: Past Traditions, Current Issues and Future Prospects* [ed. Menachem Mor; Lanham/New York/London: University Press of America, 1992] 24-37; and Fredriksen, "Judaism," 532-48; Goodman, *Mission and Conversion*, 38-90.

subversion, Christianity's unwillingness to acknowledge the legitimacy of other religions was sure to arouse suspicion.[144]

Even more contemptible, however, was the refusal of Christians to participate in the ceremonies of the common life, ceremonies that were both civic and religious in nature. The Roman attitude would later be codified in an imperial command, which was summarized by Paternus, proconsul of Africa, at Cyprian's first trial in 257: "Those who do not profess the Roman religion must not refuse to take part in Roman religious ceremonies."[145] It is little wonder, therefore, that hostility should have been aroused against the Christians of Asia Minor, who had forsaken their traditional religions in favor of a cult of recent origin and then refused to participate fully in the public life of their society.[146]

---

[144]See Stephen Benko, *Pagan Rome and the Early Christians* (Bloomington: Indiana University Press, 1984) 1-29; G. E. M. de Ste Croix, "Why Were the Early Christians Persecuted?" *Past and Present* 26 (November 1963) 24-31; W. H. C. Frend, *Martyrdom and Persecution in the Early Church: A Study of a Conflict from the Maccabees to Donatus* (New York: New York University Press, 1967) 77-93; Garnsey and Saller, *Roman Empire*, 163-77; MacMullen, *Paganism*, 1-4; A. D. Nock, *Conversion: The Old and the New in Religion from Alexander the Great to Augustine of Hippo* (London/New York/Toronto: Oxford University Press, 1933; reprint, Lanham: University Press of America, 1988) 66-137; Smallwood, *Jews under Roman Rule*, 124; and Wilken, *Christians*, 63-64. On Greco-Roman criticism of Eastern religions (including Judaism), see Balch, *Wives*, 65-80. For Roman criticisms of Christianity in the first one hundred years of Christian history, whether directly stated (by Roman writers), indirectly reflected (in Christian responses), or implied (in Greco-Roman views of religion in general), see Benko, *Pagan Rome*, 1-29; and Wilken, *Christians*, 1-93. Of course, one should distinguish between the attitudes toward Christianity portrayed in Roman writings and actual Roman policy toward Christians. Roman policy was basically irenic until the stability of a society was put at risk due to conflicts between Christians and their neighbors. Nevertheless, however irenic Rome generally appeared, the criticisms of Roman writers indicate a widespread disdain for Christianity in the Empire.

[145]De Ste Croix, "Why Were the Early Christians Persecuted?" 31; translating the following, rendering the main clause negatively: "eos qui Romanam religionem non colunt, debere Romanas caeremonias recognoscere" (*Acts of Saint Cyprian* 1 [CSEL 3/3. cx]).

[146]See Balch, *Wives*, 86; Goppelt, *I Peter*, 39-41; Schutter, *Hermeneutic*, 11-12.

The Form of Their Suffering

The form in which this hostility expressed itself is more difficult to specify. We have already seen that the suffering to which 1 Peter refers cannot be identified with any full-blown imperial persecution of Christians.[147] What is most striking about 1 Peter's statements concerning the lot of its intended audience is their lack of specificity. Missing are such technical terms for persecution as διωγμός and θλῖψις and the technical term for formal accusation, κατηγορία.[148] The suffering of the communities is, for the most part, referred to in the most general terms: πάσχω (2:19, 20; 3:14, 17; 4:1, 15-16, 19; 5:10), παθήματα (4:13; 5:9), ὑποφέρειν λύπας (2:19), λυπηθῆναι ποικίλοις πειρασμοῖς (1:6), and ἡ πύρωσις πρὸς πειρασμόν (4:12). When the letter turns to more concrete characterizations of this suffering, the language used is that of slanderous or accusatory speech: ἐπηράζω (3:16), καταλαλέω (2:12; 3:16), ὀνειδίζω (4:14), αἰτεῖν λόγον (3:15), and βλασφημέω (4:4). This second group of terms clearly indicates verbal abuse of Christians by their neighbors. Furthermore, the injunction of 3:15 to be prepared to provide an ἀπολογία to anyone demanding an account of one's hope may well refer to judicial proceedings, in which case some or all instances of the other speech terms may also refer to accusations brought against Christians in the courts. We must determine, therefore, whether the slanderous speech of which 1 Peter writes might have occurred in informal settings, in the courts, or both. In addition, we must take up a question adumbrated above, in connection with Pliny's correspondence with Trajan, and ask whether some from the communities addressed may have been executed for their faith.

As an entrée into these questions, we shall evaluate the most sustained argument to date in favor of the position that 1 Peter presupposes legal proceedings against its readers, that offered by William L. Schutter in his *Hermeneutic and Composition in I Peter*. Schutter finds in three passages indications that the letter's intended

---

[147]See above, pp. 19-20, 49-50.

[148]Kelly, *Epistles of Peter*, 10; cf. Schelkle, *Petrusbriefe*, 8; Selwyn, *Epistle of St. Peter*, 53.

readers are being brought to trial by the procedure *cognitio extra ordinem*, the same procedure by which Christians would later be tried by Pliny: 1 Pet 2:14-15 refers to the *imperium* by which provincial governors were empowered to try potentially capital cases; 3:13-17, although formulated in a sufficiently general manner as to be applicable to informal settings as well as to forensic contexts, reflects the proceedings of *cognitio extra ordinem*; and 4:15 implies that some Christians had been convicted of the crimes listed, including murder.[149] A brief examination of these passages will facilitate our critique of Schutter's thesis.

(1) The positioning of the words about governors in 2:14-15 is crucial, as Schutter recognizes. In 2:12, the readers are enjoined to maintain good behavior (τὴν ἀναστροφὴν ... καλήν) in order that, in case their gentile neighbors speak against them (καταλαλοῦσιν) as wrongdoers (κακοποιῶν), the former will see the readers' good works (τῶν καλῶν ἔργων) and will, consequently, glorify God in the eschaton.[150] Then, in rather stereotyped fashion, the letter exhorts submission to the institutional authorities, specifically the emperor and his governors, and explains, again in stereotypical terms, that the function of these governors is to punish (ἐκδίκησιν) wrongdoers (κακοποιῶν) and to praise (ἔπαινον) those who do good (ἀγαθοποιῶν) (2:13-14).[151] Finally, in 2:15, 1 Peter harks back to the exhortation in v. 12 to do good works in the face of accusations of wrongdoing, and to the description in v. 14 of the governors' task to punish wrongdoers and to praise those who do good; the readers are told that it is God's will that they, precisely by being doers of good (ἀγαθοποιοῦντας), should silence the ignorance of their foolish accusers (2:14-15).

The question to be addressed here is whether these verses have in view a specific juridical situation. In 2:14, the word ἐκδίκησιν, used to describe one function of the Roman governors, is to be

---

[149]Schutter, *Hermeneutic*, 14-17.

[150]ἐν ᾧ, as in 3:16, is a temporal construction that is best rendered "in case" (so Michaels, *1 Peter*, 117; Kelly, *Epistles of Peter*, 105; contra Goppelt, who translates it "wherein" [*I Peter*, 159 n. 18]); cf. Selwyn's "in the very act of" (*Epistle of St. Peter*, 170). For the interpretation of this eschatological doxology, see below, pp. 159-60.

[151]The closest parallel is Rom 13:1-4; cf. Tit 3:1, 8.

interpreted in light of the juridical sense it bears in its extrabiblical usage; magistrates, according to 1 Peter, were given the responsibility and power to prosecute criminal cases.[152] It was by virtue of their prosecutorial mandate that governors fulfilled their function of preserving social order. In this light, ἔπαινον *may* invoke the juridical concept of acquittal and exoneration (as Schutter argues), but this is by no means a necessary implication of the juridical term ἐκδίκησιν.[153] Certainly the easier reading is to take ἔπαινον in its more general sense of commendation.[154] Regardless of how ἔπαινον

---

[152]So Gottlob Schrenk, "ἐκδικέω, ἔκδικος, ἐκδίκησις," *TDNT* 2. 446; cf. Best, *I Peter*, 114; Goppelt, who translates εἰς ἐκδίκησιν "to prosecute" (*I Peter*, 185). For the juridical meaning of the ἐκδικ- word group see Schrenk, "ἐκδικέω," 442-46.

[153]Schutter argues that ἔπαινον refers to "the *laudatio* he [the governor] pronounced to clear the name of the accused" who was found innocent (*Hermeneutic*, 16 n. 72). Best argues that the parallelism between the two members of the purpose clause in v. 14 indicates that the second should be interpreted in legal-juridical terms in accordance with the first (*I Peter*, 114). While the juridical function of the governor is clearly presupposed in the first member, since it was by legal proceedings that magistrates punished evildoers, the second member does not necessarily point to the juridical context. A more likely context is the governor's function of bestowing commendation on worthy persons (Goppelt, *I Peter*, 185-86). Winter argues that what is in view here is the public recognition of benefactors of a city by means of both a ceremony in which the rulers would praise the benefactor and the erection of an inscription commemorating the act of benefaction. Winter points to numerous inscriptions recording the commendation (often using the ἐπαιν- family) of people for public benefactions (often designated as "the good" or "good deed[s]") (*Seek the Welfare*, 26-40). Although this inscriptional evidence does point to the kinds of associations that praise of rulers would evoke in a first-century reader, there is no reason to insist (as Winter does) that 1 Peter invokes this procedure to encourage the addressees to make the kinds of exceptional contributions to their cities that will issue in public recognition. To be sure, the question of whether one acts in accordance with the social order and in ways that promote the common good is very much at issue in the letter. First Peter is not, however, concerned with the exceptional deeds of prominent, well-to-do citizens but with the responsibilities of all members of society—including those liminal members in the Christian communities—to do good rather than evil. Goppelt correctly says of 1 Peter's use of this tradition: "Here it is used formulaically of merely civic recognition and thereby the legal protection that all who conduct themselves properly can expect" (*I Peter*, 186). Similarly, Kelly argues that 1 Peter "is simply reminding them, in a quite general way, that governments are inclined to look approvingly on well conducted citizens" (*Epistles of Peter*, 109).

[154]So Kelly, *Epistles of Peter*, 109.

is read, however, the first member of this purpose clause clearly refers to the magistrates' juridical function of sentencing criminals. Schutter, therefore, is probably correct in arguing that these verses reflect a situation not unlike that of the procedure *cognitio extra ordinem*, by which provincial magistrates adjudicated the cases of individuals who had been accused by their fellows of criminal activities.[155] Although καταλαλέω (2:12) is not a technical term for formal accusation and no specific charges are mentioned, it does appear that the intended readers are being enjoined to exhibit such behavior as would, in a trial before the governor, give the lie to the charges that they were wrongdoers, with the result that their accusers would be discredited and the governor's verdict would be acquittal and exoneration. Whether 1 Peter envisions such trials of Christians as present realities or even imminent probabilities, however, is quite another matter. Given the letter's preoccupation with slander and accusations of wrongdoing and the indication in 4:4 that actual abuse is in view, we can be certain that 2:12-15 presupposes that the addressees are being slanderously accused of wrongdoing, whether or not these accusations are being made in the courts.

(2) Turning now to Schutter's second passage, two aspects of 1 Pet 3:13-17 are striking: the use in 3:15 of the word ἀπολογία and the similarity of the terminology of vv. 16b-17a with that of 1 Pet 2:12-15. The latter phenomenon suggests that a similar situation is in view in both 2:12-15 and 3:16-17. The question here is whether 3:15 can help to clarify the nature of that situation. The word ἀπολογία ultimately derives from the juridical sphere and is often used as a technical term to denote a legal defense. As J. N. D. Kelly points out, however, if legal proceedings are in view here, they are not necessarily capital trials before the provincial governor; the language of 3:15 "is at least equally compatible with petty prosecutions before civic magistrates."[156] Furthermore, the word ἀπολογία is frequently used less formally in nonjuridical contexts (as in 1 Cor

---

[155]On the procedure *cognitio extra ordinem*, see Adolf Berger and Barry Nicholas, "Law and Procedure, Roman," *OCD*, 588-89; de Ste Croix, "Why Were the Early Christians Persecuted?" 11-17; Jones, *Criminal Courts*, 101-18; Sherwin-White, *Roman Law*, 1-23.

[156]Kelly, *Epistles of Peter*, 29.

9:3 and 2 Cor 7:11). The phrase αἰτεῖν λόγον, although not inappropriate to the juridical setting, is not a technical term for legal examination or accusation.[157] The adverb ἀεί and the possibility that the query for an ἀπολογία might come from anyone, moreover, suggest routine, informal contacts rather than formal legal proceedings.[158] Furthermore, in a *cognitio extra ordinem* proceeding, the accused was interrogated by and would respond to the magistrate rather than just anyone.[159] Despite the use of the word ἀπολογία, therefore, 1 Pet 3:13-17 does not appear to have been formulated with specific reference to formal *cognitio extra ordinem* proceedings. This is not to say that the exhortations in 3:13-17 could not have applied just as well to legal proceedings—whether in provincial Roman or local civic courts—as to everyday, informal encounters; indeed, in light of 2:12-15, the possibility remains that criminal trials may have been of some concern to 1 Peter.[160] It does not appear, however, that such trials were a primary concern.

(3) Finally, Schutter sees 1 Pet 4:14-16 as evidence that some Christians had already been tried and sentenced for "'murder, theft,' and various transgressions against the public welfare." In Schutter's opinion, it was this precedent that brought entire Christian communities under suspicion of the tendency to *flagitia*, which resulted in prosecutions of innocent Christians on the basis of a presumed connection between Christianity and actual criminal activity.[161] Goppelt, on the other hand, thinks that 4:14-16 indicates that some Asia Minor Christians had been brought to trial on the basis of slanderous accusations that they had committed such crimes as

---

[157] Michaels, *1 Peter*, 188.

[158] Cf. Balch, *Wives*, 94; Best, *1 Peter*, 134; Goppelt, *1 Peter*, 244; Kelly, *Epistles of Peter*, 143; Michaels, *1 Peter*, 188.

[159] Although the original charge could have been brought by any subject of the Empire—who might have even been summoned to state the accusation in court—it was the magistrate who conducted the formal trial (Berger and Nicholas, "Law and Procedure," 589; cf. Jones, *Criminal Courts*, 113-14). Of course, the exhortation in 1 Pet 3:15 would still apply to the magistrate who, in the particular case of a trial, would be the "anyone who asks."

[160] Cf. Balch, who says of 3:15, that "the writer of 1 Peter seems to view the judicial trial of Christians as a possibility, not as a present reality" (*Wives*, 95).

[161] Schutter, *Hermeneutic*, 16-17.

murder and theft, and when the charges proved groundless, they were condemned nevertheless—solely for being Christians.[162]

Of the offenders listed in 4:15, the first two clearly denote criminals. The third, κακοποιός, does not refer to any specific act but to criminal activity in general, as in 1 Pet 2:12, 14, where its plural is contrasted with ἀγαθοποιῶν, and in 1 Pet 3:17, where the same contrast is expressed with the participial forms of the two words.[163] The meaning of the fourth term, ἀλλοτριεπίσκοπος—which is not attested elsewhere prior to the fifth century CE—is much disputed. For our purposes, it will suffice to note that there is no precedent for understanding ἀλλοτριεπίσκοπος to be a criminal charge; indeed, the repeated ὡς would appear to set this term apart from the previous three.[164] Finally, in vivid contrast to the offenses listed in 4:15 (note the εἰ δέ and the repeated ὡς), 4:16 considers the possibility of suffering simply for being a Christian, quite apart from any wrongdoing.

Against Schutter, there is no reason to think that 4:15 presupposes that some Christians of Asia Minor had actually committed or been wrongly convicted of the crime of theft, much less that of murder. As J. N. D. Kelly points out, these two crimes come from a stock catalogue and are invoked here to underscore the contrast between suffering the just penalty of the law and suffering undeservedly as a Christian amid a hostile society.[165] The third and fourth terms may denote possible behaviors against which the readers need to be warned, but it is only the fifth "offense"—that of being a Christian—with which the letter is ultimately concerned. Having already considered the likelihood of suffering in the name of Christ in v. 14, the letter again takes up such suffering in v. 16, after contrasting it with suffering the just penalty of criminal activity in v. 15. This juxtaposition of the unjust suffering of the Christian with

---

[162]Goppelt, *I Peter*, 39, 311.

[163]See Goppelt, *I Peter*, 325-26 n. 36; Kelly, *Epistles of Peter*, 188.

[164]See Hermann Wolfgang Beyer, "ἐπισκέπτομαι, ἐπισκοπέω, ἐπισκοπή," *TDNT* 2. 620-22. Ca. 500 CE, in Pseudo-Dionysius *Ep.* 8 (*PG* 3. 1089c), the word ἀλλοτριεπίσκοπος clearly refers to a bishop transgressing the bounds of his office (Beyer, "ἐπισκέπτομαι," 621 n. 12).

[165]Kelly, *Epistles of Peter*, 189.

the deserved suffering of the convicted criminal, however, does not necessarily mean that the intended audience is facing the threat of prosecution, whether on such charges as murder and theft or on the charge of adherence to Christianity. Apart from the references to murderers and thieves, nothing in this passage points explicitly to the realm of legal proceedings. It is worth noting here that, although Christians were charged before Pliny with various unnamed crimes, Pliny found them innocent of these charges. Of course, Pliny also executed some of the Christians brought before him, but these executions were not the result of convictions of *flagitia*.[166]

In conclusion, 1 Peter envisions a situation of extreme hostility toward Christians on the part of their neighbors, a perfectly intelligible state of affairs in light of the poor reputation Christianity had in the eyes of the Romans. The pervasive concern for doing good rather than doing wrong in the face of slanderous accusations of wrongdoing indicates that 1 Peter agrees with the larger society's standard of behavior in accordance with the good but disagrees on what constitutes good and bad behaviors. The letter may even envision sporadic charges being brought against Christians by their detractors, and the prosecution of the accused by local authorities or Roman magistrates. In particular, the connection in 2:12-15 of the governors' prosecutorial function with the exhortation to the kind of right behavior that should silence one's accusers seems to point subtly in this direction. To reckon with the possibility of criminal prosecutions of some of 1 Peter's addressees, moreover, we need not assume an exact correspondence between their situation and the later one depicted in Pliny's correspondence with Trajan, in which being a Christian was itself a crime. The hostility of non-Christians toward Christians that is presupposed in 1 Peter—and reflected in Roman writings of the first two centuries CE—may have occasionally led to conflicts or even public disturbances that resulted in criminal prosecutions of those who seemed to constitute a threat to the peace.[167] First Peter may well reckon with such possibilities. That the letter assumes that Christians had already been condemned to

---

[166] See de Ste Croix, "Rejoinder," 30-31.
[167] Goppelt, *I Peter*, 327-28.

death, however, whether on the charge of murder or on the charge of being Christian, seems highly unlikely. It is simply inconceivable that so grave a situation would not have been more clearly reflected in the letter. What *is* clearly reflected in 1 Peter is a situation of sustained verbal abuse and slanderous accusation of Christians by their nonbelieving neighbors. In the next section, I shall examine the significance the letter attaches to this situation.

Their Honor at Risk

In my view, the key to understanding the problem of suffering in 1 Peter lies in the letter's use of the language of honor and dishonor. The bare statistics alone are impressive: If we consider only the most obvious words from the honor semantic field, we find the δοξ- root fourteen times in the letter, the τιμ- root six times, and ἔπαινος twice. Accompanying these terms are several that denote dishonoring or shaming, most notably καταισχύνω (twice) and αἰσχύνομαι (once). For assistance in uncovering the significance of 1 Peter's use of these terms and others, I shall consult the social-scientific research on the values of honor and shame in Mediterranean societies.

For more than three decades cultural anthropologists have been using, debating, and refining a model of Mediterranean societies—both ancient and modern—that views the key cultural values of these societies in terms of codes of honor and shame.[168] "Honor and

---

[168]In what follows I shall sketch the basic features of the model in the most general terms. For the arguments concerning the origins of the honor-shame dynamic in the Mediterranean and the fine points of the model in its various permutations from place to place and from time to time, see especially J. G. Peristiany, ed., *Honour and Shame: The Values of Mediterranean Society* (Chicago: University of Chicago Press, 1966; Midway Reprint, 1974); Jane Schneider, "Of Vigilance and Virgins: Honor, Shame and Access to Resources in Mediterranean Societies," *Ethnology* 9 (1971) 1-24; John Davis, *People of the Mediterranean: An Essay in Comparative Social Anthropology* (Library of Man; London: Routledge & Kegan Paul, 1977) 89-101; Jeremy Boissevain, "Towards a Social Anthropology of the Mediterranean," *Current Anthropology* 20 (1979) 81-93; David D. Gilmore, "Anthropology of the Mediterranean Area," *Annual Review of Anthropology* 11 (1982) 175-205; David D. Gilmore, ed., *Honor and Shame and the Unity of the Mediterranean* (Washington: American Anthropological Association, 1987); J. G. Peristiany and Julian A. Pitt-Rivers, eds.,

shame are reciprocal moral values representing primordial integration of individual to 'group.' They reflect, respectively, the conferral of public esteem upon the person and the sensitivity to public opinion upon which the former depends."[169] The notions of honor and shame provide the connection between the ideals of a society and the individual's aspiration and ability to embody those ideals. Honor and shame are thus "the reflection of the social personality in the mirror of social ideals."[170] The person who aspires to fulfill certain ideals of his or her society, claims to have achieved that aspiration, and has that claim validated in the court of public opinion is honorable. The one whom society deems honorable is thereby granted a certain social status and can expect to be treated in accordance with that status.[171] Honor, therefore, establishes status.[172] To be dishonored or shamed, on the other hand, is to have one's

---

Honor and Grace in Anthropology (Cambridge Studies in Social and Cultural Anthropology 76; Cambridge: Cambridge University Press, 1992). Especially important here is the seminal articulation of the model by Julian A. Pitt-Rivers in "Honour and Social Status," *Honour and Shame: The Values of Mediterranean Society*, 21-77. For summaries of the state of the discipline of Mediterranean anthropological studies, see Gilmore, "Anthropology"; and idem, "Introduction: The Shame of Dishonor," *Honor and Shame and the Unity of the Mediterranean*, 2-21. Finally, Bruce J. Malina has synthesized much of this material and more to articulate an honor-shame model for interpreters of the NT in *The New Testament World: Insights from Cultural Anthropology* (Rev. ed.; Louisville: Westminster/John Knox, 1993) 28-62; see also Malina and Jerome H. Neyrey, "Honor and Shame in Luke-Acts: Pivotal Values of the Mediterranean World," *The Social World of Luke-Acts: Models for Interpretation* (ed. Jerome H. Neyrey; Peabody: Hendrickson, 1991), esp. 25-46.

[169]Gilmore, "Introduction," 3; see also Pitt-Rivers's classic formulations in his 1966 study, "Honour and Social Status": "Honour is the value of a person in his own eyes, but also in the eyes of his society. It is his estimation of his own worth, his *claim* to pride, but it is also the acknowledgement of that claim, his excellence recognized by society, his *right* to pride" (21). Shame is "a concern for repute, both as a sentiment and also as the public recognition of that sentiment. It is what makes a person sensitive to the pressure exerted by public opinion. In these senses it is synonymous with honour" (42).

[170]J. G. Peristiany, Introduction to *Honour and Shame: The Values of Mediterranean Society*, 9.

[171]Pitt-Rivers, "Honour and Social Status," 21-22.

[172]Of course, for the well-born the reverse is true: status establishes honor. Even the well-born person's honor, however, can be challenged and must be evaluated in the court of public opinion (Pitt-Rivers, "Honour and Social Status," 23).

claim to honor rejected by society and so to fall short of the status and role to which one has aspired.[173]

In relatively small-scale societies characterized by face-to-face interactions between individuals, honor and shame are a constant preoccupation.[174] Since one's claim to moral excellence and its attendant honor is relative to similar claims made by others in a society, such claims are always implicitly claims to excel over others.[175] This is not to say that *every* social encounter constitutes a challenge to honor or that Mediterranean societies are so hierarchical that no two persons within them may be of equal rank.[176] Indeed, some societies—such as rural peasant societies—consist largely of equals whose mutual respect is the highest honor attainable. It is, however, precisely within such societies of equals, in which few if any dare hold out hope for formal bestowal of honors by the powers that be, much less any elevation in the hierarchy of social rank, that competition for relative honor is so important. In such societies, implicit and explicit challenges to honor constantly arise, providing the occasion for either the enhancement or the loss of honor, depending upon the outcome of the challenge.[177] Whereas the cultural scripts by which such challenges are formulated differ from society to society, it is always the society as a whole that establishes the rules of the game and so functions as the arbiter of claims and challenges to honor.[178]

Furthermore, just as individuals have honor, so honor is an attribute of social collectives. Groups of all sizes, from the family to the nation, have their own collective honor. As members of such groups, individuals share in the honor of the larger whole. Conversely, if one individual is dishonored, the honor of the entire group is compromised. Furthermore, a single individual, whether the father

---

[173]Pitt-Rivers, "Honour and Social Status," 72.

[174]Peristiany, Introduction to *Honour and Shame*, 11.

[175]Pitt-Rivers, "Honour and Social Status," 23.

[176]Malina appears to be going a bit too far when he claims that "in the first-century Mediterranean world, every social interaction that takes place outside one's family or outside one's circle of friends is perceived as a challenge to honor, a mutual attempt to acquire honor from one's social equal" (*New Testament World*, 37).

[177]Pitt-Rivers, "Honour and Social Status," 23.

[178]Pitt-Rivers, "Honour and Social Status," 27.

in the family or the leader of the nation, embodies and is responsible for the honor of the whole, and the individuals' honor is in part a function of their fidelity to the head of the group. The patronage system that was virtually ubiquitous in late antiquity depended upon precisely this bond of mutual obligation between patron and client.[179]

What appears to be the most distinctive feature of the Mediterranean variant of the honor-shame system is the role played by gender distinctions.[180] Most of what has been said above concerning honor and shame in Mediterranean societies actually applies predominantly to adult males. The honor of females in such societies is tied closely to their significant males, first to the father and brothers in their family of origin and then to the husband and sons in their family of procreation. Females embody the family's shame, which is expressed primarily as female sexual purity. Male honor is closely allied with the concept of manliness or masculinity, so that an affront to the sexual purity of a woman constitutes a challenge not to her honor but to her husband's (or her father's or son's). When a female is sexually violated, it is the male responsible for her who is shamed; her lost chastity symbolizes his emasculation.[181]

When 1 Peter is read in light of this model, a remarkable correspondence appears between the general features of the model and the letter's depiction of the social situation of its intended readers. Indeed, although the precise nature and intensity of the

---

[179] Pitt-Rivers, "Honour and Social Status," 35-36.

[180] Much of the debate among anthropologists of the Mediterranean over the last thirty years has centered on two issues: (1) what is distinctive about the Mediterranean version of the honor-shame dynamic (since people in most, if not all, societies appear to seek honor while attempting to avoid dishonor) and (2) the role of gender distinctions in the Mediterranean system. It appears now that it is precisely the role of gender in the Mediterranean honor-shame system that makes it unique, or at least distinctive. "Mediterranean honor . . . is a 'libidinized' social reputation; and it is this eroticized aspect of honor—albeit unconscious or implicit—that seems to make the Mediterranean variant distinctive" (Gilmore, "Introduction," 11).

[181] On the gender specificity of the Mediterranean system of honor and shame see Carol Delaney, "Seeds of Honor, Fields of Shame," *Honor and Shame and the Unity of the Mediterranean* (ed. David D. Gilmore; Washington: American Anthropological Association, 1987) 35-48; Gilmore, "Introduction," 3-17; Malina, *New Testament World*, 48-53; Pitt-Rivers, "Honour and Social Status," 42-71; Schneider, "Of Vigilance," 17-22.

addressees' suffering remains elusive, the consequences of that suffering in terms of their own self-worth and social status become visible with the help of the honor-shame model. Goppelt, some fifteen years ago, articulated the essence of the matter without fully developing his insight: The verbal hostility directed at the intended readers of 1 Peter, Goppelt explains, "is more than personal insult: It takes from them the public respect [*bürgerliche Ehre*] on which existence in society depended."[182] The following examination of the letter's characterization of the conflict situation of its intended readers will both confirm Goppelt's judgment and allow his seminal insight to reach fruition.[183]

The social world within which 1 Peter and its Christian addressees were located was highly structured, both by law and by convention. Roman society was *legally* stratified according to a hierarchy of ranks or orders—senators, equestrians, decurions, freeborn persons, slave-born freed persons, and slaves—with birth and wealth being the primary ingredients in rank. All members of the first two orders and most decurions (all of which together represented only a small fraction of the population of the Empire), along with many free persons occupied the legally recognized position of citizen.[184] Within each order (and, to a far lesser extent, across orders), were many gradations of social status. Social status, unlike rank, was a matter not of law but of the *social estimation* of a

---

[182]Goppelt, *I Peter*, 39.

[183]In this sense I am taking up one aspect of a challenge articulated by Elliott in *What Is Social-Scientific Criticism?* After offering a thumbnail sketch of the situation and strategy of the letter, he explains that a more complete analysis would have to include "social and cultural features of the environment that are encoded in the text . . . including [among many others] the values and scripts concerning honor and shame" (79). Elliott himself has now taken his own analysis a step further in an article that appeared too late to be considered in the present monograph: "Disgraced Yet Graced: The Gospel according to 1 Peter in the Key of Honor and Shame," *BTB* 25 (1995) 166-78.

[184]Garnsey and Saller, *Roman Empire*, 112-18. In the first three centuries CE, only about six hundred persons were senators. The number of decurions was much larger; in general, decurions were the top one hundred males of each city. For these figures, see Hopkins, "Élite Mobility," 103.

Suffering and Disgrace

person's prestige based on custom and convention.[185] As Peter Garnsey and Richard Saller explain, "A Roman's status was based on the social estimation of his honour, the perception of those around him as to his prestige."[186] Cicero, in a speech composed in the first century BCE, demonstrates both the paramount value of honor and the dependence of honor on social recognition:

> The highest, truest glory [*gloria*] depends upon the following three things: the affection, the confidence, and the mingled admiration and esteem [*honore*] of the people. . . .
> The third, then, of the three conditions I named as essential to glory [*gloriam*] is that we be accounted worthy of the esteem [*honore*] and admiration of our fellow men. (*Off.* 2.9, 11)[187]

And one was accounted worthy of esteem largely in terms of the degree to which one behaved in a manner befitting one's position in the social order.[188]

The concern for honor and shame that pervades Roman society is, not surprisingly perhaps, characteristic of 1 Peter as well. Another look at the three passages Schutter adduces in support of his argument that legal proceedings are in view in 1 Peter will reveal that each one reflects a preoccupation with honor and shame, and each contains the language of challenge and response that is appropriate to such a concern.

---

[185] Garnsey and Saller, *Roman Empire*, 109-25. Cf. Ramsay MacMullen, *Roman Social Relations: 50 B.C. to A.D. 284* (New Haven/London: Yale University Press, 1974) 88-94; Meeks, *Urban Christians*, 53-55.

[186] Garnsey and Saller, *Roman Empire*, 118.

[187] Trans. Walter Miller (LCL); cited by T. Martin, *Metaphor and Composition*, 108-10.

[188] See Meeks's characterization of the place of honor and shame in Roman society: "The exchange of goods, services, and prestige, in proportion to the socially assigned 'worth' of each participant, was the process that, Aristotle suggested, made ancient society work. . . . Honor and shame were the reciprocal sentiments that enforced the unwritten rules of these continual transactions. It is enough for Epictetus to say, in his hypothetical example of a man seizing a role for which he was unsuited, that Thersites would have put himself to shame before 'a multitude of witnesses' [*Disc.* 3.22.1-8]" (Wayne A. Meeks, *The Moral World of the First Christians* [LEC 6; Philadelphia: Westminster, 1986] 37).

(1) In 1 Pet 2:12-15, the addressees' antagonists are the nonbelieving "gentiles" outside the Petrine communities. The challenge to the believers' honor consists in the gentiles' "defaming" (καταλαλέω) the addressees by accusing them of being "wrongdoers" (2:12). At issue, therefore, is whether the addressees' behavior (ἀναστροφή) conforms to the ideals of society. Without detailing precisely what such behavior entails, it is clear that two kinds of conduct are contrasted. The one falls short of the societal standards and is called wrongdoing; those who exhibit such behavior are subject to punishment by the guardian of the public welfare, the emperor's prefect (2:14). The other behavior conforms to the ideals of society, and so is called "doing good"; it brings praise (ἔπαινος)—the formal bestowal of honor—from the Roman prefect (2:14). First Peter enjoins its readers to "do good" (2:12, 15), that is, to behave in a manner that issues in commendation rather than censure, in honor rather than dishonor. Then the accusers will be silenced as their ignorance is exposed by the praiseworthy conduct of those whom they have slandered (2:15). The result of this challenge, therefore, will be honor retained for the Petrine Christians and ignominy for their challengers, whose accusations will have been found to be groundless.

(2) Nowhere in 1 Peter does the honor-dishonor dynamic come to clearer expression than in 3:13-16. Here the letter anticipates that its intended readers will suffer at the hands of their neighbors in spite of—even because of—the readers' pursuit of the good (3:13), or their "good behavior in Christ" (τὴν ἀγαθὴν ἐν Χριστῷ ἀναστροφήν [3:16]). The challenge to honor here comes in the form of a face-to-face confrontation in which the nonbeliever demands of the believer an ἀπολογία for the hope he or she embraces as a believer in Christ (3:15). The command to be ready *at any time* to respond to such a challenge corresponds to the agonistic character of Mediterranean honor-and-shame societies in which challenges to honor can arise in any social encounter. The addressees are enjoined to offer the apology demanded and to make their response "with gentleness and respect" (μετὰ πραΰτητος καὶ φόβου), maintaining a "good conscience" (συνείδησιν . . . ἀγαθήν) and exhibiting "good behavior in Christ" (3:16). The challenge, however, is not merely the

Suffering and Disgrace 101

demand to account for religious faith; echoing 2:12, the hostile nonbelievers are envisioned as defaming (καταλαλέω) the Petrine addressees and reviling (ἐπηρεάζω) their good behavior in Christ (3:16). As the outcome of this confrontation, assuming that the readers follow the letter's prescribed course of action, the letter anticipates the failure of the attempted defamation, so that the accusers rather than the accused will find themselves dishonored (καταισχυνθῆναι [v. 16]).

(3) The challenge to honor in 4:14 is expressed with the verb ὀνειδίζω, a virtual synonym of the word ἐπηρεάζω used in 3:16. In 4:14, there is no explicit defamation based on the charge of improper conduct but rather the general notion of reviling someone simply for being a believer in Christ. On the other hand, 4:15 probably does reflect the letter's assumption that charges of wrongdoing or mischief making (though probably not of murder or theft) had been brought against some members of the communities addressed (possibly though not necessarily in the courts).[189] Certainly the informal charge of wrongdoing is presupposed in the two passages discussed above. Here, however, the confrontation between nonbelievers and believers is couched in the most general terms as the reproach of the former against the latter based solely on religious differences. The general nature of the accusation is echoed in 4:16, where the letter envisions its readers as suffering simply because they are Christians, apart from any specific, legally proscribed acts of wrongdoing. That honor is at stake in this confrontation is clear from 4:16, where 1 Peter commands the one who suffers as a Christian not to be ashamed (μὴ αἰσχυνέσθω).

The concern reflected in these three passages for maintaining honor in the face of threats from outside the Christian communities permeates the letter. Because these Christians have withdrawn from certain aspects of the common public life that they deem inappropriate to their faith, they are reviled (βλασφημέω) by their neighbors (4:4).[190] In 3:9, the addressees are instructed not to respond in kind

---

[189]See above, pp. 91-94.

[190]Although the religious connotations of βλασφημέω are not to be denied here, the object of this hostile speech is not God but the intended recipients of the letter. In this sense, the word harks back to its original meaning, which was basically

when reproached (λοιδορία); in stark contrast to the defamation (καταλαλέω) they encounter (2:12; 3:16), they are to speak well (εὐλογέω) of their detractors. In the face of such widespread hostility, the letter quotes Isa 28:16 to assure its readers that no one who believes in Christ will be put to shame (καταισχυνθῆναι). Servants are instructed to submit to their masters "with complete respect" (ἐν παντὶ φόβῳ [2:18]) and are promised God's commendation (χάρις παρὰ θεῷ), if not that of their society (2:20).

These passages together portray a situation of recurring confrontations between the intended readers and their nonbelieving neighbors in which the addressees were being reviled and falsely accused of engaging in antisocial behaviors. Consistent with the honor-shame model, the letter views the reputation of both parties, the accuser and the accused, as at risk in these confrontations. Such encounters constitute challenges to honor and, as such, cannot be resolved without one side being shamed. What 1 Peter hopes for is that the challengers will be dishonored rather than the letter's readers. The strategy by which 1 Peter aims to realize this hope will be examined in the next two chapters. There we shall discover in the letter's answer to the plight of its addressees still more evidence for the appropriateness of the honor-shame model to the task of interpreting 1 Peter.

First, however, we must make a final inquiry into how well the honor-shame model fits the data of 1 Peter. Since the role of gender appears to be the distinctive feature of the honor-shame system in Mediterranean societies,[191] then 1 Peter must show signs of the peculiar Mediterranean view of the relationship of honor and shame to gender distinctions if the model is to be applied fruitfully to 1 Peter rather than foisted upon it. Affirmative evidence is found in 3:1-7. The Mediterranean value of female moral—especially

---

synonymous with, though perhaps a bit stronger than, two other words used by 1 Peter in reference to the hostile speech of the addressees' antagonists: λοιδορία and ὀνειδίζω. See Hermann Wolfgang Beyer, "βλασφημέω, βλασφημία, βλάσφημος," *TDNT* 1. 621, 623; cf. BAGD, 142.

[191]See above, p. 115.

sexual—purity (ἡ ἁγνὴ ἀναστροφή)[192] and the ideal of the submission of wife to husband are reflected vv. 1-2 and 5-6.[193] Alongside the injunction to females of submissive behavior, the letter prescribes dress proper to female shame in vv. 3-5. And the role of the male as the embodiment and custodian of the honor (τιμή) of his wife is presupposed in v. 7. The extent to which the letter embraces these values and ideals and/or critiques them will be addressed in chapter 4. That they are reflected at all, however, is conclusive evidence that the honor-shame value system typical of Mediterranean societies provides the social-symbolic context—or at least a key element of that context—within which 1 Peter is to be interpreted.

The essence of the problem addressed in 1 Peter, therefore, is the pervasive threat to honor inherent in the relentless verbal attacks of non-Christians against the letter's addressees. For the intended readers, adherence to Christ had issued in conflicts with their neighbors that threatened to undermine their place in society. To return to Goppelt's incisive formulation, the calumny directed at the Petrine Christians "is more than personal insult: It takes from them the public respect on which existence in society depended."[194] In a world in which one's honor and attendant social status were of the utmost importance, the letter depicts a situation in which its addressees were finding their Christian faith to be a threat to their place and well-being in society.[195] In sociological terms, life in their

---

[192] The adjective ἁγνή here is moral rather than cultic. Given its specific application to wives, it should probably be rendered "chaste," reflecting that supreme attribute of the moral woman in the Mediterranean world (as in 4 Macc 18:7; 2 Cor 11:2; and Tit 2:5). See BAGD, 12 and the literature cited there.

[193] For the topos concerning submission of wives to husbands in Greco-Roman rhetoric see Balch, *Wives*, 23-62, 95-99, 143-49. Balch does not, however, connect the submission of wives with the honor-shame system.

[194] Goppelt, *I Peter*, 39; quoted above, p. 98.

[195] Cf. Troy Martin's statement of the problem that "sets up the rhetorical situation" for the author of 1 Peter: "The realization of the expected δόξα has not occurred. In fact, the recipients' former 'δόξα' has been eroded, and they are now being perceived as shameful (2:12; 4:4)" (*Metaphor and Composition*, 111). He then characterizes 1 Peter's response to this problem as follows: "The eschatological material in this document functions rhetorically to resolve this problem and persuade the readers to continue to follow the conduct prescribed" (*Metaphor and Composition*, 113). My position differs from Martin's in several respects. First, I want to maintain

world had become problematic. It is this socially perilous situation that 1 Peter calls "suffering." Such is the rhetorical situation to which the letter is addressed. Nor has the present investigation uncovered any reason to doubt that this rhetorical situation reflected, at least in its general contours, the actual historical situation of Christian communities of Asia Minor during the last three decades of the first century.[196]

---

the distinction in principle between rhetorical situation and actual situation. Second and more important, rather than leaving δόξα untranslated, I would render it "honor," thus giving the term sociopolitical specificity in light of the honor-shame model. Third, Martin's statement of the letter's resolution of this situation, as I shall demonstrate in chaps. 4-5, is far too simplistic. It is not primarily eschatology that provides the answer to the problem of the threat to honor; 1 Peter insists that the addressees are *not* in fact shameful, that their honor has *not* in fact eroded, and the letter provides a way of retaining and recognizing honor within the communities of believers in the face of the counterclaims made by outsiders.

[196]It should be noted here that a number of scholars go a step further than I have gone to argue that the accusations of wrongdoing being brought against 1 Peter's addressees were specifically concerned with the disruption of the hierarchical household structure that occurred when slaves and/or wives converted to Christianity and forsook the religious practices of the *paterfamilias*. The definitive articulation of this position is Balch, *Wives*, 81-121. See also David L. Balch, "Early Christian Criticism of Patriarchal Authority: I Peter 2:11–3:12," *USQR* 39 (1984) 161-73; Kathleen E. Corley, "1 Peter," *Searching the Scriptures*, vol. 2, *A Feminist Commentary* (ed. Elisabeth Schüssler Fiorenza; New York: Crossroad, 1994) 350-54; Elisabeth Schüssler Fiorenza, *In Memory of Her: A Feminist Theological Reconstruction of Christian Origins* (10th anniversary ed.; New York: Crossroad, 1994) 260-66. I do not find this thesis supported by the evidence of 1 Peter: (1) The explicit statements about the confrontations between the addressees and their antagonists are far too general to be limited to the issue of the place within the household of women and slaves. (2) The words to slaves in particular seem to be formulated not so much to instruct actual slaves as to show their experience to be exemplary for all the addressees. (3) The words to wives are sufficiently stereotyped as to preclude the need to set them within the context of specific criticisms of Christian disruption of household order. (4) Moreover, this thesis gives too prominent a place to the household code, which actually occupies only a few verses of 1 Peter. Certainly, the vilification of the addressees presupposed in 1 Peter might have included accusations that women and slaves were doing wrong by forsaking their household religions, but such a situation is not explicit in the letter, nor is it required to make sense of 1 Peter.

Conclusions

In this chapter, I have undertaken to explicate the sociohistorical context of 1 Peter and its intended readers, with special emphasis on the nature of the suffering addressed in the letter. I began by investigating the questions of the letter's authorship, date, and provenance. Although the data do not admit of definitive answers to these questions, the evidence suggests the likelihood that 1 Peter is a pseudonymous letter that originated in Rome sometime during the period 75-105 CE. These considerations, however, yield little information concerning the sociohistorical context of the letter's intended readers. Accepting the post-Petrine date for the letter as a working hypothesis does preclude identifying the suffering addressed in the letter with the situation immediately prior to Nero's campaign against the Christians of Rome, but an organized imperial persecution of Christians—whether actual or impending—does not appear to be the concern of the letter in any case.

I then turned attention to 1 Peter's intended audience and found no reason to doubt that the letter was actually addressed to Christians in the four Roman provinces of Asia Minor named in 1:1. As for the ethnic composition of the communities addressed, the letter directs itself to gentiles who had converted to Christianity, despite the virtual certainty that at least some of the actual Christian communities in Asia Minor at the time were mixed congregations of Jews and gentiles. This address to gentiles appears to have been a function of the letter's understanding that gentile believers were suffering at the hands of unbelieving gentiles who did not look favorably on the conversion of some of their number to a new, foreign religion. Finally, as regards the social status of the addressees, a detailed examination of the evidence in 1 Peter in light of other sources from late antiquity and the secondary literature on Greco-Roman social history forced the conclusion that Elliott and Tàrrech are incorrect in insisting that the addressees were literally resident aliens, probably rural peasants. On the contrary, the words πάροικοι, παροικία, παρεπίδημοι, and διασπορά are used *metaphorically* by 1 Peter to designate the ambiguous socioreligious situation of its gentile Christian addressees in terms of the LXX people of God.

Finally, after locating the source of the conflict in the antipathy Roman society held for religions, such as Christianity, whose adherents tended to withdraw from certain activities of the common life, I then inquired into the nature of the "suffering" presupposed in 1 Peter. The letter envisions hostility expressed verbally in the form of reproach and false accusations of criminal activity against its intended audience. Although the letter's language is sufficiently general to allow for the possibility of judicial proceedings, 1 Peter's focus falls on the kind of informal hostile speech that could be encountered in common, everyday social interactions. In light of the honor-shame model constructed by anthropologists of the Mediterranean, the nature of the suffering engendered by this hostile speech came into sharper relief. The slanderous accusation and verbal challenges directed at 1 Peter's addressees actually constituted a threat to their honor and social status. The suffering with which 1 Peter deals, therefore, is the relentless attack on honor in the form of slander in general and false accusations of wrongdoing in particular.

In terms of the sociology of knowledge, 1 Peter is addressing a situation of conflict between the social world and the symbolic universe of its addressees, a conflict that itself issues from a more fundamental clash of symbolic universes. The antagonists of the Petrine addressees, although living side by side with them, can be said to inhabit a different symbolic universe. Recall that resocialization—as in the case of religious conversion—is only successful to the extent that a symmetry is established between the external and internal worlds of the one(s) being resocialized. For the Petrine addressees, the success of their resocialization into the world of Christianity is now very much in doubt. Their existence in society has become problematic due to their allegiance to the symbolic universe of Christianity. Their beliefs have issued in actions that are differently valued by their unbelieving neighbors, who consequently revile them. The task that falls to 1 Peter, therefore, is to attempt a resolution of the conflict between social world and symbolic universe. Since an adjustment to the former is well beyond the letter's range of possibilities, the answer, it would appear, must lie in some manipulation of the latter. What is needed is a legitimation of the addressees' symbolic universe that would render life within a hostile society intelligible and tolerable. In the next two chapters, I shall examine the strategy 1 Peter adopts to accomplish this task.

CHAPTER 4

THE SOLUTION, PART ONE: THE LIMINALITY OF CHRISTIAN LIFE

In the previous chapter, I concluded that the problem addressed in 1 Peter is the threat to the honor of the letter's addressees inherent in the verbal abuse directed at them by their non-Christian antagonists. I suggested, therefore, that the problem may be viewed, from the standpoint of the sociology of knowledge, as one of conflict between the addressees' social world and their symbolic universe, a conflict that issued from the clash of their symbolic universe with that of their antagonists. In terms of the sociology of knowledge, it would appear that the letter's task is to offer its intended readers a legitimation of the symbolic universe into which they had been initiated at conversion but which has since become problematic for them. Interestingly, 1 Peter itself states the situation in similar terms, not once but twice in chap. 1—in vv. 13-17 and in vv. 18-22.

Symbolic-Universe Maintenance/Legitimation

In 1:13, after recounting the salvation-producing effects of the disclosure of Christ in the gospel message, the letter gives its readers the threefold injunction to "gird up the loins of your mind [τῆς διανοίας], be sober [νήφοντες], and set your hope fully upon the grace that is coming to you in the revelation of Jesus Christ."[1] The

---

[1] Most scholars translate the aorist participle ἀναζωσάμενοι and the present participle νήφοντες as imperatives (see, e.g., the NRSV; Beare, *Epistle of Peter*, 95; Brox, *Petrusbrief*, 72-73; Goppelt, *I Peter*, 105; Kelly, *Epistles of Peter*, 64-66; Selwyn, *Epistle of St. Peter*, 139-40.) The imperatival force of the participles here can

letter, in effect, reminds its readers of the state of affairs created by the proclamation of the Christ event and then insists that its readers *acknowledge* this state of affairs and *think* accordingly. In 1:14-17, the letter also enjoins *conduct* appropriate to this knowledge of reality (ἀναστροφή [1:15], ἀναστράφητε [1:17]). Contrasted with this knowledge of reality and its concomitant behavior is the intended readers' previous view of things, which the letter characterizes as "ignorance" (ἄγνοια), and their previous way of life, which the letter denounces as "being conformed to lusts" (1:14).

Then, in 1:18, the letter again appeals to what its addressees already know about reality (εἰδότες), and, in 1:18-21, it again summarizes the salient points of that reality in terms of God's salvation-creating action in Christ. The letter also reiterates the contrast between pre-Christian and Christian behavior; the intended readers' present Christian behavior is set over against the "futile behavior" of their non-Christian past (1:18, 22). And the Christian construction of reality is called "truth" (ἀλήθεια) in 1:22.

First Peter thus contrasts two competing realities, or perceptions of reality, along with the behaviors of the individuals who subscribe to one of these realities or the other. The one construction of reality is the truth, whereas the other is ignorance. Both are said to characterize the letter's intended readers, but at different times in their lives. Later (in 4:3-4), 1 Peter will state explicitly what is only implied here, namely, that this clash is not merely one between the intended readers' past and present knowledge and behavior but also between their present knowledge and behavior and those of their opponents. 1 Peter is writing to legitimate its addressees' knowledge

---

be attributed to their coordination with the following finite verb, the imperative ἐλπίσατε. See Ernest De Witt Burton, *Syntax of the Moods and Tenses in New Testament Greek* (3d ed.; Chicago: University of Chicago Press, 1900; reprint, Grand Rapids: Kregel, 1976) § 450; J. Harold Greenlee, *A Concise Exegetical Grammar of New Testament Greek* (4th ed.; Grand Rapids: Eerdmans, 1979) 67; cf. BDF, § 421. David Daube recognizes this possibility, but thinks it just as likely that Hebrew or Aramaic influence may explain the imperatival use of these participles (Daube, "Participle and Imperative in 1 Peter," in Selwyn, *Epistle of St. Peter*, 482). Indeed, in several places in 1 Peter (2:18; 3:1, 7, 9) participles unconnected with imperatives clearly have imperatival force (see Daube, "Participle and Imperative," 482-88; Brox, *Petrusbrief*, 73-74).

The Liminality of Christian Life

and conduct in the face of opposition from non-Christians who, as it were, inhabit a different symbolic universe with a competing knowledge of reality and a competing set of behaviors.

Common to both symbolic universes—in fact, pervasive throughout the first-century Mediterranean world—was the honor-shame value system. It is not the value placed on honor and shame that separates 1 Peter and its addressees from the antagonists; if this were the case, 1 Peter could simply denigrate the value of honor, thereby attenuating (although not relieving altogether) the "suffering" of its intended readers. Along with the addressees and their opponents, however, 1 Peter *presupposes* the honor-shame dynamic. Far from dismissing the challenges to honor, therefore, 1 Peter recognizes them to be a profound threat to the social viability of its addressees. What 1 Peter attempts to do is to fashion a legitimation of the symbolic universe of its addressees, one that will establish alternative criteria by which to evaluate the social phenomena that are currently seen, both by the intended readers and by their antagonists, as threats to the honor of the addressees.

We have seen in chapter 3 that, in societies characterized by the honor-shame system, an individual's honor was a function of two variables: (1) the individual's own claim to honor and (2) the evaluation of that claim by society. These two factors roughly correspond to two aspects of Berger and Luckmann's analysis of the sociology of knowledge: (1') the maintenance or legitimation of a symbolic universe in the face of threats to it and (2') the community's role in providing the plausibility structure for the individual. Of course, this dual correlation—of (1) the individual's claim to honor with (1') symbolic-universe maintenance or legitimation and of (2) society as arbiter of the individual's claim to honor with (2') society as mediator of a plausibility structure—is far from exact. It is, however, sufficiently close to suggest an organizing principle for the remainder of this monograph. Taking the second pair first, in this chapter, I shall examine what 1 Peter has to say about the identity of the Christian community as the social collective that, amid a hostile society, both renders the Christian world plausible for its individual members and ratifies their honor. Then, taking up the first pair of correlates, in chapter 5, I shall explore how 1 Peter employs the symbol of the suffering and glorified Christ to legitimate the symbolic universe of its intended readers and to (re)order their understanding of how honor is acquired and dishonor avoided within the community of Christ's followers.

Christian Existence as Liminal

In chapter 1, I summarized the debate between David L. Balch and John H. Elliott concerning the kind of relationship 1 Peter wants its addressees to have with their non-Christian contemporaries, and I promised to offer an alternative to the opposing positions articulated by Balch and Elliott. In the following pages, I shall argue that 1 Peter offers its readers a "liminal" self-identity, that is, an identity that is neither assimilationist nor sectarian, neither firmly ensconced within the larger society nor entirely removed from it. To set the stage for my proposal, I shall briefly revisit the Balch-Elliott debate and then examine three responses to it.

Balch, Elliott, and Their Critics

Balch, we have seen, interprets 1 Peter as urging its readers to assimilate to the larger society in order to silence their critics. The household code figures prominently in 1 Peter's strategy, according to Balch; by invoking the Greco-Roman ideal for the administration of the household, the letter upholds the conventions of Roman society as the norm for its Christian minority communities. Elliott, on the other hand, insists that the letter is designed to empower its readers to resist assimilation and to maintain their group solidarity and distinctive identity as the household of God so that they can provide compelling witness to their faith in the face of hostility from their neighbors. I noted earlier that both positions, although diametrically opposed, find support in the letter.[2]

Charles H. Talbert recognizes this ambiguity in 1 Peter and, over against the "either-or" positions of Elliott and Balch, proposes a "both-and." Based on sociologist George Homas's analysis of

---

[2]See above, pp. 18-22.

group behavior, Talbert argues that 1 Peter seeks *both* internal cohesion (Elliott) and social adaptability (Balch) for its addressees. The letter's emphasis on the common experiences of Christians (e.g., rebirth and election) and on Christian suffering serves to promote cohesion, while its emphasis on behavior that accords with Greco-Roman ideals serves to promote adaptability. Without both internal cohesion and some degree of acceptance by society, Talbert says, the Christian groups could not hope to survive for long.[3]

Talbert's proposal would appear prima facie to be more reasonable than the extreme positions taken by Balch and Elliott. Indeed, Balch recognizes that internal social cohesion is necessary to the communities' survival, just as Elliott recognizes that 1 Peter holds some values in common with Greco-Roman society.[4] Nevertheless, Balch and Elliott remain at odds over the main thrust of the letter, and, in polemically formulating their arguments, they sometimes overstate their cases.[5] One wonders, for example, whether Balch has not misrepresented Elliott's view when he says: "If the boundaries of Petrine Christianity were as closed as Elliott suggests, the missionary interest reflected in 1 Peter as a whole would be inexplicable."[6] In fact, Elliott goes to great lengths to characterize the Petrine communities not just as sects but as *conversionist* sects. Elliott, to cite an example from the other side of the dispute, insists that "nothing in 1 Peter . . . indicates an interest in promoting social assimilation"; even where Elliott acknowledges that some values and patterns of behavior are held in common by 1 Peter and the larger society, he does not admit of any adoption of Greco-Roman social ideals by 1 Peter. Rather, almost as if the points

---

[3]Charles H. Talbert, "Once Again: The Plan of 1 Peter," *Perspectives on First Peter* (ed. Charles H. Talbert; NABPRSSS 9; Macon: Mercer University Press, 1986) 146-48.

[4]See, e.g., Balch, "Hellenization/Acculturation," 100-1; Elliott, "1 Peter, Its Situation and Strategy," 73.

[5]I am speaking here of the essays Balch and Elliott wrote in response to each other's 1981 books on 1 Peter; in these essays, each sharpens his thesis in response to what is clearly perceived to be an opposing position (Balch, "Hellenization/ Acculturation"; Elliott, "1 Peter, Its Situation and Strategy"). Already in the original books, of course, the essentials of their positions are present, but not in so polemical a form.

[6]Balch, "Hellenization/Acculturation," 84.

of correspondence between 1 Peter's ethic and that of Greco-Roman society were purely coincidental, Elliott avers that "the avoidance of evil and the doing of good is behavior consonant with both societal and divine norms."[7] The strength of Talbert's thesis is its ability to recognize a degree of validity in both Balch's and Elliott's positions.

The weakness of Talbert's proposal, in my view, lies in its acceptance of the basic terms of the debate as set out by Balch and Elliott. In essence, Talbert argues that Balch and Elliott are both correct, and he proposes a sociological model by which to synthesize their (anti)theses. If one agreed with Talbert that Balch and Elliott are both correct, except insofar as each insists that his position precludes the other's, then Talbert's synthesis would be eminently more attractive than either Balch's or Elliott's.

In this chapter, however, I shall argue that neither Balch nor Elliott is entirely correct. In brief, I do not think the data in the letter support Balch's reading of 1 Peter as urging assimilation to society, although I do find that 1 Peter's symbolic universe has much in common with that of the society at large, in particular the honor-shame system and parenetic elements that presuppose a hierarchical social structure and, therefore, tend toward conformity to the larger society. Elliott, I think, has the stronger argument, but it too fails to persuade at a number of points. His misreading of the πάροικοι and παρεπίδημοι terminology has already been noted in chapter 3 and will be treated in greater depth below; I shall also argue that the letter evinces little missionary interest and is not as indifferent to the ideals of Greco-Roman society as Elliott thinks. So, to the extent that my criticisms of Balch and Elliott prove persuasive, Talbert's thesis loses much of its force.

Lauri Thurén offers another middle way between the extremes represented by Balch and Elliott. Thurén agrees with Talbert that both positions are solidly based in the text of 1 Peter and that any group wishing to survive in a hostile society must both maintain its social cohesion and exhibit some adaptability. He thinks it implausible, however, "that the same group is simultaneously tempted both to assimilate and to dissimilate, so that the author has to emphasize

---

[7]Elliott, "1 Peter, Its Situation and Strategy," 72-73.

both problems in the same short letter."⁸ Thurén's solution is to posit not a homogeneous group with two opposite problems (as he thinks Talbert does) but two different implied audiences, one comprised of people who were tempted to assimilate in order to avoid persecution and the other of people who were tempted to precisely the opposite response to social pressures—to behave badly by rejecting all societal standards and by returning hostility for hostility. The first group is encouraged to continue to live a life that is at odds with society but in accord with Christian faith. First Peter tries to show that the paradoxical situation of being both elected (by God) and rejected (by society) is normal for Christian life and that this status is of immeasurable value. The second group is told not to disdain the values of the larger society but to be good, well-integrated citizens. The letter instructs them not to seek revenge on their enemies but to bless them in order to win them to the faith.⁹

The strength of Thurén's thesis over against Talbert's lies in Thurén's refusal to pose the question in terms of internal cohesion versus adaptability to society. For Thurén, the question raised by the Balch-Elliott debate is primarily one of the nature of the relationship between the Christian addressees and their non-Christian neighbors. First Peter is clearly preoccupied with this question, whereas the concern for internal group solidarity and cohesion appears to me to be suggested more by the sociological models Elliott and Talbert employ than by the explicit statements in 1 Peter.

As with Talbert before him, however, Thurén too readily allows the Balch-Elliott debate to set the terms of the subsequent discussion.¹⁰ Whereas Talbert essentially says that Balch and Elliott are both correct except insofar as they fail to notice that the two emphases of 1 Peter are directed toward different purposes (the one toward internal cohesion and the other toward external adaptability), Thurén argues that both are correct except insofar as they fail to

---

⁸Thurén, *Rhetorical Strategy*, 37-38. As we shall see, however, Thurén accepts that the author *does* "emphasize both problems in the same short letter." Thurén differs from Talbert not in arguing that only one problem is addressed but in his explanation of *why* the two problems are addressed.
⁹Thurén, *Rhetorical Strategy*, 109-25.
¹⁰See esp. Thurén, *Rhetorical Strategy*, 106.

recognize that the two emphases of the letter are directed to two different implied audiences (one that is tempted to assimilate and one that is tempted to reject society outright). In the same way that the criticisms of Balch and Elliott offered later in this chapter (and already suggested above) have negative implications for Talbert's synthesis, therefore, they also call into question key elements of Thurén's synthesis. Most important, Thurén's positing of a second implied audience, whose tendency is toward aggression and to which 1 Peter counsels assimilation to Greco-Roman ideals for missionary purposes, seems to me to be unsupportable by the text. In the same way that I cannot find the missionary emphasis Elliott sees in 1 Peter, neither can I find reflected there a concern to correct hostile, aggressive, antisocial behavior. It is one thing to find in the letter ethical norms drawn from Greco-Roman society; it is quite another to conclude that the letter is addressing an implied audience of individuals who were deliberately transgressing these norms.

Finally, Reinhard Feldmeier, as we have seen in chapter 1, presents a third response to the Balch-Elliott debate. Feldmeier agrees with Elliott that 1 Peter wants to prevent assimilation and that community coherence is called for throughout the letter,[11] but he thinks that both Elliott and Balch misrepresent 1 Peter's overall intention. The letter advocates neither a sectarian existence (Elliott) nor acculturation (Balch). Rather, 1 Peter's addressees are instructed to traverse a middle path between the twin dangers of assimilation on the one hand and sectarian flight from the world on the other. The key element in 1 Peter's strategy is the stranger (*Fremde*) motif. As strangers, the addressees are distinct from the present age, but they must not withdraw from society. They are to live as God's people within the given social structures, testifying therein to their God-given eschatological existence, which is not derived from the world and cannot be accommodated to the world. Although he admits that the Petrine ecclesiology does show some marks of the "conversionist sect," Feldmeier insists that the letter's openness to the world precludes the designation "sect." Salvation, for 1 Peter, should not be locked up within the walls of the community but communicated,

---

[11]Feldmeier, *Christen als Fremde*, 188, see esp. n. 73.

and this mediation of salvation should occur by means of Christians' behaving in accordance with generally recognized ethical precepts. Feldmeier, therefore, using Troeltschian terminology, prefers to describe the letter's "ecclesiology" as combining the *Offenheit* of a church with the *Entschiedenheit* of a sect.[12]

Whereas Talbert and Thurén think that Balch and Elliott are both correct, Feldmeier insists that they are both wrong. In order to sustain this claim, however, he must grossly caricature Elliott's position. Balch, it is true, explicitly characterizes 1 Peter as assimilationist; but Elliott certainly does not see the letter as advocating a "flight from the world." Nor does Feldmeier achieve any gain in historical understanding by eschewing Elliott's use of Bryan R. Wilson's conversionist-sect typology in favor of the far more theologically charged Troeltschian typology of sect versus church. In fact, despite Feldmeier's insistence that Elliott has gotten it wrong and that 1 Peter is more open to society than Elliott allows, I find Feldmeier's characterization of the letter's prescription for its readers' relation to society to be virtually identical to the one Elliott describes in terms of the "conversionist sect." To the extent that Feldmeier does actually describe a community profile that is more open to society than the one Elliott outlines (as opposed to simply asserting that this is the case), my reservations about the letter's missionary intention for its addressees are even more apropos of Feldmeier's thesis than they are of Elliott's.

Although I agree with Talbert, Thurén, and Feldmeier that neither Balch nor Elliott provides a satisfactory account of the kind of relationship 1 Peter wants its readers to have with the society, I am not convinced by the alternatives these three offer. Having suggested some specific criticisms of the several positions above, I shall conclude with some broader methodological observations. Balch and Elliott, I think, fail to acknowledge the genuine ambiguity of the evidence in the letter. Talbert and Thurén correctly note the ambiguity but offer solutions that are overly complicated. They essentially agree that both Balch and Elliott are correct about certain aspects of 1 Peter and that Balch's and Elliott's interpretations are

---

[12]Feldmeier, *Christen als Fremde*, 189-91.

not mutually exclusive. Talbert's synthesis is based on a proposed dual purpose, while Thurén's is based on a proposed dual audience. Feldmeier's alternative to Balch and Elliott is not so much a synthesis as a third way, and as such, it has the advantage of being simpler than Talbert's and Thurén's. Feldmeier also recognizes the ambiguity that Balch and Elliott deny. In my view, however, he too neatly resolves the ambiguities within a sophisticated theological account of 1 Peter's "ecclesiology." I share Feldmeier's interest in the self-identity the letter offers its readers and I agree that the stranger terminology is central to that self-identity, but I do not think that Feldmeier has sufficiently grounded his analysis in the social history of the late-first-century Mediterranean world or in social-scientific theory.

In the following pages, I shall offer a new interpretation of the function of 1 Peter's ambiguous statements about its intended readers' Christian identity within a hostile non-Christian society. I contend that the letter's ambiguous statements and images together construct an identity that is itself ambiguous with respect to the larger society. Followers of the Christ who suffered and was consequently glorified, the letter explains, occupy a place that is neither here nor there, neither fully within society nor completely removed from it. In the terminology of the anthropologist Victor Turner, Christian life for 1 Peter is a liminal existence. In presenting my argument, I shall first turn attention to Turner's theory of liminality, which he developed to deal with similarly ambiguous social phenomena.

Victor Turner on Liminality

Turner first worked out his theory of liminality in the context of his field work on ritual in African tribal societies.[13] The theory is

---

[13] For the original articulation of the theory, see Victor Turner, "Betwixt and Between: The Liminal Period in *Rites de Passage*," *Proceedings of the 1964 Annual Spring Meeting of the American Ethnological Society* (ed. June Helm; n.p.: American Ethnological Society, 1964) 4-20 (reprint in *The Forest of Symbols: Aspects of Ndembu Ritual* [Ithaca/London: Cornell University Press, 1967] 93-111 [hereafter, page numbers refer to the reprint]); and idem, *The Ritual Process: Structure and Anti-*

essentially an adaptation and expansion of Arnold van Gennep's seminal discussion of rites of passage. Van Gennep had argued that in any society, the life of the individual consists of a series of passages from one age or occupation or social position to another, and that such passages are frequently accompanied by special acts or ceremonies—rites of passage—that "enable the individual to pass from one defined position to another which is equally well defined."[14] Van Gennep was convinced that, throughout cultures, the underlying arrangement of rites of passage was identical. The pattern of such rites, he argued, always consisted of three periods or phases: separation, transition, and incorporation.[15] The transition phase van Gennep called the "liminal period" (from the Latin word *limen*, meaning "threshold").[16]

In developing his own theory, Turner accepted van Gennep's analysis of the nature of rites of passage. Because Turner's interest lay in the nature of *transition* within societies, he focused his attention on rites of passage that had particularly well-developed liminal phases.[17] In such rites of passage, he discovered, persons in the liminal period are "neither here nor there; they are betwixt and between the positions assigned and arrayed by law, custom, convention, and ceremonial." Given its ambiguous "in-between" nature, it is not surprising to find the liminal period ritually symbolized as, among other things, death, darkness, bisexuality, being in the womb, or solar eclipse. Persons in the liminal phase are variously represented as possessing nothing, disguised as monsters, stripped of clothing, and the like.[18] The characteristic symbolism of liminality, Turner says, is that of paradox, "or being *both* this *and* that" (e.g., both living and dead, human and animal, or male and female).[19]

Structure (Symbol, Myth, and Ritual Series; Ithaca: Cornell University Press, 1969).

[14]Arnold van Gennep, *The Rites of Passage* (trans. Monika B. Vizedom and Gabrielle L. Caffee; London: Routledge & Kegan Paul, 1960; French original, 1908) 2-3.

[15]Van Gennep, *Rites of Passage*, 191.

[16]Van Gennep, *Rites of Passage*, 10-11; Turner, *Ritual Process*, 94.

[17]Turner, "Betwixt and Between," 95.

[18]Turner, *Ritual Process*, 95.

[19]Victor Turner, "Variations on a Theme of Liminality," *Secular Ritual* (ed. Sally F. Moore and Barbara G. Myerhoff; Assen/Amsterdam: Van Gorcum, 1977) 37.

Ritual liminality thus suspends or minimizes previously recognized social differences, thereby creating an egalitarian context in which intense bonds may be formed among those in the liminal phase. Turner calls this intimate relationship between liminars *communitas*, which he defines as "society as an unstructured or rudimentarily structured and relatively undifferentiated *comitatus*, community, or even communion of equal individuals." He contrasts this modality of human interrelatedness with a second one, namely, society as "a structured, differentiated, and often hierarchical system of politico-legal-economic positions." From his observations of these two modes of human relations, Turner infers that social life is a process of alternating between structure and communitas, inequality and equality, differentiation and homogeneity.[20]

That is to say, for Turner, liminality and communitas are not merely aspects of ritual but are pervasive in human societies. Hence his differentiation between existential or spontaneous communitas, normative communitas, and ideological communitas. *Spontaneous communitas* is communitas par excellence, as defined in the previous paragraph.[21] It is a profoundly antistructural, egalitarian relationship between I and Thou in Buber's sense.[22] *Normative communitas* occurs when a group attempts to organize existential communitas in a perduring social system. It is "the attempt to capture and preserve spontaneous communitas in a system of ethical precepts and legal rules."[23] *Ideological communitas* is the effort to specify the ideal social conditions within which the experience of spontaneous communitas can flourish (as in most utopian models of society).[24] The distinction between normative and ideological communitas lies primarily in the greater theoretical sophistication of the latter.[25]

---

[20]Turner, *Ritual Process*, 96.

[21]"Communitas is, existentially speaking and in its origins, purely spontaneous and self-generating" (Victor Turner, *Dramas, Fields, and Metaphors: Symbolic Action in Human Society* [Symbol, Myth, and Ritual Series; Ithaca/London: Cornell University Press, 1974] 243).

[22]Turner, *Ritual Process*, 126-27, 132; idem, *Dramas*, 46-47.

[23]Victor Turner, *Process, Performance and Pilgrimage: A Study in Comparative Symbology* (Ranchi Anthropology Series 1; New Delhi: Concept, 1979) 151.

[24]Turner, *Ritual Process*, 132.

[25]See Turner, *Process, Performance*, 46-47.

The Liminality of Christian Life

More important for Turner (and for my investigation) is the distinction he draws between spontaneous communitas, which occurs outside structure and is ephemeral, and that communitas (whether normative or ideological) that falls within the domain of social structure and is enduring.[26] Communitas, which is by nature a spontaneous, momentary phenomenon, can only be maintained by acquiring rules; that is to say, spontaneous communitas, if it is to endure, must become normative or ideological communitas. In the transformation of spontaneous communitas into normative or ideological communitas, "free relationships between individuals become converted into norm-governed relationships between social personae."[27] When communitas is institutionalized, "the new-found idiosyncratic is legislated into yet another set of universalistic roles and statuses."[28] And the style of normative communitas within any given community is largely dependent upon how that community symbolizes the abrogation, negation, or inversion of the structure of the larger society in which its members participate in their routine, everyday lives.[29]

Communitas, Turner argues, is most evident in liminality. And like communitas, liminality is not to be restricted to the domain of ritual. Here Turner extends van Gennep's use of the term liminality to refer beyond the bounds of ritual "to any condition outside, or on the peripheries of, everyday life."[30] Ritual is but one such condition; indeed, in preliterate societies, in which leisure time is all but unknown, ritual provides the preeminent condition for liminality. In Turner's view, religious liturgies and the initiation ceremonies of clubs and fraternities perform a similar function in today's postindustrial societies.[31] In contemporary societies, liminality is also to be

---

[26]See Turner, *Ritual Process*, 132-34. See also Turner's essay "Passages, Margins, and Poverty: Religious Symbols of Communitas," written shortly after *The Ritual Process* and reprinted in *Dramas*; here Turner distinguishes between only two types of communitas: existential and normative (*Dramas*, 243 n. 2).

[27]Turner, *Ritual Process*, 132.

[28]Turner, *Process, Performance*, 44.

[29]Turner, *Process, Performance*, 45.

[30]Turner, *Dramas*, 46-47.

[31]Turner, *Ritual Process*, 138; idem, "Variations on a Theme of Liminality," 45.

found in such phenomena as good parties, commuter trains, and pubs. Furthermore, not only individuals, but groups or whole societies can experience liminal phases in which the entire social order goes through a period of transition.[32] In all such liminal conditions, which place people outside their everyday social-structural positions, communitas may spontaneously emerge.[33]

Just as communitas—which in its purest form is spontaneous—can be brought within social structure, so liminality can become an "institutionalized state." The institutionalization of liminality is the process by which transition itself becomes a permanent condition. Many characteristics of the world's religions, according to Turner, are due to the institutionalization of liminality.[34] For examples, he points especially to the monastic and mendicant orders of the world's religions, with Francis and his followers providing a particularly telling case in point. "Francis appears quite deliberately to be compelling the friars to inhabit the fringes and interstices of the social structure of their time, and to keep them in a permanently liminal state, where . . . the optimal conditions inhere for the realization of communitas." For Francis, nakedness was the "master symbol" of emancipation from social-structural bondage, and Christ was the preeminent model of nakedness.[35] Other attempts to institutionalize liminality and perpetuate communitas include enthusiastic religious sects (such as millenarians), the hippies of the 1960s, dharma bums, and rural communards. Such efforts tend to employ symbols of marginality, outsiderhood, social-structural

---

[32]Turner, *Dramas*, 47, 53. Turner often refers to the kinds of social disruptions that produce millenarian or messianic movements, without specifying precisely what form such disruptions may take (e.g., *Dramas*, 47, 248; cf. *Ritual Process*, 133). Only slightly more specific is his suggestion elsewhere that society-wide liminality may result from "crises in social processes whether these result from internal adjustments, external adaptations, or unexpected disasters (earthquakes, invasions, plagues, and the like)" ("Variations on a Theme," 44).

[33]Turner, *Dramas*, 242. Turner also argues that liminality does not necessarily generate communitas; it may also have the opposite effect: "either a Hobbesian war of all against all, or an existentialist anarchy of individuals, each 'doing his or her own thing'" (*Dramas*, 285; see also *Dramas*, 52-52). Liminality, we might say, is a necessary but not a sufficient condition for the emergence of communitas.

[34]Turner, *Ritual Process*, 107; cf. idem, *Dramas*, 261.

[35]Turner, *Ritual Process*, 145-46.

inferiority, and liminality (in the literal sense of transition from one social-structural position to another) to construct their self-identity and to characterize both their internal relations and their relations with outsiders.[36]

Critical Appropriation of Turner's Theory

The preceding analysis of Turner's theory indicates that Turner uses the term liminal in three distinct, though certainly related, senses—the literal, the ritual, and the metaphorical. (1) Liminality in its *literal* sense refers to the actual passing of an individual or group from one social-structural status or condition to another. It is precisely such passages in the lives of individuals that frequently become the occasions for rituals. In the case of initiation ceremonies, for example, the individuals participating in the rite pass through a ritual liminal phase that symbolizes the actual liminal phase that provided the occasion for the ceremony in the first place, whether the passage is from youth to adulthood, from one religion to another, or from singleness to marriage, among endless possibilities that could be cited. Liminal in its literal sense, therefore, refers to such actual moments of transition of individuals or societies.

(2) Following van Gennep, Turner often uses the word liminal to refer to the second—the transition—stage of rituals. *Ritual* liminality, as we have seen, emerges during the second phase of a rite of passage, in which previously recognized social distinctions are left behind in order to create the conditions for communitas among the individuals in the liminal phase.

(3) Liminality is used in a *metaphorical* sense when Turner refers to symbolic representations of liminality—such as nakedness, birth, and death—that are used within ritual liminality. *Ritual liminality*, one may say, employs various *metaphors* of liminality in order to facilitate communitas. Moreover, in institutionalized liminality, as in the case of monastic orders, for example, or millenarian movements, such metaphors of liminality provide groups with the images by which to construct their own liminal identity.

---

[36]Turner, *Dramas*, 243-46; idem, *Ritual Process*, 133-46.

It is this third sense of the term—the metaphorical—in which this study is primarily interested, although the first—the literal—will also prove to be of some value in explicating Christian identity according to 1 Peter. Since we have no access to the specific rites practiced by the intended readers of 1 Peter (aside from 3:21, which indicates that their baptism is presupposed), and since the letter itself evinces little interest in ritual, liminality as an aspect of ritual will play no role in the following discussion.[37] As for the literal sense of liminality, although I have demonstrated in chapter 3 that we can know next to nothing about the specific social situation of the actual readers of the letter, I have also assayed to describe the rhetorical situation of the intended readers constructed by the letter. In light of the above treatment of Turner's work, it appears that this rhetorical situation partakes of many of the characteristics of liminality. It is the third use of the term liminal, however, that is of greatest moment for my investigation. In the pages to follow I shall argue that 1 Peter employs a number of images and metaphors of liminality to fashion for its intended readers a vision of Christian existence as liminal—as neither here nor there with respect to the larger society but "betwixt and between," both in social-structural and in temporal terms.

Turner posits liminality as the condition for spontaneous communitas, and institutionalized liminality as the attempt to facilitate ongoing, normative communitas. In the present study, the concept of liminality takes precedence over that of communitas (without entirely eclipsing it, as we shall see). Turner differentiates the two as follows. Liminality is a "state," "a sphere or domain of

---

[37]This is not to say that the letter betrays no knowledge of Christian ritual, but only that ritual per se is not an object of 1 Peter's concern. The addressees' baptism is explicitly mentioned in 3:21, not to call attention to baptism as a matter of ongoing concern in the communities addressed but as the antitype in the intended readers' recent past to the saving work of God in the time of Noah. Some LXX-Jewish liturgical traditions are invoked (1:2, 19; 2:5), and 1 Peter almost certainly draws on early christological hymns, whose setting was the worshiping communities. In these cases, 1 Peter uses symbols whose primary context was liturgy, without drawing attention to their liturgical backgrounds. And in 4:9-11, the letter gives instructions concerning mutual service, very likely service to be rendered, in part, within in the context of the gathered, worshiping communities. Nothing of any specific ritual, however, is mentioned nor need be presupposed.

action or thought," whereas communitas is "a social modality."[38] In the case of 1 Peter, we cannot probe behind the letter to uncover a pristine originating moment of spontaneous communitas among the intended readers and then trace its institutionalization in normative communitas. Nor can we inquire into the modality of intra-community relations among the addressees at the time of the letter's dispatch or reception. The data are insufficient for either task; this is true both of the actual Christians of Asia Minor, about whom we can discover virtually nothing from the letter, and of the rhetorically constructed addressees, about whose intracommunity relations the letter says little. If we lack access to the "social modality" of intracommunity relations as they *are*, however, we can and will ask whether the letter's parenesis tells us anything about how 1 Peter would like them to be. Just as institutionalized liminality provides the conditions for normative communitas in Turner's theory, so in 1 Peter the directives for intracommunity relations presuppose acceptance of the letter's construction of Christian communal self-identity. Furthermore, this study is primarily concerned with how the letter answers the addressees' problem of suffering, and 1 Peter's construction of a liminal identity is directed primarily toward that end. It is not trouble within the communities addressed that occupies 1 Peter but the conflict between them and the larger society. In the following pages, therefore, I shall first inquire into the "sphere or domain of action or thought" constituted by the vision of community that 1 Peter presents its intended readers in response to their suffering, and only then turn attention to the "social modality" that is to characterize life within such a community.[39]

---

[38]Turner, *Dramas*, 52.

[39]Furthermore, the distinction between the *sphere* of liminality and the *social modality* of communitas is severely attenuated in Turner's notion of normative communitas. In the latter, communitas has itself become rule governed, so that "normative communitas" assumes to some extent the nature of sphere or domain. That is, the "norms" of normative communitas in essence create a place for the human relations they govern. And since this monograph (like 1 Peter) is more interested in the relationships between Christians and outsiders than in the relationships among Christians, the concept of liminality as the sphere of Christian life in a hostile world is the aspect of Turner's work that will most inform this study.

This part of the study will proceed as follows: First, I shall demonstrate that 1 Peter presupposes a temporal context for Christian life that is liminal in the literal sense; the addressees are living in that ambiguous time between Christ's death and resurrection on the one hand and the imminent manifestation of the fullness of his glory on the other. Second, I shall argue that the identity 1 Peter offers its readers is liminal in the metaphorical sense; as such, it is an instance of institutionalized liminality. Third, in light of the letter's vision of the liminality of Christian existence, I shall examine 1 Peter's directives for its intended readers' relations with their non-Christian antagonists. Fourth, I shall inquire into the letter's prescription for relations among believers within the communities addressed. This final step is crucial methodologically, because it will provide a means of testing the fit of Turner's theory with 1 Peter. If 1 Peter's construction of Christian communal self-identity is to be interpreted in terms of Turner's notion of institutionalized liminality, then the letter's parenesis should exhibit characteristics of normative communitas. I shall argue that this is precisely the case.

Liminality in 1 Peter

I have already suggested that the rhetorical situation addressed by 1 Peter exhibits many characteristics of liminality in the literal sense of the word. The addressees are under verbal attack by their non-Christian neighbors, and this polemical situation threatens to undermine the intended readers' social status. With respect to society at large, the addressees are being marginalized; they are being forced into a socially liminal position. Alongside the social liminality ascribed to the letter's addressees, 1 Peter exhibits "literal" liminality of another kind—temporal liminality. This temporal liminality, moreover, is characteristic not only of the lives of the letter's addressees in particular but of Christian life in the world in general. Whereas the social liminality in which the addressees find themselves constitutes the problem addressed by the letter, 1 Peter's depiction of the temporal liminality of Christian existence provides part of the letter's answer.

Temporal Liminality. The letter itself frames the question of the temporal context of Christian existence in a provocative way in 1:11. First Peter has just recounted the addressees' conversion to Christianity in 1:3-9: God, according to (κατά) the divine mercy, caused them (along with the implied author [ἡμᾶς]) to be reborn through (διά) the resurrection of Jesus Christ. As a result of their conversion, the addressees now believe in Christ; and the ultimate outcome of that belief will be their salvation "in the last time" (ἐν καιρῷ ἐσχάτῳ) [v. 5]). Israel's prophets, the letter says in 1:10, prophesied about the grace that the addressees would receive and inquired into the nature of the salvation that grace would effect. In particular, as the Spirit of Christ within them was prophesying about Christ's suffering and subsequent glory, the prophets wondered to "what time or what kind of time" (τίνα ἢ ποῖον καιρόν) these prophecies referred. The prophets' first question—"what time?"—is quickly answered by the divine disclosure (ἀπεκαλύφθη) of v. 12. God revealed to the prophets that they were not serving themselves but "you"—the readers of the letter—"now" (νῦν)—the present time of the proclamation of the gospel (εὐαγγελισαμένων). This "now," therefore, is the καιρός of the proclamation of the gospel. But the second question—"what kind of time?"—is not explicitly answered here. It remains for 1 Peter's readers, including us, to discover the answer to this question in the reading of the letter. If the time to which the prophets addressed their message turns out to be the καιρός of the proclamation of the Christ event, what kind of καιρός is this?[40]

---

[40]The NRSV translates τίνα "the person"; in this reading the prophets' question is twofold—what person or what time? The word ποῖος, of course, is ambiguous; it can function as a simple interrogative pronoun. Indeed, it is this ambiguity that leads to the NRSV reading, in which τίνα is treated as a synonym of ποῖον and so assigned a different referent to avoid redundancy. Furthermore, G. D. Kilpatrick argues that 1 Pet 1:11 follows the "general New Testament practice" of treating τίνα as an interrogative pronoun and ποῖον as an interrogative adjective, so that the question is "who is the Messiah and when will he come?" (G. D. Kilpatrick, "1 Peter 1:11 ΤΙΝΑ ῾Η ΠΟΙΟΝ ΚΑΙΡΟΝ," *NovT* 28 [1986] 91-92). The following verse, however, addresses only the question of time; the identity of the person is already contained in the summation of the content of the prophecies in v. 11. The mystery that is addressed in the divine revelation of v. 12 concerns not the person but the time prophesied about. (See Michaels, *1 Peter*, 41; cf. BAGD, 684; Brox,

The logical place to begin the search for an answer to this question is with 1 Peter's references to time in general and to its intended readers' temporal location in particular. Certainly the most programmatic expression of the letter's view of the present καιρός in relation to past and future time is the statement, in 4:7, Πάντων δὲ τὸ τέλος ἤγγικεν. The τέλος of all things, that is, the eschatological consummation expected in both early-Jewish and early-Christian tradition, is near. The word τέλος is used in this sense in two other places in the letter—1:9 and 4:17.[41] In the former, τέλος designates the eschatological outcome of faith (τῆς πίστεως) in Christ (εἰς ὅν [1:8]), namely, σωτηρίαν. In the latter, τέλος designates the eschatological result of refusal to obey (ἀπειθούντων) the gospel. In all three verses, therefore, what is clearly in view is the eschaton, when God will bring history to an end and mete out punishment or grant salvation, depending upon one's response to the gospel of God's act in Christ. And 1 Pet 4:7 unequivocally states that this eschatological moment is near. It would appear, therefore, that a partial answer to the second question posed in 1 Pet 1:11 is that the letter's present καιρός is time on the cusp of the eschaton; but the letter has much more to say about what kind of time this is.

The word καιρός first occurs in 1 Peter in 1:5, where it is situated between two other key terms—ἔσχατος and ἀποκαλύπτω. Believers are being kept by God's power, according to 1:5, "for salvation ready to be revealed in the last time" (ἐν καιρῷ ἐσχάτῳ). This view of salvation is quite literally an apocalyptic-eschatological

---

Petrusbrief, 69 n. 231.) BDF wonders whether the combination is a deliberate tautology for emphasis (BDF, § 298 [2]). But translating ποῖον as "what kind of" is consistent with the only other appearance of ποῖος in 1 Peter—in 2:20 (see BAGD, 684). Moreover, I want to argue that however one translates ποῖον, 1:11 in particular and 1 Peter in general are greatly concerned with the nature of the temporal context of Christian life, and the question of time posed in 1:11 concerns not only location on a time line but the nature of God's activity in the Christian communities and the world, both in and beyond history. That is to say, I find in the τίνα ἢ ποῖον of 1:11 a question (whether explicit or implicit) that is contemplated throughout the letter. For ποῖον καιρόν as a question about the manner of time or the circumstances attending the time in view, see Brox, *Petrusbrief*, 68-70; Goppelt, *I Peter*, 98; Kelly, *Epistles of Peter*, 60; Michaels, *1 Peter*, 41-42; Selwyn, *Epistle of St. Peter*, 135.

[41]Τέλος is also used adverbially to mean "finally" in 3:8.

The Liminality of Christian Life

one. Presumably God is the actor implicit in the passive form ἀποκαλυφθῆναι; the same God who is presently preserving believers will, in the last καιρός, reveal their salvation. Although 1:5 gives no explicit indication of how near or remote the καιρὸς ἔσχατος is, the adjective ἑτοίμην, which modifies σωτηρίαν, suggests the possibility that the last time is rather near: Eschatological salvation is, even now, ready to be revealed.[42] Indeed, in light of the use of τέλος in 1:9 and 4:7, 1 Pet 1:5 should also be read as implying not only the present readiness of salvation but also its imminence. And this readiness/nearness of salvation has its counterpart in 5:1, where the implied author characterizes himself as a "sharer in the glory that is about to be revealed" (ὁ . . . τῆς μελλούσης ἀποκαλύπτεσθαι δόξης κοινωνός). Just as ἑτοίμην in 1:5 signals the imminence of the revelation of salvation, so in 5:1 the participle μελλούσης indicates that God's revelation of the glory that is Christ's as a result of Christ's suffering and that awaits believers in Christ is expected momentarily.[43] According to 1 Pet 1:5, therefore, the present time—the καιρός of the proclamation of Christ (1:11)—is not the final, decisive moment, although that final moment is not far off.[44]

The word καιρός appears in two other places in the letter—in 4:17 and 5:6. The former is situated in the context of several admonitions concerning proper Christian conduct in the face of persecution. After 1 Peter enjoins its addressees to rejoice in suffering (4:13) and to glorify God (4:16), 4:17 provides the basis (ὅτι) for these imperatives—ὁ καιρὸς τοῦ ἄρξασθαι τὸ κρίμα ἀπὸ τοῦ οἴκου τοῦ θεοῦ. Here καιρός functions as the predicate nominative of an unexpressed copula,[45] and the genitive articular

---

[42]"God's salvation exists already in his [sic] saving intent. It is present but not yet visible; it needs only to be 'revealed,' and the moment of its revelation is very near" (Michaels, *1 Peter*, 23).

[43]On μέλλω as indicating imminence and not merely futurity, see BAGD, 501. Michaels sees the emphasis here on futurity (*1 Peter*, 282), a position I find untenable in light of, e.g., 1 Pet 4:5, 7, 17; 5:10.

[44]Cf. Goppelt, *I Peter*, 88 n. 29: "Even the ἔσχατος καιρός in 1:5 is not . . . the 'end time,' in the sense of the already present time extending to the parousia, but the point in time at which the end occurs." Cf. Goppelt, *I Peter*, 118 n. 67.

[45]Goppelt, *I Peter*, 329; Michaels, *1 Peter*, 270.

infinitive specifies the nature of this καιρός in terms of its purpose.[46] The present, 1 Peter says, is the time of the beginning of God's judgment. Whereas in 1:5 the καιρός in view is clearly future, although the adjective ἑτοίμην suggests that this future is very near, in 4:17 καιρός refers to the letter's present time. The present καιρός, although not the last καιρός, is the time for the beginning of God's judgment of the world. Both early-Jewish and early-Christian tradition located God's universal judgment in the last time.[47] The present, therefore, although not yet the eschaton, is the time for the beginning of (at least one of) the eschatological events.

First Peter 4:5 is instructive on this point. Here 1 Peter uses the adverb ἑτοίμως to describe God's disposition with respect to the judgment. The letter's addressees are assured that those who currently abuse them will be called to give an account of themselves to God, "who is ready to judge the living and the dead" (τῷ ἑτοίμως ἔχοντι κρῖναι ζῶντας καὶ νεκρούς). God's present readiness to judge in 4:5 corresponds to the readiness of the eschatological σωτηρία in 1:5, and this correspondence suggests that God's judgment, like salvation, is imminent. This suggestion of imminent eschatological judgment in 4:5, furthermore, corresponds to the present as the καιρός of the beginning of judgment in 4:17 and, more generally, to the nearness of the end of all things in 4:7.

The fourth and final appearance of καιρός in 1 Peter comes in 5:6. Here the letter commands its readers to humble themselves before God in order that God might exalt them ἐν καιρῷ. As in 1:5, 1:11, and 4:17, καιρός in 5:6 refers not to a period of time in the sense of that which can be measured by clock or calendar, but to a moment invested with meaning and purpose by the decision and action of God. The NRSV does well to render ἐν καιρῷ "in due time." No explicit, unambiguous reference to chronology occurs in this passage, although the adjective ὀλίγον in 5:10 should probably be taken as a reference to the duration of suffering (rather than to the

---

[46]BDF, § 400 (1).

[47]See, e.g., Richard H. Hiers, "Day of Christ," *ABD* 2. 76-79; idem, "Day of Judgment," *ABD* 2. 79-82; Christopher Rowland, *The Open Heaven: A Study of Apocalyptic in Judaism and Early Christianity* (New York: Crossroad, 1982) 156-89, esp. 156-76.

The Liminality of Christian Life   131

intensity of suffering).⁴⁸ Even if we suspend judgment on the meaning of ὀλίγον in 5:10, however, the passages discussed in the previous paragraphs indicate that the καιρός of the exalting of believers by God is the imminent future καιρὸς ἔσχατος.

On the basis of the above examination of 1 Peter's use of the words καιρός, τέλος, and ἑτοίμην/ἑτοίμως, we may now draw the provisional conclusion that 1 Peter views the present καιρός not as the καιρὸς ἔσχατος proper but as a time so near the καιρὸς ἔσχατος that it can be said to be the time of the beginning of the events of the καιρὸς ἔσχατος. Our investigation is not yet at an end, however.

The word ἔσχατος, which first occurs in 1:5 (in the phrase ἐν καιρῷ ἐσχάτῳ), appears in 1:20 for the second and final time in the letter, here in connection with one of three occurrences of the word χρόνος. Christ, according to 1:20, was predestined before the foundation of the world and manifested, on account of the addressees, ἐπ' ἐσχάτου τῶν χρόνων. The latter construction is unique in early-Jewish and early-Christian literature, although it closely resembles such phrases as ἐπ' ἐσχάτων τῶν ἡμερῶν (Gen 49:1; Hos 3:5; Mic 4:1; Jer 37:24; Ezek 38:16; Dan 10:14 [θ']; 2 Pet 3:3; 2 Clem. 14:2; Barn. 12:9; 16:5), ἐπ' ἐσχάτου τῶν ἡμερῶν (Num 24:14; Jer 23:20; 25:19; Dan 10:14; Heb 1:2), ἐπ' ἐσχάτῳ τῶν ἡμερῶν (Deut 4:30), and ἐπ' ἐσχάτου τοῦ χρόνου (Jude 18). These phrases refer either generally to the future or specifically to the eschaton,⁴⁹ and ἐπ' ἐσχάτου τῶν χρόνων in 1 Pet 1:20 should be interpreted similarly. Unlike the καιρὸς ἔσχατος (1:5), which is clearly future albeit very near (4:7), the ἔσχατος τῶν χρόνων has already begun, at the manifestation of Christ. The expression ἐσχάτου τῶν χρόνων indicates a view of history as a series of epochs—χρόνοι—and Christ's appearance as occurring at the end

---

⁴⁸In 1:6 and 5:10 ὀλίγος probably refers to suffering for a short time rather than to suffering a small amount. Since the case for the temporal use of the adjective can only be made on the basis of what the letter says elsewhere, however, it would be circular argumentation to cite 1 Peter's use of ὀλίγος as evidence for the nearness of the καιρὸς ἔσχατος. See BAGD, 563; Goppelt, *I Peter*, 89, esp. n. 35, 365; Michaels, *1 Peter*, 28, 302.

⁴⁹Harold W. Attridge, *The Epistle to the Hebrews: A Commentary on the Epistle to the Hebrews* (Hermeneia; Philadelphia: Fortress, 1989) 39.

of these periods.⁵⁰ That a καιρὸς ἔσχατος and a τέλος are still expected, however, is evidence that ἐπ' ἐσχάτου τῶν χρόνων should be taken to indicate not the end point of history but the beginning of the end. While the last καιρός lies in the near future, 1 Peter views the present as the very end of the series of χρόνοι comprising history. As such, the present too is, according to 1:11, a decisive moment—a καιρός—the καιρός of the gospel. We might say that the letter's eschatology is realized in the sense that the end of the final historical epoch (ἔσχατος τῶν χρόνων) has already begun, and future in the sense that the final moment (καιρὸς ἔσχατος)—the consummation (τέλος)—is still to come.⁵¹

The other two occurrences of χρόνος in 1 Peter are particularly telling because they refer to the temporal duration of historical Christian existence at the end of the χρόνοι of history. The intended readers' existence in society is characterized, in 1:17, as a "time of exile" (τὸν τῆς παροικίας ὑμῶν χρόνον) and, in 4:2, "as the remaining time in the flesh" (τὸν ἐπίλοιπον ἐν σαρκὶ ... χρόνον). Both phrases—especially the latter—imply but a short duration of the present condition of Christian life, which accords with what we have found elsewhere in the letter concerning the time remaining at the end of the last χρόνος of history.

Two short but significant words appear in several of 1 Peter's characterizations of the temporal context of the lives of its addressees. Five times 1 Peter uses the word νῦν to contrast sharply the *previous* life of its intended readers with their *present*, postconversion existence. The most programmatic of these is found in a verse already considered above—1:12. Here 1 Peter brings together salvation history and the personal history of its readers by explaining that the καιρός of Christ and the gospel—the καιρός the prophets announced—is the now of the readers' reception of the

---

⁵⁰Michaels, *1 Peter*, 68. Gerhard Delling's comment on 4 Ezra's "the end of times" is apropos, for it characterizes the apocalyptic view of time in relation to God's will: "'End of the times' means end of the cosmic time(s) that God has ordained, ... not the end of time as such" ("χρόνος," *TDNT* 9. 591 n. 58). First Peter 1:20 displays a similar understanding of history: Before the foundation of the κόσμος, God had already ordained that Christ would appear at precisely the end of the epochs of history. See also Kelly, *Epistles of Peter*, 26.

⁵¹Cf. Beare, *Epistle of Peter*, 106-7.

gospel. The present, furthermore, is the now of God's merciful reconstitution of the addressees as God's own people (2:10), the now of their return to Christ (2:25), the now of the baptism that saves them (3:21). Whereas νῦν appears in contexts that contrast the present with the past, the letter twice uses the word ἄρτι to contrast the present with the future.[52] In light of their ready-to-be-revealed salvation (1:5), the readers are said to be rejoicing even though now they may have to suffer (1:6). Similarly, the addressees are described as rejoicing and believing in Christ even though now they cannot yet see him (1:8; cf. 1:7, 13; 4:13; 5:1).[53]

By way of expanding my earlier provisional answer to the second question of 1:11, we may say that the present καιρός is the time for Christians to believe and rejoice in contrast to their past, in light of their future, and in spite of their present. This stance, moreover, is consonant with the letter's emphasis on hope and faith.

For 1 Peter, hope and belief constitute the twofold disposition of Christians in the midst of a hostile society. Immediately following the letter's prescript, 1:3-9 signals the primacy of both faith and hope in the letter's construal of Christian life. That to which believers have been born again is a "living hope" (ἐλπίδα ζῶσαν), that is, an "inheritance kept in heaven" (κληρονομίαν ... τετηρημένην ἐν οὐρανοῖς) (1:3-4). The referent of this hope and inheritance, as we have already seen above, is eschatological salvation (1:5, 9). Four times in 1:5-9 1 Peter refers to Christian faith, which, like hope, is oriented toward the eschatological disclosure of salvation and of Christ (cf. 2:6-7). The first formal imperative in the letter, in 1:13, is the command to hope.[54] Having just reminded its readers, in 1:3, of the living hope that God engendered in them, the letter now

---

[52]So Michaels, *1 Peter*, 28.

[53]While ἀγαλλιᾶσθε in 1:6 and ἀγαπᾶτε and ἀγαλλιᾶσθε in 1:8 are either indicatives or imperatives in form, their context demands reading them as imperatives. 1:3-12 comprises one long, complex sentence that begins as the letter's thanksgiving (in v. 3) and functions as the material ground for the imperatives of vv. 13-14, which are introduced with διό (although further warrants follow in vv. 16, 18-19, etc.). The aorist imperative ἐλπίσατε, in 1:13, is, therefore, the first formal imperative in the letter; it determines the imperatival force of the preceding participles ἀναζωσάμενοι and νήφοντες (also in v. 13).

[54]See above, pp. 109-10 n. 1.

commands, in 1:13, that they set their hope fully on the divine grace coming to them at the revelation of Jesus Christ. And in 1:21, hope in God stands alongside faith in God as the outcome in human life of God's raising and glorifying Christ. In 3:15, the letter envisions its addressees being called by their accusers to account for their hope; hope here symbolizes that which is distinctive of Christian life vis-à-vis the larger society. Finally, in 5:9, strength of faith is the means by which the addressees will be able to resist the devil.

In conclusion, the present καιρός is the now of the preaching and acceptance (particularly by 1 Peter's addressees) of the gospel. And what kind of καιρός is this? In the first place, this καιρός falls at the end of the last epoch of history, an end that is marked as such by the appearance of Christ, but it is not yet the last καιρός, which lies in the immediate future and will be marked by the final disclosure of Christ and his glory. In the imminent future καιρὸς ἔσχατος, God will bring history to its consummation, which includes pronouncing judgment upon the disobedient, who tormented the Petrine addressees, and granting salvation to believers. In the present καιρός at the very end of the last historical epoch, just before the καιρὸς ἔσχατος, Christian life is of but a short duration and is fraught with suffering at the hands of hostile nonbelievers. Amid such hostility, the characteristic stance of Christians is one of faith and hope; and faith and hope issue in rejoicing and perseverance.

Christian life is thus an existence "betwixt and between" history and the eschaton. A more temporally liminal view of Christian existence can scarcely be imagined. The temporal context of Christian life is the end-before-the-end that was introduced at Christ's manifestation on earth and will be consummated at the revelation of his glory. First Peter's depiction of the temporal liminality of Christian life contains within it one very important element of the letter's total answer to the problem of the suffering of its addressees. The duration of their suffering will be short; the imminent appearance of their salvation is beyond doubt. (Without this temporal framework, the letter's answer to the problem of suffering probably would not have stood a chance of winning the day with many actual late-first-century Christians in Asia Minor who were suffering for their faith.) But the letter does much more than

The Liminality of Christian Life

assure its readers that their salvation is near. In the next stage of this investigation, I shall examine how the letter symbolizes a communal liminal identity appropriate to the actual temporal liminality of Christian life.

Metaphorical Liminality. The metaphors 1 Peter uses in its symbolic construction of an identity for its readers appear to be derived, roughly speaking, from two sources: the LXX, that is, the scriptures of early Christianity, on the one hand and the everyday social world of the Roman Empire on the other. What is of greater interest to this study than the origin of the metaphors, however, is the associations they would have evoked in the minds of the letter's intended readers. The task set for the following pages, therefore, is to explicate the function of the various metaphors by which the letter designates its addressees. Toward this end, I shall seek to explain how each individual metaphor contributes to the whole and how the metaphors, individually and collectively, might have been understood by the late-first-century gentile believers in Christ who make up the letter's intended audience. Although these intended readers would have been informed by—would have had their symbolic universes shaped by—both the LXX and the social, economic, and political realities of first-century Greco-Roman society, the metaphors 1 Peter uses appear, for the most part, to have been intended to resonate primarily with either one of these provinces of meaning or the other. In what follows, I shall first discuss those images and metaphors by which 1 Peter associates its readers with LXX Israel and then turn to images that are more evocative of the social world of late antiquity.

(1) Liminal Images Evoking LXX Israel. The groundwork for this part of the study has already been laid in chapter 3, where I examined 1 Peter's use of the words παροικία, πάροικοι, παρεπίδημοι, διασπορά, and ἐκλεκτοί. All five, I argued, derive from the LXX, and their significance in 1 Peter is, therefore, to be interpreted against the backdrop of their LXX use. In the LXX, these words refer to God's people, whether Israel's forebears, Israel, Judah, or individual Israelites. The first four terms—παροικία, πάροικοι, παρεπίδημοι, and διασπορά—usually refer to the

literal alienness or strangerhood of God's people during periods of temporary sojourns in lands not their own; furthermore, παροικία, πάροικοι, and παρεπίδημοι are already used metaphorically in the Psalms. Although 1 Peter does *not* use the words παροικία, πάροικοι, παρεπίδημοι, and διασπορά to designate its addressees as *literal* resident aliens and/or temporary sojourners (contra Elliott), these words clearly *do* reflect to some extent the letter's perception of its intended readers' sociopolitical situation. First Peter, I concluded, adopts these words, which originally characterized the LXX people of God in various situations of literal and/or figurative foreignness, and applies them metaphorically to its Christian addressees. I shall now examine the role these terms play in the letter's symbolic construction of an identity for its addressees.

I begin where the letter begins, with 1:1. In typical Greco-Roman epistolary fashion, 1 Peter opens with a prescript that identifies, first, the sender of the letter and, then, the intended recipients.[55] What is unusual about this prescript is that the first three words identifying the letter's addressees were not to be taken literally.[56] Rather, the words ἐκλεκτοῖς παρεπιδήμοις διασπορᾶς constitute a metaphor that introduces, at the very inception of the letter, an important aim of 1 Peter, namely, to present the addressees with a self-identity by which to legitimate and understand their existence as minority communities amid a hostile society. If the function of a Greco-Roman letter's adscript was to identify its intended recipients, then already in the opening words of 1 Peter, the

---

[55]See, e.g., David E. Aune, *The New Testament in Its Literary Environment* (LEC 6; Philadelphia: Westminster, 1987) 162-65, 174-80; Stanley Kent Stowers, *Letter Writing in Greco-Roman Antiquity* (LEC 5; Philadelphia: Westminster, 1986) 20.

[56]Of course, many letters composed in antiquity contain elements of the prescript that did not literally designate the actual authors and/or recipients. Such was the case, e.g., in pseudepigraphic personal letters, novelistic letters, and letters embedded in larger narratives (see Aune, *New Testament*, 167-70). What separates 1 Peter from these kinds of letters, however, is that 1 Peter's adscript was intended to be read *by its original recipients* as metaphorical. In this regard, 1 Peter is extremely unusual among letters of late antiquity. Interestingly, another exception is to be found in the NT document immediately preceding 1 Peter, namely, James (and very likely another in a document that follows shortly, i.e., 2 John).

readers are invited to understand themselves in terms of God's dispersed LXX people.⁵⁷

Not a few commentators correctly note that the juxtaposition of ἐκλεκτοῖς and παρεπιδήμοις (which is unique in biblical literature)⁵⁸ affirms for the addressees that they are God's chosen and informs them that being God's chosen entails an alien existence in society.⁵⁹ In Michaels's words, "The addressees are 'strangers' because of (not despite) being chosen."⁶⁰ The metaphor ἐκλεκτοῖς παρεπιδήμοις διασπορᾶς, thus, expresses, in terms of the LXX people of God, the letter's fundamental conception of Christian existence as liminal with respect to society at large. By thus clarifying the relation between the addressees' divine election and their social alienation, the adscript sets the stage for what is to follow and provides the lens through which its readers are to view the other LXX terms for Israel that 1 Peter will apply metaphorically to them.

The Christian-as-alien motif is next encountered in 1:17, in the phrase τὸν τῆς παροικίας ὑμῶν χρόνον. Since the adscript, 1 Pet 1:2-12 has rooted its addressees' election in the purposes and action of God and reminded its readers that their salvation was secured by the resurrection of Christ and will be disclosed at the eschatological revelation of Christ. Until then, they are said to be believing, rejoicing, and hoping, sustained by God's power and secure in the knowledge of their future inheritance. Although their present lot is suffering, the letter assures them that what they have received in their acceptance of the gospel proclamation was the object of both the prophets' interest and the angels' longing. The διό of v. 13 then

---

⁵⁷On the function of the prescript, see T. Martin, *Metaphor and Composition*, 42-47. Victor Paul Furnish correctly notes that the emphasis in 1 Peter's prescript falls on the identification of the addressees, "due to the author's description of what it means for the addressees to be Christians where they are in those provinces" ("Elect Sojourners in Christ: An Approach to the Theology of I Peter," *PSTJ* 28/3 [Spring 1975] 2-3). Cf. Goppelt's statement that the words used in the adscript "direct attention to the theme of the letter" (*I Peter*, 62).

⁵⁸Michaels, *1 Peter*, 6.

⁵⁹E.g., Best, *I Peter*, 70; Feldmeier, *Christen als Fremde*, 104, 176-77; Furnish, "Elect Sojourners," 4 (although Furnish explicitly couches the alienness in terms of temporary sojourning in this world); Michaels, *1 Peter*, 6-7.

⁶⁰Michaels, *1 Peter*, 6.

introduces a series of commands. In light of the foregoing recital of how things are between the addressees and God on the one hand and between the addressees and their non-Christian neighbors on the other, 1 Peter instructs its readers to gird up their minds, to be sober, to set their hope fully on the coming grace, not to be conformed to the former passions, to be holy, and to conduct themselves in the fear of God who judges all impartially, τὸν τῆς παροικίας ὑμῶν χρόνον (1:17), that is, "during the time of your alien residence." With this temporal phrase, 1 Peter symbolizes the intersection of temporal liminality and social liminality. The social liminality of the intended readers' present situation is both temporally delimited as a χρόνος—a period of time—and metaphorically valorized in terms of the alien residence of the LXX people of God.[61] Both aspects of this dual process are important to the letter's strategy. In the midst of a parenetic section in which the intended readers are commanded not to revert to their previous way of life but, in the words of the Levitical code, to be holy as God is holy (1:15-16), this brief prepositional phrase both assures them that the precarious situation in which they find themselves will not last forever and legitimates precisely this difficult existence with reference to the social alienation experienced by God's elect in the LXX.

In 1 Pet 2:4-10, several terms familiar from the Greek scriptures are applied to the letter's addressees. We begin with v. 5, where 1 Peter tells its addressees that, like living stones, they are being built into a spiritual οἶκος.[62] As if the figurative nature of this imagery were not clear enough, the letter signals its intent first by the ὡς preceding λίθοι and then by the adjective πνευματικός following οἶκος (as well as the πνευματικάς that modifies θυσίας shortly thereafter).[63] The imagery of living stones being built into an

---

[61]See above, pp. 77-79.

[62]Commentators are divided over whether to read οἰκοδομεῖσθε as an indicative or an imperative. Although I read οἰκοδομεῖσθε as an indicative, my interpretation of the function of this verse would not be materially effected by translating the verb as an imperative. In either case, an identity for the addressees is presented, whether in terms of that which God *is* doing with them or that which God *intends* to do with them if they obey the imperative.

[63]I do not think that πνευματικός here should be rendered "metaphorical," as if it were being used as a technical term for distinguishing literal language from

οἶκος is suggested by, but fits only loosely with, the references to Christ as the stone rejected by humanity but precious to God and chosen by God to be the cornerstone (2:4, 6-8).[64] Whereas Christ is the living stone in v. 4 and the stone in vv. 6-8, believers are the living stones in v. 5. And if the logic connecting v. 5 to vv. 4 and 6-8 is elusive, the structure of v. 5 itself is far from clear. Two things are certain: The readers are to see themselves as the living stones being built into an οἶκος πνευματικός, and εἰς indicates that the purpose of this process of building is that a holy priesthood should offer spiritual sacrifices to God through Jesus Christ. What is problematic in terms of the grammatical structure of the sentence is the identity of the ἱεράτευμα ἅγιον. Despite the difficulty of seeing oneself as both building block and priest, v. 9 shows that this is precisely what is being asked of the readers in v. 4. The βασίλειον ἱεράτευμα/ἔθνος ἅγιον of v. 9 is identical to the ἱεράτευμα ἅγιον of v. 4.[65] Both οἶκος and ἱεράτευμα are metaphors for the addressees.

The essential question raised by 2:4 concerns the significance of the οικ- terminology. Elliott, as I have noted in chapter 1, thinks the οἶκος motif is all important to 1 Peter's strategy; it is the primary means by which the letter addresses its readers' dilemma. First Peter, according to Elliott, offers its readers a home for the homeless.[66] Although I shall postpone a sustained critique of Elliott's proposal

---

figurative. I suspect that Elliott is correct that πνευματικός reflects the early-Christian notion of that which is characteristic of or due to the Spirit of God (John H. Elliott, *The Elect and the Holy: An Exegetical Examination of I Peter 2:4-10 and the Phrase βασίλειον ἱεράτευμα* [NovTSup 12; Leiden: Brill, 1966] 153-57; cf. Best, *I Peter*, 102; Goppelt, *I Peter*, 140; Kelly, *Epistles of Peter*, 90; Michaels, *1 Peter*, 100). Even so, both the house into which believers are being built and the sacrifices referred to in the phrase "spiritual sacrifices" are metaphorical.

[64]On early-Christian application of Isa 8:14; 28:16; and Ps 117:22 to Christ, see Elliott, *Elect and the Holy*, 28-33; Goppelt, *I Peter*, 138, 144.

[65]I shall argue below that οἶκος here refers to the temple, so that the readers are symbolized as both the stones of the temple and the priests officiating within the temple. Even if we were to grant Elliott's argument that οἶκος here means household, however, the mixing of the metaphors of living stones and priests would remain, despite Elliott's assertion that "Peter is not guilty of an abrupt mixture of imagery but rather must be credited with an apt choice of words" (*Elect and the Holy*, 162).

[66]See above, pp. 10-12.

until later in this chapter, several observations must be made here in connection with 2:5, where we encounter the first two occurrences of words in the οικ- family and one of only two occurrences in the letter of οἶκος.

(1) The imagery of 2:5a is clearly architectural: What is being built of stones is some sort of edifice, whether a house or a temple. In *The Elect and the Holy*, Elliott goes to great lengths to argue that οἶκος here does not refer to the temple but should be rendered "house." Then, however, based on his finding of a household motif in 4:10 and in 4:17, "where τοῦ οἴκου τοῦ θεοῦ obviously denotes not a temple but the Christian congregation in the communal sense," he insists that the notion of *household* must be present in 2:5 as well. Because he cannot simply ignore the unmistakable architectural language of construction in 2:5—where, indeed, he has already acknowledged that a house is in view—he resorts to arguing that both the ideas of house and of household are present in 2:5, and so he translates οἶκος by the hybrid "house(hold)."[67] Although I agree with Elliott that οἶκος in 4:17 denotes not temple but household,[68] the logic of his contrasting of the temple with the Christian community in 4:17 is fallacious: Of course it is the Christian communities that are designated by the metaphor οἶκος, both in 4:17 and in 2:5; but this observation says nothing about how οἶκος should be translated in either verse. Although household imagery is present in the letter—earlier in the metaphors of children and father in 1:14-17 and later in the οἶκος of 4:17—in 2:5 it most certainly is not; what is in view here is an edifice. The question is whether this edifice is the temple or a house.

(2) Despite Elliott's protestations to the contrary, the purpose clause introduced by εἰς discloses the cultic associations of the entire metaphor complex in 2:5.[69] The reason these living stones are being

---

[67]Elliott, *Elect and the Holy*, 158-59. In support of his position, Elliott here cites Beare, *Epistle of Peter*, 122; he could also have cited Otto Michel, "οἶκος, οἰκία, οἰκεῖος," *TDNT* 5. 142.

[68]See below, pp. 143-46.

[69]See Best, *I Peter*, 101; Feldmeier, *Christen als Fremde*, 205; Goppelt, *I Peter*, 140-41; Kelly, *Epistles of Peter*, 90; Michaels, *1 Peter*, 100; Selwyn, *Epistle of St. Peter*, 159-60.

built into an οἶκος is so that the addressees, as a holy priesthood, may offer spiritual sacrifices to God. Both the architectural nature of the metaphor in the main clause and the temple associations of the purpose clause must be given their due weight. This is by no means to insist on translating οἶκος as "temple," but it is to reject Elliott's rendering, "house(hold)," a term that both excludes the temple associations that are clearly in view in the purpose clause and embodies Elliott's less-than-persuasive claim that 2:5 is part of a pervasive household motif.

(3) The metaphor in 2:5 is not that of a completed οἶκος but of an οἶκος being built. At the very least, therefore, Elliott's thesis should be tempered by the realization that the οἶκος of 1 Pet 2:5 is not a finished structure but one still being assembled. The addressees are individually symbolized as the materials for a building that is presently under construction. Whereas the metaphors of the elect sojourners of the diaspora (1:1) and of their alien residence (1:17) are closely related and together evoke the image of the LXX people of God in hostile surroundings, the metaphor of the construction of an οἶκος for a priesthood evokes quite a different set of LXX associations. Nevertheless, all three metaphors have one thing in common: They are images of liminality. While the liminality inherent in the metaphors of 1:1 and 1:17 is the social liminality of the dispersed or wandering people of God, the liminality of the building metaphor inheres in the *process* quality of the image. The readers are, as it were, a people en route; they are neither what they were prior to conversion nor what they will yet be; and in the interim, they are to understand themselves as constituent parts of a greater whole that God is now constructing.[70]

If 2:5 depicts the readers as in the process of being built into an οἶκος in order that they may become a holy priesthood offering spiritual sacrifices, 2:9 states that they already are both priesthood and holy. While the designation ἱεράτευμα ἅγιον (2:5)—which

---

[70] Michel overinterprets the imagery of 2:5—indeed he calls it "a great primitive Christian allegory"—when he says that the figure of living stones being built into an οἶκος suggests the "spiritual integration of the individual into the community" ("οἶκος," 142). The intended readers of 1 Peter have already been integrated into the community; their conversion and baptism clearly lie in the past.

appears to be original to this letter—is suggested by Exod 19:6, the four epithets applied to the addressees in 2:9 are drawn directly from Exod 19:6 and Isa 43:20-21. Both Exod 19:6 and Isa 43:20-21 occur in lengthy passages that celebrate the divine deliverance of God's people and proclaim their unique status as God's own; and the epithets 1 Peter draws from these passages fulfill a similar function in the letter. Over against those who do not believe (2:7), who disobey the word and consequently trip over the stone that is Christ (2:8), 1 Peter states that, just as God's LXX people experienced divine deliverance from their subjugation to peoples who rejected God, the letter's addressees' faithful response to Christ does not result in their being put to shame before their accusers (2:7) but in their becoming an elect race, a royal priesthood, a holy nation, a people of God's own (2:9).

Just as the εἰς clause in 2:5 specifies, in terms of the LXX cult, the function assigned to the addressees as ἱεράτευμα ἅγιον, so the ὅπως clause in 2:9 specifies, in terms partially drawn from Isa 43:21, the vocation to which God has called the readers. In both the offering of spiritual sacrifices (2:5) and the declaration of God's virtuous deeds (2:9), what seems to be in view is the praise of God implicit in a public life conducted in accordance with the letter's standards for Christian behavior (see 2:12).

The contrast of 2:9 between unbelievers and believers is transposed in 2:10 into a contrast between the intended readers' former and present conditions. Here the letter invokes Hosea (1:6, 9; 2:25), in which God's merciful appointment of Israel as God's own people is symbolized in the narrative of Hosea, Gomer, and their children. And just as 2:9 declares the current status of the addressees before God, 2:10 states that they have already received God's mercy and so been transformed into God's people.

Unlike the metaphors of LXX Israel appearing in 1:1, 1:17, and 2:5, the images of 2:9-10 are not themselves metaphors of liminality. These images express what the addressees have already become as a result of God's action and their faithful response. These metaphors perform the important function of symbolizing, again in terms of biblical Israel, the addressees' categorical otherness with respect to the larger society in which they were once full-fledged participants and within which they now find themselves as members of minority communities under threat. In this regard it is important to recognize that the terms 1 Pet 2:9 takes from Isaiah 43 were themselves parts of a lengthy prophecy delivered to God's people in captivity, that is, in a profoundly liminal παροικία situation. In terms of their status before God, the intended readers' position is not at all ambiguous; but in terms of their place in society, the liminality inscribed in the adscript remains. They are called the elect race in 2:9, but 1:1 has already disclosed that divine election results in social liminality; they are said to be a royal priesthood in 2:9, but 2:5 has earlier depicted them as a priesthood still in the making. As if to assert that their temporal and social liminality is not eclipsed by their secure status before God, moreover, 2:11 immediately returns to metaphors of liminality as it addresses the question of how the intended readers should behave amid a hostile society.

In 2:11 the letter introduces a parenetic section with the verb παρακαλέω, followed by the particle ὡς and the metaphor(s) of liminality πάροικοι καὶ παρεπίδημοι. The latter, as we have seen in chapter 3, is an unmistakable allusion to Gen 23:4, where Abraham describes himself as a πάροικος καὶ παρεπίδημος. Here, then, is the final explicit appearance in the letter of the believer-as-alien motif. First Peter urges certain kinds of behavior upon its readers as people in a socially liminal position analogous to that of Abraham. Whereas Abraham was a πάροικος καὶ παρεπίδημος among the Hittites, the addressees are such among unbelieving gentiles, as 2:12 makes clear. The behavior commanded, although not explained in detail, is to abstain from the fleshly passions that war against the soul, while maintaining good behavior. And, as if to add specificity to the vocation urged in 2:5 and 2:9, the purpose of the conduct to which the addressees are called is ultimately that those who slander them might recognize their good behavior and glorify God (2:12).[71]

Finally, in 4:17 the word οἶκος is again used metaphorically, here with reference not merely to the addressees (as in 2:5) but,

---

[71] For more on 2:9, 12, and 1 Peter's view of the responsibilities of its addressees toward non-Christians, see below, pp. 156-69.

presumably, to all Christians (ἡμῶν). Even more explicitly than in 2:5, the word οἶκος in 4:17 evokes a LXX reference to the temple, namely, Ezek 9:6. Unlike οἶκος in 1 Pet 2:5, however, it does not appear that the οἶκος of 4:17 is meant to designate the intended readers as the metaphorical temple. While God's judgment is said in Ezek 9:6 to have begun with the elders who were outside the οἶκος=temple (ἀπὸ τῶν ἀνδρῶν τῶν πρεσβυτέρων, οἳ ἦσαν ἔσω ἐν τῷ οἴκῳ), in 1 Pet 4:17 judgment is said to be about to begin with the οἶκος of God (ἀπὸ τοῦ οἴκου τοῦ θεοῦ). The prepositional phrases introduced by ἀπό in both verses indicate the people with whom God's judgment begins. In Ezek 9:6, it is the elders who will be judged first; in 1 Pet 4:17, it is the οἶκος τοῦ θεοῦ. The word οἶκος in Ezek 9:6 is situated a full nine words after ἀπό, in a relative clause specifying the location of the elders. In 1 Pet 4:17, οἶκος appears with its article immediately after ἀπό. This asymmetrical correspondence between the prepositional phrases introduced by ἀπό suggests that οἶκος in 4:17, while echoing the οἶκος of Ezek 9:6, does not intend a metaphorical transfer of temple as the marker of a geographical place in Ezek 9:6 to temple as the group of believers in 1 Pet 4:17. Rather, it appears that οἶκος in 1 Pet 4:17 is to be understood as "household"; the Christian community is here pictured not as the metaphorical temple but as the metaphorical family of God. Indeed, in the immediate context of Ezek 9:6, the word οἶκος is twice used in a similar fashion to denote God's people—the οἶκος of Judah in Ezek 8:17 and the οἶκος of Israel and Judah in Ezek 9:9. Just as the three occurrences of οἶκος in Ezekiel 8-9 alternate between the meanings metaphorical household and literal temple, so 1 Peter uses the word metaphorically to refer to its addressees as the temple in 2:5 and then in 4:17 with reference to them as the household of God.[72]

---

[72]Indeed, it appears that the ideas of Christians as temple and as family emerged early in the development of Christian tradition, although the former is elsewhere expressed not with οἶκος but with ναός (in 1 Cor 3:16-17; 6:19; 2 Cor 6:16; Eph 2:21); the latter is already presupposed in Gal 6:10 (οἰκεῖοι τῆς πίστεως) and Eph 2:19 (οἰκεῖοι τοῦ θεοῦ) and is more fully developed later, in 1 Tim 3:15 and Heb 3:6. Cf. Michel, "οἶκος," 125-28. In his discussion of these and other passages in *Home* (189-200), Elliott seems to me to go beyond the evidence in arguing for a "household constitution and ideology of the Christian movement" that "provided the theoretical

The important question for this study, however, is not whether οἶκος in 4:17 associates the addressees with the temple or with a household but whether and how this instance of the οἶκος metaphor contributes to the letter's symbolic construction of a liminal identity for its intended readers. Although the metaphor of God's οἶκος in 4:17—whether understood as household, as temple, or as both at once—is not itself a liminal metaphor, the larger imagery of which it is a part is profoundly liminal. Whereas earlier in the letter the readers are assured in the midst of their suffering that the future will bring salvation, vindication, and honor for them (1:3-9, 13, 21; 2:12) and dishonor for their antagonists (3:16; 4:5), 1 Pet 4:17 introduces the startling notion that their suffering is to be viewed as God's judgment, which begins with believers and only then proceeds to nonbelievers.[73] The οἶκος of God in this context neither provides safety and security for its members nor strengthens the symbolic boundary separating believer from nonbeliever. Paradoxically, the hostility of the larger society toward Christians (4:16) is here symbolized as God's judgment, and the difference between Christians and non-Christians is pictured in the following verse (4:18) not as a categorical distinction but as a difference of degree. Both will be judged, the rhetorical question of 4:18 implies, but unbelievers will be judged much more harshly. In the concluding exhortation of 4:19, 1 Peter urges those who suffer *according to God's will* to do good and entrust themselves to God, the faithful creator.

In this context, what does it mean to be a member of God's οἶκος? It means that one's undeserved suffering at the hands of non-Christians is to be understood as God's judgment, in the face of which one is to continue to trust God as the faithful creator. The social liminality that gave rise to this letter in the first place is here

---

model and the practical basis for the articulation and institutionalization of the Christian vision of communal salvation" (199).

[73]This is not to say that there is no implied threat of punishment accompanying the various parenetic statements in the letter; in 1:14-17, e.g., an obvious (though not quite explicit) threat of judgment follows the command to be holy. Furthermore, in 4:12, suffering is viewed as a πύρωσις whose purpose is to test believers. Similarly, the much debated 4:1-2 may well speak of a purgative effect of suffering. But each of these is quite another matter from explicitly saying, as 1 Pet 4:16-17 does, that suffering for being a Christian is itself God's judgment.

transmuted into a kind of theological liminality. Beginning with the first verse of the letter, 1 Peter has embraced its addressees' social liminality, symbolically transforming it via several metaphors into the characteristic mode of Christian existence during the temporally liminal καιρός between Christ's glorification and that of his followers. Now, in a passage (4:12-19) in which so many concerns and motifs of the letter converge—the calumny that constitutes the addressees' "suffering," suffering interpreted as a sharing in Christ's suffering, the spirit of δόχα and of Christ presently resting on those who suffer as they await the joyful eschatological disclosure of Christ's δόχα, doing good amid suffering, the nearness of the eschaton implied in the imminence of judgment—1 Peter thrusts the addressees as the οἶκος of God into a more thoroughly liminal situation than that with which they began. Not only does divine election mean election to a socially liminal existence characterized by undeserved suffering at the hands of nonbelievers, but precisely this suffering is God's means of judging the elect. The hostility of nonbelievers toward believers constitutes God's personal act of judgment of God's people.

To be sure, the letter's emphasis in 4:17b-18 falls not on the judgment of believers but on the much harsher judgment that awaits the ungodly, and the exhortation the letter derives from this argument from the lesser to the greater is that those who suffer according to God's will should entrust themselves to God, the faithful creator, as they do good (v. 19). The implication of v. 19 would appear to be that those who do right have nothing to fear from the creator, who is both trustworthy and faithful. Although the letter certainly does not emphasize the notion of unjust suffering as divine judgment, this notion is, nevertheless, present, and it introduces into the letter an element of ambiguity in the relationship between God and the elect that, in my view, is not fully integrated into what the letter has to say elsewhere about God's disposition toward God's people. Even 1 Peter's depiction of the relation between its addressees and their faithful creator, therefore, is characterized by a kind of liminality.

(2) Other Images of Liminality. Alongside the LXX images that contribute to 1 Peter's symbolic construction of an identity for its addressees, the letter also uses several images of liminality that

are more evocative of the everyday world of Greco-Roman society than they are of LXX traditions. The first of these is found in 1:14-17, where the intended readers are addressed "as obedient children" (ὡς τέκνα ὑπακοῆς) who invoke God as their father. Although I do not think that 1 Peter's calling its addressees children and God their father here is part of an overarching household motif (as Elliott argues),[74] this terminology clearly does resonate with the Roman preoccupation with the household and its governance.[75] In the Greco-Roman world, as in the Hebrew earlier, children were situated at the lowest rung of the social ladder. They had essentially no place in adult society beyond the household, and within the household, they were utterly dependent upon the head of the household—the *paterfamilias*.[76] They were, therefore, expected to be subservient to the *paterfamilias* and to render him unquestioned obedience, a duty that was not left behind when the child reached maturity. Thus, Epictetus says of one's obligation to one's father: "One is called upon to take care of him, to give way to him in all things, to submit when he reviles or strikes you. 'But he is a bad father.' Did nature, then, bring you into relationship with a *good* father? No, but simply with a father" (*Ench.* 30).[77]

It was only through education, moreover, that children could be led out of their ignorance and immaturity into adulthood and full

---

[74]Elliott, *Home*, 202.

[75]See Keith R. Bradley, *Discovering the Roman Family* (New York/Oxford: Oxford University Press, 1991); and Suzanne Dixon, *The Roman Family* (Baltimore/London: Johns Hopkins University Press, 1992).

[76]This is not to say, however, that children were immediately dependent on their fathers—or even their parents—for their social and material needs; quite the opposite is the case. Many members of the household participated in the raising of children; and the *pater familias* who could afford it would often hire someone or assign a slave to be a child's primary caregiver and tutor. See Bradley, *Discovering*, 3-12, 37-75.

[77]Trans. W. A. Oldfather (LCL); see also Epictetus *Disc.* 2.10.7 On the obedience a child owes the father, see also Balch, *Wives*, 7, 17, and the sources cited there. This tradition can be traced back as far as Plato, who says that children should be submissive to both father and mother, who have the right to rule over their offspring (*Resp.* 425B; *Leg.* 690A).

participation in the larger society.⁷⁸ Indeed, adult slaves enjoyed considerably more opportunities to engage in the social, commercial, and political affairs of Greco-Roman society than did children.⁷⁹ Interestingly, one device by which slaves were dehumanized (a device replicated repeatedly throughout history, including in the United States) was the custom of addressing adult male slaves as "boy" (παῖς/*puer*).⁸⁰ First Peter's designation of its intended readers as children, therefore, metaphorically places them at the margin of society—even outside society except insofar as the *paterfamilias* represents his entire household to society—and, within the household, in a position of total dependence upon and obligation toward their father.

The children/father metaphor occurs in a parenetic section in which the addressees are exhorted to conduct themselves ἐν φόβῳ during their period of alien residence (παροικία). Alongside the metaphor of the believer as alien in a hostile society—a metaphor of social liminality—1 Peter uses the domestic metaphors of children and father to inscribe the believer's position of liminality before God. Whatever their status in the society at large, or even within the believing communities, all the addressees are children in the family

---

⁷⁸See H. I. Marrou, *A History of Education in Antiquity* (trans. George Lamb; Madison: University of Wisconsin Press, 1956; French original, 1948) 218-19; cited by Warren Carter, *Households and Discipleship: A Study of Matthew 19-20* (JSNTSup 103; Sheffield: JSOT Press, 1994) 107; and Beryl Rawson, "Adult-Child Relationships in Roman Society," *Marriage, Divorce, and Children in Ancient Rome* (ed. Beryl Rawson; Oxford: Clarendon, 1991) 17-30; on the role of the pedagogue, see Bradley, *Discovering*, 48-64.

⁷⁹On the participation of slaves in Greco-Roman society, see Dale B. Martin, *Slavery as Salvation: The Metaphor of Slavery in Pauline Christianity* (New Haven/London: Yale University Press, 1990) 1-49. Indeed, until they reached maturity, children were often placed under the tutelage of slaves; see Bradley, *Discovering*, 48-64.

⁸⁰M. I. Finley, *Ancient Slavery and Modern Ideology* (New York: Penguin, 1980) 96. The tradition that children and slaves occupy similar positions of subordination goes back at least as far as Plato and is a regular feature of Greco-Roman parenesis of the late first century. (Women are also generally assigned a place of subordination, but to a lesser extent, for although subject to their husbands, they are superior to children and slaves.) See, e.g., Plato *Resp.* 431C, 433D; Aristotle *Pol.* 1253b.7-8; 1254a.22-24; 1254b.13-21; 1260a.9-14; Philo *Decal.* 165-67; *Spec. leg.* 2.225-27, 233; Col 3:18-25; Eph 5:22; 6:1, 5.

of God.[81] And just as the *paterfamilias* demanded complete obedience, so the addressees are to render obedience to God their father. This is not to say that the addressees are thereby symbolically placed in either a precarious position with respect to God or, as in 4:17, an ambiguous position. Although the power of the *pater* over his *familia* was virtually absolute, and both exposure of infants and infanticide—especially of females and deformed children—were not uncommon,[82] Jewish and Greco-Roman sources are rife with instruction that fathers should protect and provide for their families and govern their households justly.[83] As in the case of the model *paterfamilias*, so God as father demands obedience from the addressees as children but can be trusted not to dispense punishment arbitrarily but to do so appropriately and impartially (ἀπροσωπολήμπτως [1:17]). God's demand, moreover, is not capricious but arises from God's own character as holy (1:16) and from God's gracious action in Christ to ransom the addressees from

---

[81]In 2:17 and 5:9, the letter enlarges the scope of the metaphor of children in God's household by designating all Christians the world over as ἡ ἀδελφότης.

[82]For the power of the father over his children (*patria potestas*), see Carter, *Households*, 102-3; Emiel Eyben, "Fathers and Sons," *Marriage, Divorce, and Children in Ancient Rome* (ed. Beryl Rawson; Oxford: Clarendon, 1991) 114-43; Garnsey and Saller, *Roman Empire*, 136-38; T. Martin, *Metaphor and Composition*, 169-72; Richard Saller, "Corporal Punishment, Authority, and Obedience in the Roman Household," *Marriage, Divorce, and Children in Ancient Rome* (ed. Beryl Rawson; Oxford: Clarendon, 1991) 144-65. For the primary sources for infanticide in antiquity, see Carter, *Households*, 102-3, esp. n. 5. Garnsey and Saller caution that not all babies who were exposed died, and that exposure is not the same as infanticide, since the literary sources clearly reveal the expectation that exposed infants would not die but be picked up and enslaved (*Roman Empire*, 138).

[83]The instruction to fathers not to be overbearing or unjust in their treatment of the members of their households—especially their children—is embodied in the NT household codes in Eph 6:4; Col 3:21. For the emphasis in the Greco-Roman world on paternal benevolence and parental affection for and delight in children, see, e.g., Hierocles *On Duties* (=Stobaeus) 4.22.24 (trans.: Abraham J. Malherbe, *Moral Exhortation: A Greco-Roman Sourcebook* [LEC 4; Philadelphia: Westminster, 1986] 101); *Ps.-Phoc.* 207; Pseudo-Plutarch *De Liberis Educandis* (=Plutarch *Mor.*) 7E; see also Carter, *Households*, 108-12; Saller, "Corporal Punishment," 144-65. J. Gaudemet explains, "Der 'pater familias' ist ... kein Tyrann mit unumschränkter Macht. Er ist Organ des Verbandes, den er regiert ... ; er muss seine Vorrechte im Interesse des Verbandes ausüben" ("Familie I (Familienrecht)," *RAC* 7. 331; cited by T. Martin, *Metaphor and Composition*, 171 n. 119).

the futility of their past behavior in accordance with ancestral tradition (1:18-19; cf. 1:14).

The second non-LXX metaphor of liminality appears in 2:2, where the addressees, "as newborn babies" (ὡς ἀρτιγέννητα βρέφη), are instructed to "long for the pure spiritual milk in order that, by it, you may grow up into salvation." While evoking associations similar to those called forth by the metaphor of the obedient child, the metaphor of the newborn baby symbolizes an even greater degree of liminality. Here it is not a question of whether or not to obey one's father but of whether or not to survive past infancy, a real concern given the high infant mortality rate in the Roman Empire. It is estimated that as many as one third of infants died in their first year, and only one half reached their fifth birthday.[84] If the addressees are to grow from infancy to reach the maturity of salvation, 1 Peter says, they must be nourished by the pure spiritual milk, presumably the word of the Lord by which they were born anew (1:23-25), that is, the proclamation of Christ, whose resurrection is the means by which God accomplished their rebirth (1:3).[85] If the metaphor of children stresses the common obligation the addressees have to obey their father, the metaphor of newborn babies underscores their absolute dependence on God.

The letter has already twice referred its addressees' conversion and initiation into the Christian community as a rebirth (using the word ἀναγεννάω [1:3, 23]). Victor Turner cites the symbols of gestation, (re)birth, and the suckling of infants as common to initiation rites of many cultures.[86] Rebirth supplies a profoundly liminal image for an adult's initiation into a religion, for it symbolizes that moment of transition from being a fetus within one's mother to becoming a member of the human community. The metaphor of rebirth was almost certainly familiar to the addressees, possibly as a part of their baptismal catechesis and/or liturgy. Whether or not the

---

[84]B. Frier, "Roman Life Expectancy: Ulpian's Evidence," *Harvard Studies in Classical Philology* 86 (1982) 213-51. Garnsey and Saller's estimates are slightly lower: "a quarter or more" died before the age of one, with as many as one half not reaching their tenth year (*Roman Empire*, 138).

[85]Cf. Tàrrech, "Le milieu," 344-45.

[86]E.g., Turner, "Betwixt and Between," 96, 99.

image would have evoked the memory of their baptism, it certainly would have called to mind their conversion and incorporation into the community of believers.⁸⁷ By means of the metaphors of infancy and of childhood, 1 Peter extends the familiar metaphor of rebirth in order to characterize the present situation of its addressees as a liminal condition. They are all utterly reliant on God their father: Like children, they are obligated to obey God; like newborn babies, they are dependent upon the nourishment of God's word proclaimed by and among the people of God.

Finally, in 2:16 the letter applies to its addressees two metaphors drawn from the structure of Greco-Roman society itself. They are to conduct themselves "as free persons . . . but as slaves of God" (ὡς ἐλεύθεροι . . . ὡς θεοῦ δοῦλοι). The institution of slavery provides 1 Peter with a powerful metaphor of liminality for Christian existence before God.⁸⁸ In *Slavery and Social Death: A Comparative Study*, Orlando Patterson demonstrates that slavery, in general and within the Roman Empire in particular, was a kind of institutionalized marginality.⁸⁹ Although ostensibly human beings, slaves were in fact mere property, utterly devoid of honor and, so,

---

⁸⁷In favor of a baptismal background to the rebirth metaphor are, among others, Goppelt, *I Peter*, 84; Kelly, *Epistles of Peter*, 47-49; and Windisch, *Die katholischen Briefe*, 59. Against a baptismal context, see Friedrich Büchsel, "γεννάω, γήννημα, γεννητός," *TDNT* 1. 674. Selwyn is ambivalent about the matter (*Epistle of St. Peter*, 123), as is Best (*I Peter*, 75).

⁸⁸The self-designation of Israel as slaves of the Lord in the LXX (e.g., Pss 18:12, 14; 26:9; Isa 48:20) and the early-Christian tradition reflected in Paul's designation of himself as an apostle and of Christians generally as slaves of Christ (Rom 1:1; 1 Cor 7:22; Gal 1:10; Phil 1:1; cf. Eph 6:6; Jas 1:1; 2 Pet 1:1) may well lie behind 1 Peter's usage. Given, however, the context in which 1 Peter uses the metaphor of slavery—i.e., a discussion of the obligation of the letter's readers to the institutions of society—it is not the LXX or the early-Christian tradition but the everyday experience of life in the Greco-Roman world that seems to me to provide the associations that would make the metaphor work for the intended readers.

⁸⁹Orlando Patterson, *Slavery and Social Death: A Comparative Study* (Cambridge/ London: Harvard University Press, 1982) 1-101, 334-42, esp. 30-32, 40, 46, 79-94, 337. The following have also informed my treatment of slavery: Keith R. Bradley, *Slaves and Masters in the Roman Empire: A Study in Social Control* (New York/ Oxford: Oxford University Press, 1987); Carter, *Households*, 172-89; Saller, "Corporal Punishment," 144-65; Thomas E. J. Wiedemann, *Slavery* (Oxford: Clarendon, 1987).

outside the social order. Slaves thus occupied the liminal state of social death; indeed, in Roman law, the slave was *pro nullo*.[90] Although they participated in the affairs of society, they were not members of society but, rather, functionaries of their masters, empowered only to attend to their masters' affairs. "In Roman law, slaves were classified as chattel, not persons, as a 'speaking tool' (*instrumentum vocale*) that could be bought and sold or punished at the will of the masters."[91] The slave owner's authority, in fact, derived from the slave's legal and social liminality. "The slave came to obey him not only out of fear, but out of the basic need to exist as a quasi-person, however marginal and vicarious that existence might be."[92] The slave, a socially liminal being in the literal sense, thus provides the perfect metaphor of liminality.[93]

Indeed, a few lines after its use of the word δοῦλοι, 1 Peter, in 2:18, instructs slaves suffering at the hands of unjust masters to remain submissive to their masters and then, in vv. 19-25, offers the warrant for this instruction in terms that are applicable not merely to slaves but to all the intended readers. The slave who suffers unjustly is thereby upheld as the paradigm for Christian suffering in a hostile society.[94] In 2:18, it is a particular type of slave—the domestic (οἱ οἰκέται)—that is specifically addressed, but the social position in the Roman Empire of the household slave was no different in principle from that of any other slave. That all readers are implicitly

---

[90]Patterson, *Slavery and Social Death*, 40. Patterson incisively traces the developments in Roman law by which the slave was denied personhood and classified as a thing (*res*), the object of the absolute ownership (*dominium*) of the master, whose personhood was affirmed (*persona*). The result was that by the end of the Republic, the most common conception of the slave among Romans was that of a thing, "the idea of 'thingness' in law being emphasized as never before, specifically for this purpose. The slave was above all a res, *the only human res*" (*Slavery and Social Death*, 30-32).

[91]Garnsey and Saller, *Roman Empire*, 116. Cf. Aristotle's notion of the slave as an "animate instrument" (*Pol.* 1253b-1254a).

[92]Patterson, *Slavery and Social Death*, 46.

[93]"In a world where the citizen was at the center of human activity, slavery represented the opposite pole of minimum participation in humanity, and the slave came to symbolize the boundary of social existence" (Wiedemann, *Slavery*, 3; I owe this reference to Carter, *Households*, 178).

[94]Cf. Achtemeier, "Newborn Babes," 229; Feldmeier, *Christen als Fremde*, 145.

addressed in this instruction to domestic slaves is shown by the generalizing τις of 2:19[95] and by the many points of correspondence between the material in 2:19-25 and similar statements directed to the entire readership elsewhere in the letter.[96] The liminality implied in the resident alien/temporary sojourner metaphor is greatly enhanced by the metaphor of slaves who are cruelly treated by their owners and can do nothing other than continue to submit to them.

In 2:16, however, the addressees are not addressed merely as slaves but as slaves and free persons (ἐλεύθεροι) simultaneously. If the slave metaphor implies an extreme degree of liminality, the juxtaposition of the metaphors of the slave and the free person creates a still more profound level of liminality. The addressees are both slave and free, which means, following the logic of Greco-Roman social structure, that they are fully neither one nor the other. A freeborn person could have become a slave, and a slave could have been freed (although the δοῦλος would have thereby become not an ἐλεύθερος but an ἀπελεύθερος or ἐξελεύθερος), but one could not be both at once. In fact, the Roman laws of manumission reveal just how liminal the slave's position was, for at the stroke the master's pen, the slave could be transformed from mere property to human being—even a Roman citizen.[97] As if the metaphor of the slave were not liminal enough, the letter metaphorically assigns its readers to two incompatible social ranks: slave and free person.

A comparison of 2:11-17 with 1:13-21 shows that the addressees are free persons in the sense that God, through Christ's death, has ransomed them from the futile behavior typical of unbelieving gentiles (1:18-19) so that they can now abstain from fleshly passions (2:11). Although free from the futility of "gentile" behavior, however, they are not free of their obligation to live responsibly within society by "exhibiting good conduct" (2:12) or "doing right" (2:12, 14), by subjecting themselves to the emperor and to his governors (2:13-14), and by honoring all people, especially the

---

[95]Michaels, *1 Peter*, 139.

[96]Compare 2:19-20 with 3:9, 14-17; compare 2:21-24 with 3:18; 4:1, 13-16; compare ἐν φόβῳ of 1:17 with ἐν παντὶ φόβῳ of 2:18. For other parallels, see Elliott, *Home*, 205-8; Tàrrech, "Le milieu," 123 nn. 95-96.

[97]Finley, *Ancient Slavery*, 96-97.

emperor (2:17). These social obligations, moreover, arise not from Greco-Roman society's claim upon the addressees but from God's claim upon them. They are δοῦλοι of God. For them to presume to be free of such social obligations would be to use their God-given freedom as a pretext for wrongdoing. The parenetic significance of the liminality of being at the same time metaphorical free persons and metaphorical slaves of God thus emerges: If the πάροικοι and παρεπίδημοι metaphors of 2:11 symbolize the addressees' otherness—their alienation—vis-à-vis the larger society, whose way of life they have rejected and whose hostility they must consequently endure, the metaphors of free persons and slaves in 2:16 reconstitute their relation to society in terms of their obligation as God's slaves to respect the emperor and his representatives and not to engage in the kinds of antisocial behaviors that governors are to punish.

In conclusion, in response to its addressees' socially liminal situation as members of religious minority communities within a hostile society, 1 Peter offers them a liminal identity constructed by various metaphors of marginality, social-structural inferiority, process, and/or transition. Most prominent among these is a group of metaphors that establish associations between the addressees and the biblical people of God. Through the metaphors of the elect transients of the diaspora, resident aliens and transients, alien residence, holy priesthood, chosen race, royal priesthood, holy nation, people for God's own possession, and people of God, the addressees are called upon to view themselves in terms of LXX Israel, God's own people whose election resulted in a socially liminal existence amid diverse societies over the course of centuries. The addressees' election by God and rejection by society are thus to be understood as the replication of the experience of the biblical people of God.

The readers' present position as God's people and their future salvation and vindication are secured by God's past act in Christ, which became effective for them at their conversion. In the words of the prophet Hosea, their conversion has constituted them as God's people (1 Pet 2:10). Their previous existence can now be seen retrospectively as that of a nonpeople: They were living in darkness (2:9), enslaved by ignorance to passions (1:14), and, so, conducting

The Liminality of Christian Life 155

themselves in the futile ways of their ancestral customs (1:18), namely, licentiousness, passions, drunkenness, revels, carousing, lawless idolatry, and wild profligacy (4:3-4). Their break with the past is also signified in the metaphors of rebirth and of children in the household of God. These metaphors together symbolize the social liminality of the people of God in a non-Christian world.

This break with the past, moreover, demands a new construal of the believers' responsibility to the society in which they were once full participants but which now stands in opposition to them. This new relationship is symbolized in the liminality of being simultaneously free and slave. The readers are free persons but are enslaved to God, which means that their freedom must never be construed as license to do wrong. Their obligation as God's slaves to obey God without question entails a decisive break with all that is considered wrongdoing, but it also entails the obligation to do right (2:15), which includes the Greco-Roman requisites of honoring all persons, especially the emperor (2:16). The prescribed behavior in accordance with Greco-Roman social conventions, therefore, is to be rendered not out of recognition of society's claim but in obedience to God's demand.

There is also a kind of liminality *within* the people of God. Whereas the addressees' relation to God is never in question, the metaphors of nursing infants, of children, of slaves, and of the house under construction all symbolize the readers' position of absolute dependence on and obligation to God. And the metaphor of the household of God where judgment begins (4:17) uncharacteristically assigns the larger society's hostility toward the addressees to God's own act of judgment. While the readers' past conversion, present position before God, and future salvation are never in doubt, they now must reckon with the paradox that their undeserved suffering is not only the result of God's election and according to God's will but also God's personal act of judgment. Still, even in this passage, the accent falls not on the judgment of the addressees but on the far greater judgment about to befall their antagonists.

The metaphors examined above function together to legitimize the addressees' social liminality. They are neither fully integrated members of society nor entirely removed from it. They have made a clean break with the past and yet their obedience to God entails conduct in accordance with certain societal conventions. For those readers who accept 1 Peter's constellation of metaphors as constitutive of their identity, social alienation is valorized as the will of God, as the corollary to their divine election, and as the authentic expression of the vocation to which God has called them as God's own people. Their social liminality, thus, need not be a threat to their personal integrity, as long as they recognize that they are members of an alternative social entity and that this alternative community provides their plausibility structure over against the claims—and threats—of the larger society.

In this section of my study, I have focused on the self-identity 1 Peter offers its readers, and have characterized this self-identity, using Victor Turner's terminology, as liminal. That is to say, the self-identity is constructed by means of metaphors that evoke liminal associations between the readers and the symbolic universes of the LXX and the Greco-Roman world. Two tasks remain. The first concerns the vocation to which the addressees are called and their responsibility to the larger society. If they accept the letter's symbolic self-identity as their own, how are the readers to behave among those outside their communities? The second task is to examine the nature of the relations that are to obtain among believers within these communities.

Extracommunity Relations. Before turning to those passages that explicitly address the dispositions and behaviors the addressees are to exhibit toward non-Christians, I shall first attend to 1 Peter's general parenetic directive of 2:1. Here the letter instructs its addressees to put away (ἀποθέμενοι) all evil (κακίαν) and all deceit (δόλον) and hypocrisy (ὑποκρίσεις) and envy (φθόνους) and all slander (καταλαλιάς). Situated between the affirmation of the addressees' rebirth through God's word (1:23-25) and the command that they long for the pure spiritual milk so as to grow up into salvation (2:2-3), the injunction of 2:1 uses the popular Greco-Roman topos of the vice list to characterize, in general terms, the

The Liminality of Christian Life

kinds of behaviors that Christians should avoid.[98] Both the introductory word, ἀποτίθημι, and the five vices listed reflect early-Christian parenetic tradition.[99] First Peter 2:1, furthermore, is indebted to Psalm 33 (LXX): Ps 33:9 is quoted in 1 Pet 2:3, and the combination κακία and δόλος in 2:1 recalls the pair κακός and δόλος in Ps 33:14. Hypocrisy and envy do not elsewhere occupy 1 Peter; the latter does not occur at all outside 2:1, and the former is only alluded to a few verses earlier, in the adjective ἀνυπόκριτος of 1:22. The other three words, however, along with their relatives and synonyms, will appear again and again throughout the remainder of the letter, sometimes in contexts that explicitly address the relation between believers and nonbelievers.[100] In 2:1, however, 1 Peter does not yet connect these attitudes and actions to any specific situation but, rather, formulates, in the most general way, a Christian alternative to the addressees' erstwhile behavior according to the passions of their former ignorance (1:14).

In 2:9, as we have already seen, 1 Peter states as the purpose of God's action in making the addressees God's own: "in order that you may declare [ἐξαγγείλητε] the mighty deeds [τὰς ἀρετάς] of the one who called you out of darkness into that one's marvelous light." Elliott and Feldmeier understand this clause as a call to mission by which the readers are commissioned to proclaim to non-Christians God's mighty deeds. Both Elliott and Feldmeier invoke 1 Pet 2:12 in support of their interpretation of 2:9. In their view, 2:12 envisions a future when those who have been converted as a result of the missionary proclamation enjoined in 2:9 will glorify God on the

---

[98] Cf. Michaels, who asks whether the Christian's attitude toward society or toward other Christians is in view here. His response is that both are in view: "Without stating explicitly what he is doing, Peter now begins to speak concretely of how Christians should conduct themselves at every level, both among themselves and in the wider society" (*1 Peter*, 85).

[99] See Selwyn, *Epistle of St. Peter*, 393-97; cf. Goppelt, *I Peter*, 128; Michaels, *1 Peter*, 83.

[100] The κακ- group: 2:12, 14, 15, 16; 3:9, 10, 11, 12, 13, 17; the δολ- group: 2:22; 3:10; the καταλαλ- group: 2:12; 3:16; cf. (ἀντε)λοιδορέω (2:23); λοιδορία (3:9); βλασφημέω (4:4); and ὀνειδίζω (4:14).

eschatological "day of visitation."[101] I shall evaluate this interpretation of 2:12 momentarily; but first, I shall address the evangelistic interpretation of 2:9.

In my view, Balch, in appendix two of *Let Wives Be Submissive*, presents the definitive refutation of Elliott's (and now also Feldmeier's) interpretation of 1 Pet 2:9.[102] Although Balch's entire argument need not be recounted here, the more important points are as follows: (1) When ἐξαγγέλλω is used in the LXX of the proclamation of God's deeds or God's praises, the proclaiming is not to outsiders for purposes of proselytizing but to God in worship (e.g., Pss 55:9; 70:15; 106:22; Sir 18:4). (2) Both in Exod 19:6, which 1 Pet 2:9 quotes, and in the interpretation of Exod 19:6 given in Rev 1:6 and 5:10, the task of the priesthood God has formed is directed toward God and not toward outsiders. (3) First Peter does not elsewhere refer to its addressees' task as missionary preaching. (4) What is said about nonbelievers in 2:4-10 is that they have rejected the Lord (2:4), they do not believe (2:7), and they have stumbled over the rock that is Christ *as they were destined (by God) to do* (2:8). To these arguments I would add the obvious point that the purpose clause of 2:9, like the three words preceding it—λαὸς εἰς περιποίησιν—is derived from Isa 43:21, whose purpose clause appears to refer to Israel's vocation of proclaiming God's mighty acts *to God, in worship.*[103] Indeed, in Isa 43:22-24 God rebukes the people precisely because they did not fulfill their obligation as the elect to bring offerings and sacrifices to God. Furthermore, when the gentiles *are* mentioned earlier in Isaiah 43—in vv. 3, 4, 8, 9, and 14—they are presented not as peoples to be missionized but as hostile enemies whose oppression of God's people has been, or will soon be, ended, and in the midst of whom God's people is called to testify to the one true God, not for the purpose of persuading the nations but in order to expose their error and to vindicate Israel's

---

[101]Elliott, "1 Peter, Its Situation and Strategy," 69, 72; Feldmeier, *Christen als Fremde*, 167, 181, 186; cf. Elliott, *Elect and the Holy*, 42-43.

[102]Balch, *Wives*, 132-36.

[103]In Isa 43:21 the notion of purpose is conveyed by the infinitive rather than by ὅπως with the subjunctive, and the verb used is διηγέομαι rather than 1 Peter's ἐξαγγέλλω; 1 Peter's modifications do not alter the sense of the clause.

The Liminality of Christian Life   159

God (vv. 8-13). Just as God's LXX people is said in Isaiah to have been charged with the task of proclaiming God's mighty deeds in worship and in the midst of their antagonists, so have 1 Peter's intended readers. This interpretation is confirmed by the purpose clause of 2:5, which states that God's intention in transforming the addressees into a holy priesthood is that they should offer spiritual sacrifices to God (cf. Pss 49:13-14, 23; 50:17-19; 140:2).[104] This is not to say that 2:5 refers only to ritual acts of worship performed in the gathered communities but that the actions performed in discharging the responsibilities of this priestly commission are conceived of as God-directed acts of worship.

Moreover, if Elliott's and Feldmeier's accounts of 2:9 fail to persuade, their interpretation of 2:12 (which undergirds the former) is even less convincing, although, it must be noted, their understanding of 2:12 is shared by most commentators.[105] Against the majority opinion, W. C. van Unnik incisively points out that "there is nothing said [in 2:12] of the conversion of the Gentiles, only of their praise."[106] In fact, the context, as we have seen above, indicates not only that the "gentiles" are disobedient but that their refusal to believe the gospel was foreordained by God (2:7-8).[107] The "day of visitation" is clearly a reference to the eschatological moment when God will judge the wicked and vindicate the righteous (see, e.g., Isa 10:3; Jer 6:15; 10:15).[108] We saw earlier that 1 Peter expects the

---

[104]Elliott's interpretation of the purpose clause of 2:5 as implying "a pronounced missionary impulse" (*Elect*, 183) seems to me to be even wider of the mark than his interpretation of 2:9. Like the latter, the former is decisively refuted by Balch (*Wives*, 132-33). Indeed, in his response to Balch—"1 Peter, Its Situation and Strategy"—Elliott does not invoke 2:5 in support of his position.

[105]Brox, *Petrusbrief*, 114-15; Goppelt, *I Peter*, 160-62; Kelly, *Epistles of Peter*, 106; Michaels, *1 Peter*, 118-20; Selwyn, *Epistle of St. Peter*, 170-71; Thurén, *Rhetorical Strategy*, 107. Beare thinks that 2:12 suggests "the attractive thought that even in the dread hour of Judgment there may be mercy for those whose eyes are at last opened to the revelation of the divine glory in the beauty of the Christian character which they now slander" (*Epistle of Peter*, 138).

[106]W. C. van Unnik, "The Teaching of Good Works in I Peter," *NTS* 1 (1954-55) 105.

[107]So Balch, *Wives*, 87.

[108]On this point commentators agree. See, e.g., Brox, *Petrusbrief*, 114-15; Goppelt, *I Peter*, 160; Selwyn, *Epistle of St. Peter*, 171; van Unnik, "Teaching," 104.

"day of visitation" to bring both retribution against nonbelievers (4:5, 17-18) and the full disclosure of Christ's δόξα (4:13), along with believers' participation in that δόξα (1:7; 5:10). In 2:12, 1 Peter says that the eschaton will also be a time when those who are currently harassing the letter's addressees will render δόξα to God, and that the occasion for their ascription of δόξα to God will be their recognition of the believers' good deeds. This reference to good deeds recalls 1:17, where God is said to be the one who judges according to deeds. What is in view in 2:12, therefore, is the eschatological judgment, when even disobedient nonbelievers will recognize that those whom they had been denouncing as wrongdoers (κακοποιοί) had in fact been doing good all along. Just as the opponents will, in the end, have to give an account to God for their hostile behavior, according to 4:5, so in 2:12 these gentiles are envisioned as responding in the only appropriate fashion when they are finally made to recognize the good behavior of God's people—by rendering God δόξα. Whether this expectation is to be understood in terms of the eschatological gathering and salvation of the nations or as what von Rad calls the "doxology of judgment"—an acknowledgement of God's δόξα by those who are condemned—is unclear.[109] In either case, it does not appear that 1 Peter is here issuing a call to mission in the expectation that proper behavior will lead to the conversion of nonbelievers.

The conduct enjoined in 2:12 is set over against the "fleshly passions" of the previous verse and, by implication, the "passions" of the former ignorance of 1:14 and the "passions" and other vices

---

[109] For the expectation in early-Jewish literature of an eschatological salvation of the nations, see E. P. Sanders, *Jesus and Judaism* (Philadelphia: Fortress, 1985) 213-18. Sanders cites, e.g., Isa 2:2-3; 45:13-25; 49:6-7; Mic 4:1-2; Zech 2:11; Tob 14:6-7; *Pss. Sol.* 17:34-35; *1 Enoch* 90:30-33; *Sib. Or.* 3:669-731. For the "doxology of judgment," see Balch, *Wives*, 87; citing Gerhard von Rad, *Old Testament Theology* (New York/Hagerstown/San Francisco/London: Harper & Row, 1962-65) 1. 357-58. Similar ideas are present in *1 Enoch* 62-63 (cited by van Unnik, "Teaching," 105) and Rev 11:13 (cited by Balch, *Wives*, 87); cf. also Josh 7:19 (cited by von Rad, *Theology*, 1. 358). At the very least, what is envisioned is an eschatological moment when all nations will recognize God's self-disclosure and therefore join the people of God in praising God. Cf. the use made of Isa 45:23 in the last stanza of the Christ hymn of Phil 2:5-11.

characteristic of nonbelieving gentiles of 4:2-4. As we have seen, this contrast between the behavior proper to Christians and that behavior characteristic of gentile nonbelief does not indicate a complete rejection of the standards of proper behavior that obtained in Greco-Roman society. Quite the contrary, in 2:12 and elsewhere the letter enjoins doing good, that is, conduct in accordance with the standards presupposed in the provincial governor's imperium; doing good *should* result in the governor's commendation rather than his punishment (2:14; cf. Rom 13:1-4) and in the silencing of slanderous accusations of wrongdoing (2:15). Of course, the letter reckons with the likelihood that these positive results will not usually be forthcoming.[110] In part, this expectation is due to the discrepancy between society's definition of the good and the understanding of the good that was shared by 1 Peter and the communities addressed. As I argued in chapter 3, it was likely religious and quasi-religious civic celebrations that provided the principal area of disagreement over what constituted "doing good." Although 1 Peter and the larger society agreed on the abstract principle of doing good, some behaviors generally considered good by the larger society had already been rejected by the addressees, who judged those behaviors to be part of the futility of their "gentile" past. The letter supports this rejection and urges that its readers not capitulate to pressures to resume those activities, which it labels with the pejoratives of 4:3-4, despite the abuse they are experiencing as a result of their abstaining from such conduct (v. 4). In 4:12-14, the addressees are told to expect the reproach of non-Christians; the addressees are not to commit the specific crimes of murder and theft or to engage in wrongdoing (4:15), but they should anticipate being slandered nonetheless—not for any specific misdeeds but simply for being Christians (4:16).

In 2:13, the specific virtue of subjection to authority, especially to the emperor and his governors, is enjoined. This injunction is entirely consonant with the Greco-Roman concern with social order and acknowledges that subjection is the proper disposition to those

---

[110] See above, pp. 83-94.

in authority.[111] This attitude toward rulers appears to have been adapted early and widely in Christian tradition, as is indicated by a comparison of 2:13-17 with Rom 13:1-7, 1 Tim 2:1-3, and Tit 3:1-3. We have seen above that the mandate of 2:16 to conduct oneself according to the society's standard of the good is based not on acknowledgement of society's claim on Christians but on Christians' obligation to the God whose slaves they are. Similarly, in 2:13, subjection to the secular authorities is enjoined not in recognition of imperial claims on Christians but "on account of the Lord" (διὰ τὸν κύριον). It is this critical principle, variously worded in 2:13 and 2:16, that provides the warrant for 1 Peter's rejection of some socially accepted behaviors within the context of the letter's affirmation of subjection to imperial authority and, more generally, of doing good. Indeed, it is God's will that by doing good, the letter's addressees should silence their critics (2:15). Doing good, moreover, is the *only* course of action God has willed the addressees to pursue in order to silence their accusers. Failing this course of action, it is God's will that they endure the calumny (3:17; 4:2, 19).

Concluding the parenetic section of 2:11-17 is the fourfold command to honor all people, to love the ἀδελφότητα, to fear God, and to honor the emperor (2:17). The different verbs used with the various objects differentiate the addressees' responsibilities to the four parties mentioned.[112] Although all people are to be honored, fellow Christians are owed the further obligation of love, as was already commanded in 1:22 and will be again in 4:8.[113] To this we shall return in the next section. To God, φόβος is the proper disposition, in keeping with the LXX and early-Christian tradition of fearing the Lord (e.g., Ps 2:11; 34:10; Sir 1:11-30; Acts 9:31; Eph 5:21) and with 1 Peter's earlier injunction to the addressees to conduct themselves ἐν φόβῳ as children before God, their father and

---

[111]See August Strobel, "Zum Verständnis von Rom. 13," *ZNW* 47 (1956) 87.

[112]This is not to say that honor was not also due both to fellow Christians and to God. The former are surely included in the all of the first injunction, and the honor due God is a common theme in the LXX (e.g., Isa 29:13; Prov 3:9). In this passage, however, 1 Peter is clearly distinguishing between the obligations Christians have toward God and their fellow believers and those they have toward non-Christians.

[113]Michaels, *1 Peter*, 130.

judge (1:17).[114] Whereas the first injunction applies both to relationships within Christian communities and to the relations of Christians with non-Christians, only the fourth injunction is expressly limited to the relationship between Christians and an outsider to their communities, namely, the emperor. By instructing its readers to honor (τιμάω) all people and the emperor, the letter is encouraging behavior consonant with its overall acceptance of the conventions of Greco-Roman society, where social order and individual and collective honor were of paramount importance.[115] The specific Christian commitments to the ἀδελφότητα and to God, however, indicate the liminality of the addressees, whose most important relationships and duties, 1 Peter insists, are to their fellow Christians and to their God.

In 3:9, it is said that the readers have been called to an existence in which they are treated badly and slandered but must refuse to respond in kind, rendering instead the good word (εὐλογοῦντες) in order that they might inherit a good word (εὐλογίαν) from God. This notion of God's call to a suffering existence corresponds to the election motif examined earlier and to the anticipation of suffering according to God's will in 3:17, 4:2, and 4:19. Although 3:9 occurs immediately after an injunction that is clearly directed toward intracommunity relations (3:8), and although the first part of the injunction of v. 9 (μὴ ἀποδιδόντες κακὸν ἀντὶ κακοῦ) is formulated in quite general terms, the second part of the injunction (λοιδορίαν ἀντὶ λοιδορίας) vividly recalls 1 Peter's portrayal of Christ's response to suffering in 2:23, which, as we have seen, functions as the paradigm for slaves'—and by implication the entire intended audience's—response to unjust suffering at the hands of non-Christians. Those addressed in 2:21 are called to precisely the kind of nonretaliatory enduring of suffering that Christ exhibited. Christ, when reviled, did not revile in return (ὃς λοιδορούμενος

---

[114] It may be that 1 Peter here is deliberately setting this distinction between the fear owed God and the honor owed the emperor over against the command to fear both God and king in Prov 24:21 (so Michaels, *1 Peter*, 131).

[115] See S. Aalen, "Glory, Honour," *The New International Dictionary of New Testament Theology*, vol. 2 (ed. Colin Brown; Grand Rapids: Zondervan, 1976) 48-51.

οὐκ ἀντελοιδόρει) (2:33a); so the addressees should not return reviling for reviling (λοιδορίαν ἀντὶ λοιδορίας) (3:9).

As the warrant for the parenesis of 3:9, 1 Pet 3:10-12 quotes Ps 33:13-17, where both κακός and δόλος are proscribed. As we saw above, this pair first appeared in the general parenesis of 2:1 (as κακία and δόλος); now that general parenesis is applied specifically to the question of the addressees' extracommunity relations. The proscription of δόλος, moreover, like the parenesis of 3:9, recalls the description of Christ in chap. 2. Just as Christ did no sin (ἁμαρτία) and spoke no guile (δόλος) (2:22), the addressees, in the words of the Psalmist, must keep their tongues from evil (κακία) and their lips from speaking guile (δόλος). They must turn away from evil (κακία) and act in accordance with the good (ἀγαθός) (3:11). The warrant for these injunctions is stated in terms of God's disposition toward those who do them: Whereas God's face is turned against evildoers, God's eyes are on the just and God's ears are open to their prayers (3:12).

In light of this affirmation, it would appear that the rhetorical question that opens the next section—"And if you are zealous for the good, who will be the one who harms you?" (3:13)—is to be answered, "Certainly not God." In the face of unjust suffering, 3:14-15 proscribes fear of the antagonists and prescribes, instead, reverencing Christ as Lord in one's heart. In response to challenges from non-Christians, the addressees should always be prepared to give an ἀπολογία for their hope, and to do it with gentleness and fear (μετὰ πραΰτητος καὶ φόβου), maintaining a good conscience (συνείδησις ἀγαθή) (3:16). Gentleness, probably directed toward the accusers, is to characterize the nature of the response. In light of the proscriptions of fear in 3:14 and 3:6 and of the injunctions to fear God in 1:17 and 2:17, it would appear that φόβος here refers to one's disposition toward God rather than toward one's accusers. At the very least, it would appear to indicate an attitude of respect toward others that is implicit in the fear of God, just as the Christian's duty toward God implies a derivative duty to society (2:13, 16; cf. 3:17). In any case, doing good is presupposed in 3:16 and implicitly commanded in 3:17; and the purpose of rendering a proper account of one's hope is to put to shame the questioners (3:16).

I turn now to the household code. The first two elements of the household code are directed, in part, toward the regulation of extracommunity relations. First, the instruction to slaves beginning in 2:18 is at least partly and may be entirely addressed to slaves of unbelieving masters; it would be inconsistent with 1 Peter's prescriptions for Christian behavior elsewhere to conceive of Christian masters who treat their Christian slaves in an overbearing manner, cause them undeserved pain, and reward their good behavior with beatings (2:18-20). Indeed, the role suffering slaves play as paradigms for Christians who are suffering *at the hands of non-Christians* suggests that Christian slaves of non-Christian masters are in view here. Furthermore, in light of the usual household-code pattern of instruction to both masters and slaves, husbands and wives, the absence in 1 Peter of any directive to slave owners, implies that slave owners are not among the members of the intended audience. At the very least, therefore, we must conclude that the instruction to slaves is *largely* concerned with Christian slaves of non-Christian owners. In the face of harsh treatment at the hands of their owners, Christian slaves are to do good, to be submissive, and to endure unjust suffering patiently. Nor is such conduct enjoined only of slaves; implicitly in 2:18-25 and explicitly elsewhere, the letter charges all its addressees to exhibit these behaviors.

Second, although the command in 3:1a that wives submit to their husbands is clearly not directed *exclusively* to believing wives of unbelieving husbands, the ἵνα clause of 3:1-2 does state the purpose of wives' submission *solely* in terms of the winning to the faith of non-Christian husbands. And although much of 3:3-6 could apply equally to wives of believers and to wives of nonbelievers, the concluding participles of v. 6 clearly refer to the situation of Christian wives of non-Christian husbands. In the first place, the implicit command for wives to do good echoes both the word to slaves in 2:20 (which I take to be directed primarily, if not exclusively, to slaves of non-Christians) and the injunctions to do good in response to the calumny of non-Christians in 2:12-15, 3:11, 3:13-17, and 4:19. Second, the proscription of fear echoes the injunction not to fear hostile nonbelievers in 3:14; furthermore, the instruction to husbands in 3:7 proscribes the kind of conduct that would evoke terror in their wives. Although the submissive behavior prescribed for wives in 3:1-6, therefore, is applicable to all wives among the addressees, the section is formulated with specific reference to wives of unbelieving husbands. These women are to adopt the disposition expected of wives in Greco-Roman society and submit to their husbands, for the express purpose of converting those husbands who are not Christians. Only here in the letter is a missionary concern evident, and here it is neither a matter of verbal proclamation—indeed husbands are to be won without a word from their wives (3:1)—nor of active outreach to outsiders to the communities but of winning over non-Christian husbands by behavior consistent with the ideals of Greco-Roman social order.[116]

Balch argues that 1 Peter's use of the household code—especially the words to slaves and to wives—is apologetic in character: Slaves and wives who converted to Christianity were refusing to worship the gods of their masters and husbands, respectively. This behavior brought the ire of society and, in response, 1 Peter counsels conformity to the ideals of Greco-Roman society, with one conspicuous exception—the letter does not call for slaves and wives to return to the worship of the gods of the *paterfamilias*. The letter writer hoped, Balch argues, that when wives and slaves assumed the roles prescribed for them in the household code tradition, the slander against Christians would stop and the agitators would be shamed by the good behavior of Christian wives and slaves within their households.[117]

> The author of 1 Peter wrote to advise the Christians who were being persecuted about how they might become socially-politically acceptable to their society. . . . The author was clearly aware, however, that even if his readers conformed socially and politically, their new and different *religious* attitudes might remain unacceptable to society (1:18; 3:13-17; 4:15-16; 5:8).[118]

---

[116]For the parallels between the injunctions of 1 Pet 3:1-6 and Greco-Roman (as well as early-Jewish) moral exhortation, see Balch, *Wives*, 95-105.
[117]Balch, *Wives*, esp. 81-116.
[118]Balch, *Wives*, 88.

The Liminality of Christian Life

In short, 1 Peter's ethic encourages its readers to acculturate to Roman society by adopting behaviors in conformity with that society in order to counter Roman slander directed against them.[119]

In my view, Balch overstates the hope 1 Peter holds out that its addressees' "doing good" will result in silencing their critics. In the first place, his distinction between social-political behavior and religious attitudes is extremely dubious. We have seen in chapter 3 that Roman society did not distinguish between the religious and the sociopolitical, and from what we have seen thus far of 1 Peter's response to the plight of its addressees, neither does this letter. So long as the Christians' convictions about God caused them to withdraw from some aspects of the public life, they would remain unacceptable socially and politically.

In all likelihood, the letter does hope that some of the calumny will be stopped. In particular, in the case of the wives of nonbelieving husbands, both the instruction to wives to be chaste, silent, and submissive and the expressed hope that some husbands will be won to the faith by such behavior seem to indicate an underlying hope that, if these women follow these directives, their suffering will be lessened. It is quite another thing, however, to see the instructions to slaves and to wives as the primary means by which 1 Peter hopes to attenuate the suffering of entire Christian communities. In particular, two considerations militate against placing the household code at the center of 1 Peter's project. First, the instruction to slaves, as we have seen, plays a paradigmatic role for the entire community. Slaves who suffer for doing right follow in Christ's footsteps, as do all Christians who behave similarly. It does not appear that the direction to slaves is formulated with even the possibility in view that their masters' hostility would decrease if they were to follow the letter's directives. The alternative to suffering for doing wrong is not being commended for doing good but *suffering* for doing good. Nor does 2:18-25 give any indication that the letter hopes to silence the slander directed against Christianity's encouragement of slaves to forsake their masters' religion. Second, the word to husbands in 3:7 can play no role whatever in Balch's alleged

---

[119]Balch, *Wives*, 119.

apologetic function of the household code; indeed, in *Let Wives Be Submissive*, 3:7 is treated only in a footnote, and then not as part of this overall strategy Balch attaches to the household code.[120] It would appear, rather, that the household code is but one parenetic tradition among many that 1 Peter uses; nor is the household code the central element of a strategy of inculcating assimilation so as to reduce suffering.

Finally, in light of the foregoing, it is necessary to add a word about 1 Pet 2:5. I noted above that this verse metaphorically states the addressees' priestly vocation as the offering of spiritual sacrifices to God, and I suggested that this does not necessarily refer only to ritual acts of worship. Indeed, the notion of metaphorical sacrifices to God was already firmly fixed in biblical (Pss 50:17-21; 140:2; Hos 6:6; Mic 6:6-8) and early-Christian tradition (Rom 12:1-2; Phil 4:18; Heb 13:16). In light of 2:9-17—especially vv. 9 and 12—and the letter's emphasis on doing good, it would appear that the offering of spiritual sacrifices in 2:5 refers to a life lived in accordance with the letter's ethic, amid a hostile society (composed of those who reject Christ, the living stone [2:4, 7-8]). Discharging one's responsibilities toward society in obedience to the will of God is viewed in 2:5 as an act of worship.

In conclusion, the liminality we observed in the letter's symbolic construction of Christian communal identity is evident also in its explicit directives concerning Christian behavior in society. Just as the addressees are marked off from their non-Christian neighbors—and family members—as God's elect diaspora people in a time of παροικία within a hostile society, so they are commanded not to return to those behaviors that they recently renounced (which 1 Peter relegates to their "gentile" past). On the other hand, they are not without responsibility to conform to certain societal standards. First Peter's explicit instructions concerning its addressees' disposition toward and relations with non-Christians largely follow stereotyped parenetic traditions of Greco-Roman literature and early-Christian tradition. The letter enjoins its readers to honor all people in general and the emperor in particular and to do good. It proscribes

---

[120] Balch, *Wives*, 114-15 n. 92.

speaking guile and returning evil for evil and reviling for reviling, and it prescribes speaking a good word in response to calumny. The addressees' responsibility to society, however, is a derivative one that emerges from their prior obligation to God. Implicit in this construal of the Christian's responsibility to society is the recognition that Christians and the larger society will not always agree on what constitutes doing the good. Hence, although 1 Peter commands the doing of good, it does not expect its addressees' good behavior to be recognized as such by society. The letter holds out slight hope that its addressees' suffering will be somewhat attenuated if they adopt its prescriptions for their relations with their antagonists, but the overarching expectation is that the calumny will not be stopped and, in fact, may well get worse. For this reason, 1 Peter looks forward to the eschatological day of reckoning when its readers will finally be vindicated before their accusers, who will then respond by rendering God glory. Nowhere does the letter command missionary proclamation to outsiders, and only in 3:1-6, in the instruction to wives, is the letter's parenesis formulated with a view to the winning of non-Christians—in this case, unbelieving husbands.

Intracommunity Relations. Although we have already found good reason to describe 1 Peter's presentation of Christian life within a hostile society as liminal, it remains to make a final inquiry into the appropriateness of using Turner's theory of liminality in this interpretation of 1 Peter. If 1 Peter's depiction of Christian existence is truly an example of institutionalized liminality, then we should find in the letter's directives for intracommunity relations at least some of the characteristics of Turner's "normative communitas." Recall that, according to Turner, if spontaneous communitas—that is, "society as an unstructured or rudimentarily structured and relatively undifferentiated *comitatus*, community, or even communion of equal individuals"[121]—is to endure, it must become normative communitas; that is to say, it must be placed under the governance of "a system of ethical precepts and legal rules."[122] What one

---

[121] Turner, *Ritual Process*, 96; quoted above, p. 120.
[122] Turner, *Process, Performance*, 151; quoted above, p. 120.

would expect to find in a situation of normative *communitas*, therefore, is a community of persons whose relationships with each other are at the same time (1) relatively unstructured and egalitarian (in comparison to their relationships with outsiders to the community) and (2) to some extent rule-governed (so that these relationships can endure). In 1 Peter's directives for Christian relations, we find precisely these two characteristics. The letter presupposes that its addressees will conform to certain social-structural norms that obtained in the larger society, but at the same time it modifies those norms by presenting an intracommunity ethic characterized by love and humility.

I begin this portion of my study by taking another look at 1 Pet 2:1 and 3:9-11. We saw above that the parenesis in these two passages, although formulated in the most general fashion and not *explicitly* directed toward the regulation of either intra- or extracommunity relations, *implicitly* addresses the latter. This is not to say that the prohibitions against evil, guile, hypocrisy, envy, slander, and returning evil treatment for evil and reviling for reviling are not also applicable to the addressees' intracommunity relations; they certainly are and would have been so understood by the intended audience. But the situation to which the majority of these general parenetic statements is directed is the addressees' conflict with their outside antagonists.

The one exception to this rule is found in the verse containing the very first imperative that explicitly addresses the readers' relationships with one another—1 Pet 1:22. Here, the adjective ἀνυπόκριτον foreshadows the prohibition of hypocrisy to come in 2:1, in effect already applying that prohibition to the addressees' intracommunity relations. The purpose for which the addressees purified their souls by obeying the truth is said to be "for sincere sibling love" (εἰς φιλαδελφίαν ἀνυπόκριτον). An explicit imperative follows: "Love one another earnestly from a pure heart" (ἐκ [καθαρᾶς] καρδίας ἀλλήλους ἀγαπήσατε ἐκτενῶς). If the aim of their purification is sincere sibling love, then the command to love one another from a pure heart seeks to ensure the realization of that objective. The importance for 1 Peter of the ethic of sibling love/mutual love is suggested already by its pride of place as the letter's first word about Christian relations. And, as we shall see, the frequent recurrence of the theme of sibling love/mutual love in the remainder of the letter confirms that it constitutes the heart of 1 Peter's ethic for life within the communities addressed.

In the next passage that addresses intracommunity relations, in fact, sibling love is again urged. In 2:17, as we have seen, the letter distinguishes between the Christian's obligation to honor all people, including the emperor, to fear God, and to love the ἀδελφότης. In this formulation, the sibling love that is to govern relations within the communities addressed characterizes the greater obligation Christians owe one another in comparison with what they owe the larger society. Whereas the notions of sibling love and mutual love occur in separate clauses in 1:22, here they are combined in the pithy imperative τὴν ἀδελφότητα ἀγαπᾶτε. We have already seen that 5:9 refers to Christians the world over as a single ἀδελφότης. Given the categorical nature of the other three injunctions in 2:17, it may be that the worldwide scope of 5:9 is also in view in the command to love the ἀδελφότης in 2:17. In any case, it is clear that the addressees' relationships with each other are to be characterized by the love appropriate to siblings, which, metaphorically speaking, they are.

In 3:8, immediately following the directive to husbands, 1 Peter draws the household code to a close with a piece of general parenesis applicable not merely to slaves or wives or husbands but to all (πάντες) the addressees. With a catena of five adjectives, the letter commands the readers to be like-minded (ὁμόφρονες), sympathetic (συμπαθεῖς), loving of their sisters and brothers (φιλάδελφοι), compassionate (εὔσπλαγχνοι), and humble (ταπεινόφρονες). In light of the importance to the letter of sibling love for one's fellow believers, we might say that the third of these adjectives, φιλάδελφοι, is fundamental to the letter's conception of Christian relations and that the adjectives on either side underscore particular manifestations of sibling love. The first and, especially, the last of these, ὁμόφρονες and ταπεινόφρονες, are particularly telling. Following hard on the household code, with its directives to slaves, wives, and husbands, the exhortations to like-mindedness and humility downplay the importance of such social-structural distinctions within the Christian communities. Not only are the intended readers all brothers and sisters who are expected to love each other and to be sympathetic and compassionate toward each other, but in particular, they are to live together harmoniously, and, far from aspiring to social distinctions, they are to be humble toward one another. One could scarcely hope to find a better example of a prescription for normative communitas.

A series of directives for life within the communities of believers is given in 4:8-11, and at the head of the list is the exhortation in 4:8 to "keep the love for one another constant." The parallelism between this exhortation and the letter's initial directive for intracommunal relations in 1:22 is unmistakable:

>   ἀλλήλους   ἀγαπήσατε   ἐκτενῶς (1:22)
>   εἰς ἑαυτοὺς ἀγάπην   ἐκτενῆ ἔχοντες (4:8)

As if to guard against the possibility that anyone could read this far and still not recognize the necessity of mutual love to the well-being of the Christian community, 1 Peter makes it explicit with the introductory prepositional phrase πρὸ πάντων, "above all." The letter then prescribes two concrete activities by which to enact such love for one another (εἰς ἑαυτούς) (v. 8): the practicing of hospitality to one another (εἰς ἀλλήλους) (v. 9 [cf. 1:22]) and the using of one's God-given gifts for each other (εἰς ἑαυτούς) (v. 10 [cf. v. 8]).

Thus far, we have focused attention on those commands that 1 Peter directs to the entire community. Several more community-wide injunctions appear in 5:5-6, but before turning to them, we must examine the preceding instructions to elders and to the young in 5:1-4. More clearly than anywhere else in the letter—including the household code—5:1-4 presupposes and implicitly endorses the replication within Christian communities of the hierarchical social structure that characterized the larger society. Whereas elsewhere in the letter, various metaphors are used to characterize the addressees as an *undifferentiated collective* vis-à-vis God and/or society, here the metaphors of the shepherds (ποιμάνατε [5:2]) and the flock (ποίμνιον [5:2-3]), like the designations "elders" (πρεσβύτεροι [5:1, 5]) and "younger ones" (νεώτεροι [5:5]), serve *to distinguish between* individuals in positions of leadership and their social-structural inferiors. The elders are shepherds who are to tend the flock, and the younger ones are to subject themselves (ὑποτάγητε) to the elders.

At the same time, however, the letter demands that the elders exercise a benevolent leadership. In particular, 5:3 sets two quite different modes of leadership over against each other: The elders are not to lord it over (κατακυριεύω) their charges but to become moral examples (τύποι) for them. By means of this antithesis, 1 Peter rejects the hierarchical construction of the shepherd-sheep or elder-younger relation as one of domination and subordination and, in so doing, reconstitutes the social-structural differentiation between elders and those in their care. For 1 Peter, the elders' social position means not domination by force but leadership by example. And, given the nature of 1 Peter's parenesis, which focuses on sibling love, one must conclude that the moral example the elders are to provide their flocks consists in their embodying love, along with such virtues as hospitality, sympathy, and even humility (cf. 3:8). Indeed, in 5:5, the letter rounds off its instructions to elders and younger ones by commanding all (πάντες) to clothe themselves with humility (ταπεινοφροσύνη). All—including the shepherding elders and the submissive younger ones—are to assume a stance of humility toward each other. And in 5:6, the command for all to humble themselves is reiterated, this time with the focus on one's position before God: The addressees are to humble themselves before God ("under God's mighty hand") in order that (ἵνα) God may exalt them in due time (ἐν καιρῷ).

So, although the letter assumes the social-structural differentiation between elders and younger ones, between shepherds and their flocks, it qualifies this structural distinction in terms of its defining ethic of mutual love and self-humbling. Precisely this kind of modified social-structural differentiation is what is to be expected in normative communitas. Some social-structural norms must be adopted if human communities are to persist; but if communitas is to be maintained, structure must be kept to a minimum. Indeed, the purpose of the social process that results in normative communitas is to avoid squelching communitas and to create the conditions within which communitas can endure. And if the relatively undifferentiated, "I-Thou" relations characteristic of *communitas* are to flourish, then the structural norms adopted cannot be such as tend to reduce individuals to mere players of stereotypical roles. What we have seen thus far of 1 Peter's treatment of intracommunity relations looks very much like what one would expect of normative *communitas* within institutionalized liminality. One passage remains to be considered: the household code.

I argued in the previous section of this chapter that the instructions to slaves in 2:18 are directed to slaves of non-Christian owners and that the words to wives in 3:1-6 are primarily, although not exclusively, directed to Christian wives of non-Christian husbands. That is to say, as regards the regulation of intracommunity relations, the directives to slaves do not apply at all, and the instructions to wives are only indirectly applicable. Both slaves and wives are commanded to subject themselves (ὑποτασσόμενοι/αι) to their superiors within their households. These injunctions to submission follow closely on the command in 2:13-14 for all members of the communities addressed to subject themselves (ὑποτάγητε) to every social institution, particularly to the emperor and his provincial governors, and the commands in 2:17 to honor all people and the emperor but to love one's fellow Christians and to fear God. The demand for the subjection of slaves to masters and of wives to husbands, therefore, is of a piece with the letter's general instruction concerning the individual Christian's obligation to submit, for the sake of God (2:13), to the social-structural conventions of Greco-Roman society.

Submission, along with paying due respect, characterizes the disposition toward society that 1 Peter prescribes for its addressees. The letter also enjoins submission of some individuals to others *within* the communities. We have already observed the two explicit cases: the command to submit to the elders in 5:5 and the command to all wives—even those married to believers—to submit to their husbands in 3:1. It is in the context of this expectation that wives will submit themselves to their husbands, moreover, that the word to husbands is given in 3:7.

Husbands are instructed to live together with their wives "according to knowledge" (κατὰ γνῶσιν); and the content of the knowledge that is to determine their behavior is that, in comparison with her husband, the wife is the "weaker vessel" (ἀσθενέστερον σκεῦος). The notion of women as weaker than men, whether physically, rationally, and/or morally, was common in antiquity.[123] The letter appears to accept this socially constructed "knowledge" of reality. It also appears to acknowledge, as we noted in chapter 3, that a married woman's honor was a function of her husband's honor. The husband, in fact, possesses the power of bestowing honor (τιμή) on his wife.

Although 1 Peter accepts the conventional hierarchical relation between husband and wife, however, it also attempts to preclude any behavior on the part of husbands toward their wives that runs counter to the letter's general Christian ethic of love and humility. In acknowledgement of the wife's status as "weaker," the husband is to bestow honor on her. The expression "bestowing honor" (ἀπονέμω τιμήν) is common in the literature of antiquity, but, so far as I can determine, 1 Peter's demand that the *husband* bestow honor on his *wife* is unique. Moreover, from the standpoint of the social-scientific analysis of honor and shame, the notion of a husband's bestowal of honor on his wife is striking. Whereas, in social-scientific terms, the husband embodies the family's honor, and the wife embodies its shame, 1 Peter calls on the husband to bestow honor on his wife. For 1 Peter, the husband's recognition that his wife is the weaker vessel must issue not in domineering behavior but in the sharing of the honor that accrues to him as a result of his position as *paterfamilias*. Moreover, if wives are to be understood as (ὡς) weaker vessels, they are also to be understood as (ὡς καί) "joint heirs of the grace of life" (συγκληρονόμοι χάριτος ζωῆς). The concept of joint heirship recalls the mention in 1:4 of the inheritance that *all* Christians—without differentiation according to social roles—have gained as a result of their conversion. The husband's recognition that his wife is the weaker vessel, therefore, must be balanced by his acknowledgement that she is his equal in terms of the reception of God's grace. In this fashion, 1 Peter transforms the presupposed

---

[123]Michaels, e.g., cites the following: Plato *Resp.* 455D, 457A; *Leg.* 781A; Thucydides *History* 2.45; *Ep. Arist.* 250; Philo *Ebr.* 55 (*1 Peter*, 169).

hierarchical relation of husband to wife into a less domineering—though by no means entirely egalitarian—one.

Like the word to elders in 5:1-5, therefore, the word to husbands in 3:7 both presupposes the structural hierarchy characteristic of Greco-Roman society and modifies it in the direction of the letter's general ethic for intracommunity relations. And, also like the word to elders, the directive to husbands is immediately followed by a word to all the addressees (πάντες) that implicitly critiques the hierarchical social structure. In 5:5-6 all are called to humility; in 3:8 it is humility, along with like-mindedness, sympathy, sibling love, and compassion, to which all are summoned.[124]

This examination of 1 Peter's directives for life within the communities addressed confirms the appropriateness of using Turner's theory of liminality in interpreting 1 Peter. We earlier discovered that the letter's symbolic construction of its addressees' communal identity corresponds to Turner's concept of institutionalized liminality; now we have found that the norms 1 Peter gives for

---

[124]Although I disagree with Balch's insistence on the centrality of the household code in 1 Peter, I concur with Balch that 1 Peter not only adopts the Roman hierarchical household structure but also modifies it (see Balch, "Early Christian Criticism," 166, 169-70). The modification, however, consists not merely in the letter's insistence that slaves and women should be able to choose their own religion but more emphatically in the letter's instruction that husbands should bestow honor on their wives and that all the addressees should exhibit toward each other humility, like-mindedness, sympathy, sibling love, and compassion. In this manner, 1 Peter both reinscribes Greco-Roman patriarchy and at the same time plants the seeds of that system's destruction. What Luise Schottroff says in her treatment of 1 Timothy may be applied with modifications to 1 Peter as well: "To establish *grades* of hatred regarding women's liberation or discrimination against women in the historical Paul (1 Cor. 11:2-16; possibly 1 Cor. 14:33-36); in the household codes of Ephesians, Colossians, and 1 Peter; and in the pastoral epistles *offers no basis for a solution to the problem*. The submission of women to men is demanded in all those texts and can in no way be justified.... But there are traces within the patriarchal systems of violence of a history of liberation, and there are texts in the New Testament in which we can hear voices of women and men who are working at liberation. First Timothy shows traces of a history of women's liberation, albeit most unwittingly and entirely contrary to its declared intentions" (*Lydia's Impatient Sisters: A Feminist Social History of Early Christianity* [trans. Barbara Rumscheidt and Martin Rumscheidt; Louisville: Westminster John Knox, 1995] 77). In the case of 1 Peter, however, I would suggest that the liberating impulse inscribed in 1:22, 2:17, 3:7-8, 4:8-11, 5:2b-3, and 5:5b-6 is by no means unwitting or against the letter's intentions.

the governance of life within these communities correspond to Turner's model of normative communitas.

Conclusions

In chapter 3, I identified the suffering addressed in 1 Peter as the relentless challenge to honor in the form of slanderous accusations brought by non-Christians against the letter's addressees. I then set out in this part of my study to uncover the nature of 1 Peter's vision of Christian community, for it is within the Christian communities that the letter expects its readers to discover the answer to the problem of their suffering. In terms of the sociology of knowledge, 1 Peter's addressees can continue to embrace the Christian symbolic universe only if their communities are symbolically constituted in such a way as to render the communities capable of mediating to the individuals the plausibility structure of their world, including especially 1 Peter's legitimation of the Christian symbolic universe that has now become problematic. In terms of the values of honor and shame, 1 Peter's addressees can remain in the faith only if their communities can provide them with alternative (sub)societies within which their honor will be acknowledged and certified in the face of threats emanating from the society at large.

In this chapter, I have argued that 1 Peter symbolically constructs by means of a variety of metaphors a liminal self-identity for its readers. Christian existence amid a hostile society, the letter urges, is an existence that is neither here nor there; the Christian community is neither fully a part of Greco-Roman society nor fully abstracted from it. Accordingly, the letter's directives for life within the larger society call for its readers to abide by societal conventions except when those conventions conflict with their Christian symbolic universe. They are to submit to the emperor and his governors and to honor the emperor and all people, but they are not to resume participation in those social activities they had rejected at their conversion as incompatible with Christian faith. That is to say, 1 Peter constructs a liminal communal identity for its readers and gives them directives appropriate to their liminality. In so doing, the letter affirms that the answer to suffering is not to be found in bowing to pressure to conform.

If the problem 1 Peter addresses is the assault on the addressees' honor, then the construction of a liminal identity is but one part of the letter's answer to the problem of suffering—in essence, the community 1 Peter symbolically constructs provides the context within which the letter's answer is intelligible and workable. The task that falls to the next chapter is to examine how 1 Peter uses the symbol of the crucified, resurrected, and glorified Christ to legitimate the symbolic universe of its addressees and to provide a means of calculating honor within the Christian communities when that honor is denied from without. Assuming that challenges to honor are to be expected, how does 1 Peter propose to ensure that its readers do not lose honor in such challenges? Given the construction of a liminal community as mediator of the plausibility structure for the addressees' world, how does the Christ symbol function within 1 Peter's symbolic universe to answer the problem of suffering?

CHAPTER 5

THE SOLUTION, PART TWO: CHRISTOLOGY AND HONOR

Already, I have had occasion to comment on some of the passages in which 1 Peter refers to Christ, particularly in the course of examining the letter's depiction of the temporal liminality of Christian life. For 1 Peter, Christ's past suffering and glorification marked the beginning of the end of history, and the future revelation of Christ's glory will mark the eschatological consummation. It is my contention that this delimiting of the world's temporal parameters is but one aspect of a larger role played in 1 Peter by the symbol of the Christ who suffered and was therefore glorified. Christ, I shall argue below, is the key to the letter's response to the suffering of its addressees. As part of this response, 1 Peter sets the eschatological limits of world history, and so of human life in the world, in order to assure the addressees that their suffering will not last indefinitely. This much we have seen above.[1] Here, it is important to note that the letter establishes the end of history not merely by asserting that the end is near or by stating that Christ's glorification implies the proximity of the eschaton but by inextricably tying the addressees' fate to the experience and destiny of Christ: The imminence of the ultimate disclosure of Christ's glory means not merely that Christian suffering is about to come to an end but that Christians are about to be vindicated by God just as Christ was. Cessation of suffering, in other words, is a function of God's eschatological vindication, both in Christ's case and in that of Christians. Just as Christ faithfully

---

[1] See above, pp. 127-35.

endured suffering and was consequently vindicated/glorified by God, so believers are assured that, in consequence of their suffering, God's vindication awaits them in the immediate future.

First Peter invokes the Christ who suffered and was consequently glorified in order to legitimate the symbolic universe of its addressees in the face of the threat posed by the hostility of non-Christians. The letter in effect superimposes Christ's experience onto that of his followers so that Christ's experience becomes the interpretive lens throught which Christian experience is viewed and the template that describes the shape of Christian life. By juxtaposing the Christian's suffering with that of Christ's, and the Christian's destiny with Christ's glorification, the letter reconfigures the relationship of suffering to honor and thereby offers its readers a means of enduring reproach without losing honor. First Peter's identification of its addressees' experience with Christ's, in other words, is the essence of the letter's response to the threat to honor routinely faced by the addressees in their daily interactions with non-Christians. In the remainder of this study, I shall elaborate this thesis through an examination of the letter's references to Christ.

First, however, I shall call attention to another function of the Christ symbol in 1 Peter, one that I have already noted without extensive comment: I refer to 1 Peter's assertion that Christ is the means by which the addressees were gathered into the people of God in the first place. Indeed, however the addressees may have construed their relationship to Christ's suffering and glorification before they received this letter: and however novel the letter's message may have seemed to them in relation to their previous conceptions: we can be certain that one notion at least was presupposed by the addressees, namely, that Christ's death and God's subsequent resurrection/glorification of Christ provided their means of salvation. Moreover, this traditional notion of Christ as the means of salvation, as we have seen, assumes a specific function in 1 Peter: Christ is the means by which God has constituted alternative, liminal communities of believers within Greco-Roman society.[2] In this sense, Christ's death and resurrection/glorification play a distinct

---

[2] See above, pp. 135-56.

(though by no means unrelated) role in 1 Peter alongside their function of providing the template for Christian experience. That is to say, although the letter's final answer to the question of its addressees' suffering is given in its symbolic linking of their honor to Christ's, this answer is only possible if the addressees have first been gathered into an alternative community in whose symbolic universe Christ plays a pivotal role and within which threats to honor coming from outside the community can be reinterpreted, by means of this symbolic universe, as honor-enhancing participation in the experience of Christ. I shall now trace through 1 Peter its development of this christological response to the problem of suffering.

1 Peter 1:3-9

Following the adscript, which twice refers to Jesus Christ (1:1-2), the first verse of the letter body (1:3) mentions Christ two times. After a brief doxology to "the God and father of our Lord Jesus Christ," the letter attributes the readers' rebirth to God's great mercy as mediated through (διά) Christ's resurrection. Verses 3 and 4 together explain what Christians have been reborn "to" (εἰς): a living hope and an inheritance that is being kept in heaven for them. Verse 5 then identifies the object of that living hope and the content of the inheritance as "salvation" (σωτηρία), and it explains that the addressees are being guarded by God's power through the agency of faith (διὰ πίστεως) for this salvation, which is even now ready to be revealed "in the last time" (ἐν καιρῷ ἐσχάτῳ). In these three verses, Christ functions as the central symbol around which the letter's soteriology and eschatology are formed. God is the actor who both causes rebirth by resurrecting Christ and preserves believers by the divine power. The salvation for which believers are being preserved, moreover, is prepared already and merely awaits the as-yet-unspecified eschatological moment of its revelation.

The problem of suffering is first addressed in 1:6. Here the suffering of the addressees is placed in the context of the temporal liminality of Christian life; their suffering, the letter says, will not last long. Verse 7 then loosely associates Christian suffering with the purification of gold by fire, without actually saying that suffering itself is purifying.³ Rather, genuine faith—literally "the genuineness of faith"—which is *already* more precious than gold that is tested by fire, will, by means of suffering, be found to result in ἔπαινον καὶ δόξαν καὶ τιμήν—praise and glory and honor. Suffering is thus given the function not of purifying but of catalyzing the disclosure of the intended results (εἰς) of faith, namely, praise and honor and glory. The eschatological moment of this "finding," moreover, is specified as the time of the revelation of Jesus Christ. The time for suffering is thus delimited as a short one (v. 6) whose end will be marked by the disclosure of Jesus Christ (v. 7).

It is instructive to note how 1 Pet 1:3-9 treats faith and faith's results. Whereas in v. 5 faith is said to be the means through which God's power will keep Christians until their salvation is revealed at the last time, and in v. 7 faith is expected to result in honor, praise, and glory in the last time, v. 9 states that salvation (σωτηρία) will be the ultimate outcome of faith. In vv. 5, 7, and 9, therefore, 1 Peter virtually equates salvation (vv. 5, 9) with the honor-praise-glory complex (v. 7); both are imminent eschatological realities, both are the results of faith, and both are implicitly the work of God. Moreover, the living hope for the soon-to-be-disclosed salvation/honor, praise, and glory gives rise already to inexpressible joy in spite of suffering (vv. 6, 8). In 1:3-9, therefore, 1 Peter begins to respond to the problem of its addressees' suffering by assuring them that their eschatological salvation/commendation is as certain as their rebirth, because both are effected by God through Christ, and that it is very near.

Of greater interest for this study, however, is the letter's broaching of the pattern of suffering followed by praise/glory/honor in chap. 1. First Peter 1:6-7 implies that the suffering-commendation sequence is typical of Christian life. Moreover, not only is commendation said to follow suffering, it is said to be the purpose for suffering. The addressees have to suffer for a brief time *in order that* (ἵνα) their faith might ultimately be shown to result in praise, honor, and glory. That is to say, the course of Christian life is not merely suffering and subsequent honor but suffering and *consequent* honor.

---

³Cf. Michaels, *1 Peter*, 30.

Christology and Honor 183

Furthermore, 1 Pet 1:7 implicitly connects Christ's glorification with that of believers: The final disclosure of Christ's glory will usher in the praise, honor, and glory of his followers.

In these opening verses of the letter body, 1 Peter begins to address the problem of suffering by asserting that suffering will soon cease at the imminent disclosure of Christ's glory and by establishing the pattern of suffering and consequent commendation/glorification as characteristic of Christian life. Thus far, 1 Peter has not explicitly connected the suffering-followed-by-glory pattern to Christ; nor has it specified the relation of the believer's glorification to Christ's (other than to correlate the former with the future disclosure of the latter). These relations will be clarified in the course of the letter.

1 Peter 1:10–2:3

The word χάρις appears in 1:10 for the first time since its stereotyped use in the greeting of 1:2. In 1:10, χάρις is virtually equated with σωτηρία: grace and salvation are the twin subjects of the message of Israel's prophets. Verses 10-11 together closely associate this prophecy of χάρις/σωτηρία with the prophecy of Christ's sufferings and glory. In v. 11, furthermore, the letter first explicitly connects the pattern of suffering followed by glorification to Christ: the content of the prophets' testimony is said to be "the sufferings of Christ and the glories after these sufferings" (τὰ εἰς Χριστὸν παθήματα καὶ τὰς μετὰ ταῦτα δόξας). Verse 13 then recalls the previously mentioned notions of hope (1:3), the coming grace (1:10), and the eschatological revelation of Christ (1:7) in a general exhortation that both concludes this paragraph and serves as a transition to the parenesis of vv. 14-17: In light of the good news (v. 12) about Christ's suffering and glorification and the grace/salvation they have effected (vv. 10-11), the addressees are therefore (διό) instructed to set their hope fully on the grace that will come to them at the revelation of Christ.

First Peter's use in this paragraph of the word χάρις is an important part of the letter's emerging response to the problem of the suffering of its addressees. Recall that 1 Pet 1:3-9 virtually equates σωτηρία, ἔπαινος, δόξα, and τιμή as designations of God's eschatological act on behalf of believers that will be realized at the revelation of Christ. First Peter 1:10 now expands this list of synonyms by identifying χάρις with σωτηρία. Furthermore, this identification of χάρις with σωτηρία is made even clearer in 1:13, where χάρις is said to attend the eschatological revelation of Christ in precisely the same way that 1:5 and 1:9 say that σωτηρία will arrive with Christ's revelation. The functional synonymity among χάρις and these other terms found in 1:5-9 prepares the way for the use of χάρις to refer to God's approval later in the letter (as we shall see below).

Turning now to the parenesis in 1:14-17, we note that 1 Peter has thus far had very little to say about suffering; in 1:6, the addressees are said to be "distressed by trials of various kinds" (λυπηθέντες ἐν ποικίλοις πειρασμοῖς), and 1:11 mentions the sufferings of Christ (τὰ εἰς Χριστὸν παθήματα). Nor is anything said explicitly in vv. 14-17 of the addressees' suffering. The metaphor of their time of παροικία (v. 17), however, points unmistakably to the abuse they are undergoing at the hands of their detractors, and the encouragement to maintain "holy" conduct and not to return to the "passions" that characterized their former "ignorance" clearly presupposes that the addressees were being pressured to resume participation in those societal activities they had forsaken at their conversion to Christianity.[4] In the face of such pressure, 1 Peter urges resistance.

As the warrant for this parenesis, 1 Peter invokes the figure of Christ in 1:18-20. At the end of the epochs of history (ἐπ' ἐσχάτου τῶν χρόνων), the letter says, Christ was manifested on account of the addressees (δι' ὑμᾶς); by Christ's precious blood (τιμίῳ αἵματι) they were ransomed from the futile behaviors of their ancestral traditions (ἐκ τῆς ματαίας ὑμῶν ἀναστροφῆς πατροπαραδότου). Here, for only the second time thus far in the letter, a word from the τιμ- group appears. In 1:7, the addressees' present suffering was expected to result in future τιμή; now, in 1:19, Christ's redemptive blood is said to be τίμιον. The adjective τίμιον, set in stark contrast to "perishable" silver and gold, conveys

---

[4]See above, pp. 61-63, 83-94.

at least the notion "precious"; but implicit in this adjective is the idea, explicitly conveyed (as we shall see below) in 2:4-7, that Christ is honored by God.[5] Whereas 1:7 and 2:4-7 enlist words from the τιμ- group to address directly the problem of the threat to honor, the use of τίμιον in 1:19 to characterize Christ's blood *implicitly* responds—or at least prepares the way for 1 Peter's response—to this threat by associating honor with Christ and, specifically, with Christ's suffering. In 1:7, the honor denied by a hostile society is promised as an imminent gift from God, to be granted in response to faithful perseverance in the face of society's hostility; in 1:19, we discover that, in advance of God's glorification of Christ (1:21), the blood that Christ shed in his redemptive (and, as we shall discover below, prototypical) suffering was itself precious, imbued with honor by God. This somewhat subtle association of honor with Christ anticipates 1 Peter's insistence in 2:4-7 that one's response to Christ bears directly on one's honor.

Several motifs we have seen earlier reappear in v. 21. The addressees are said to believe/to have faith in God and to have hope in God, and their belief and hope in God are said to result from (ὥστε) God's having raised Christ and having given him δόξα. Although no specific content is here predicated of hope, the connection between Christ's resurrection and glorification and the believer's hope implies that the object of the believer's hope is a future beyond suffering that will be similar to what Christ experienced after his suffering, that is, a future that includes resurrection and glorification. First Peter has already said that the believer's hope is based on Christ's resurrection (1:4), that the content of this hope includes future glory/honor (1:7), that believers will pass through suffering to glory/honor (1:6-7), and that Christ has already done so (1:11-12). Now, in 1:21, the content of Christian hope is implicitly identified with God's resurrection and glorification of Christ.

---

[5]Cf. Michaels, *1 Peter*, 65. Michaels says that τίμιον here "is probably to be read in light of 2:4 and 6." In view of the likelihood that any document a community deemed worthy of preserving would be read repeatedly, Michaels's position is very close to mine. I would prefer, however, to see here an intimation of what is to follow rather than to say that 1:19 is to be read in light of 2:4-6.

In gradually unfolding its answer to the problem of suffering, 1 Peter has thus far argued that (1) Christ's suffering and glorification were the means by which God effected the believers' rebirth and soon-to-be-revealed salvation; (2) Christians will receive praise, glory, and honor consequent upon their suffering; that is, Christian life conforms to the pattern of suffering followed by glory; (3) believers' reception of praise, glory, and honor/grace/salvation will occur at the revelation of Christ; and (4) Christ has already exhibited the sequence of suffering followed by glory. If 1 Peter has explicitly shown that Christ's life established the pattern of suffering followed by glory and that Christian life must follow the same course, it has not yet explicitly set forth Christ's experience as the model for Christian life. The letter has, however, hinted at what is to come by suggesting—without explicitly stating—that the second part of the christological pattern, namely, glorification, is to be replicated in the experience of Christ's followers. Nor has the letter yet elaborated a means for dealing with the challenges to honor that were the occasion for its writing. It has, however, laid the groundwork for its proposal by showing that (1) God is the one who bestows honor, both on Christ and on Christ's followers; (2) God has already granted Christ eschatological honor/glory; and (3) the blood of Christ shed for believers' redemption was, in advance of Christ's glorification, already imbued with honor, highly valued in God's sight (τίμιον).

1 Peter 2:4-10

Following the parenesis in 1:22–2:3, in which Christ is not mentioned until the very last word, namely, κύριος (and it only becomes apparent that κύριος refers to Christ when one reads the πρὸς ὅν of v. 4), 1 Peter next refers to Christ in 2:4. Here the letter draws a contrast between two evaluations of Christ, the living stone. Rejected by people, Christ is chosen and highly valued or honored (ἔντιμος) in God's sight (cf. 1:19). Then, in a remarkable transference of predicates from Christ to his followers, v. 5 likens those who come to Christ as living stones, using the same term by which Christ is designated in v. 4 (λίθος ζῶν). First Peter thus establishes (1) a correspondence between Christ and his followers and (2) a distinc-

Christology and Honor

tion between Christ and his followers on the one hand and those who reject Christ on the other.

This correspondence/distinction is elaborated in 2:6-8. Verse 6 quotes Isa 28:16, which 1 Peter takes to be prophetic of God's action in the Christ event and of the contrasting responses it evokes in human beings. As is clear from 2:4, 1 Peter identifies the chosen and honored stone/cornerstone of Isa 28:16 with Christ. The quotation of Isa 28:16 identifies belief as the proper response to Christ and emphatically promises that those who believe in him will certainly not be put to shame (οὐ μὴ καταισχυνθῇ). Here is the first of three appearances of the (κατ)αισχυν- word group in 1 Peter. In light of the other occurrences of words from this group in contexts that directly address the outsiders' attacks on the addressees' honor (namely, in 3:16 and in 4:16), it appears that already in 2:6, 1 Peter is addressing this conflict. This inference is confirmed in v. 7. Here 1 Peter places ὑμῖν first in the sentence, emphasizing that the promise of Isa 28:16 is realized precisely among these readers, for they fulfill the condition of the promise stated in the participial subject of Isa 28:16, namely, belief (ὁ πιστεύων): "To *you* who believe..." (ὑμῖν... τοῖς πιστεύουσιν). Whereas the promise of Isa 28:16 is stated negatively in terms of what will certainly not happen to believers, namely, being put to shame, v. 7 couches the fulfillment of the promise positively: Honor (ἡ τιμή) is granted to them.[6] Earlier, τιμή, along with ἔπαινος and δόξα, was promised to believers at the revelation of Christ (1:7); now, although no time frame is explicitly given in 2:7, it appears that τιμή is here conceived of as already bestowed on those who believe.[7] Verses 7b-8 proceed

---

[6] For a similar reading of v. 7, see the NJB: "To you believers it brings honour." In this regard, the NJB is to be contrasted with the NRSV, the REB, and the NAB, all of which understand τιμή as referring to the value or preciousness of Christ in the eyes of believers. Against this view, Michaels incisively explains: "In the immediate context it is not so much a question of how Christian believers perceive Christ as of how God... perceives him, and of how God consequently vindicates both Christ and his followers (Michaels, *1 Peter*, 104). The following understand v. 7 similarly: Bigg, *Commentary*, 131; Goppelt, *I Peter*, 145; Kelly, *Epistles of Peter*, 93; Selwyn, *Epistle of St. Peter*, 164.

[7] Reading the implied copula in v. 7a as present rather than future makes sense in light of a number of phenomena of the context. The distinction between those who

to contrast the bestowal of honor on those who believe in Christ with the stumbling and falling of those outside the Christian communities who neither believe in Christ nor obey the word. The same contrast is implicit in vv. 9-10, both in the many predicates applied to the addressees and, especially, in the references to conversion, for what the addressees once were—in darkness, no people, nonrecipients of God's mercy—their antagonists, by implication, still are.

In 2:4-10, therefore, 1 Peter establishes the fundamental nexus of relations and oppositions among Christ, his followers, and their detractors that will provide the means by which challenges to honor coming from non-Christians can be evaluated and countered within the Christian communities. In particular, honor is inextricably linked to Christ: One's honor is a product of one's relationship with Christ, the one honored by God. Those who place their trust in the chosen and honored (corner)stone who is Christ will not be put to shame but will receive honor both now and at the eschaton. In 3:16 and 4:16, 1 Peter will explicitly bring this theme to bear on social confrontations between believers and their antagonists, but the essential elements of the letter's response to threats to its addressees' honor are now in place.

1 Peter 2:11-17

The letter's first *explicit* reference to the hostility of non-Christians toward its intended readers occurs in 2:12. We have already seen that 2:12, among other passages, reveals that 1 Peter is addressing a situation in which its intended readers are being falsely

---

presently believe and those who do not and, consequently are *now* stumbling over Christ, the rock of stumbling implies that honor, like belief, disbelief, and stumbling, is a present reality. That is to say, both the prophecies of Isa 28:16 (1 Pet 2:7) and Isa 8:14 (1 Pet 2:8) appear to be regarded as now fulfilled among, respectively, the addressees and their opponents. Moreover, the distinction implicit in v. 9 and explicit in v. 10 between what the addressees once were and what they are now would also seem to point in the direction of the present tense in v. 7a. Goppelt understands the implied copula to be present tense (*I Peter*, 145), and Kelly rightly points out that this honor "includes (a) their privileged status here and now, on which he will dwell more fully in 9f., but also (b) their triumph over their mocking assailants and their salvation on the last day" (*Epistles of Peter*, 93).

accused by their non-Christian neighbors of being wrongdoers.[8] In response, 1 Peter prescribes good behavior in the hope that, whenever accusations are brought, the accusers will be silenced (2:15) and, ultimately, forced to acknowledge the believers' good deeds and therefore to glorify God at the eschaton (2:12). Although nothing is said explicitly in 2:12 of the competition for honor, the slanderous accusation that the addressees are wrongdoers presupposes such a situation, as becomes clear in 2:14, where the provincial governor's commendation (ἔπαινος) is said to be refused to wrongdoers but granted to those who do good. The turning of the opponents' calumny of the believers into praise of God implies that the believers' honor, presumed to be at stake in such slanderous attacks, will not be compromised by those attacks. Indeed, it is God's will that by doing good, the addressees should silence their critics (2:15).[9]

On the other hand, I have suggested earlier that the letter is not terribly optimistic about the likelihood that the addressees' critics will be silenced any time soon.[10] Indeed, in 2:12, it is only at the eschatological day of visitation that the opponents will finally render God δόξα. Moreover, although the imperative to behave properly and to do good is formulated for the purpose of silencing critics (2:15), and the function of governors is said in part to be the commendation of those who do good (2:14), the letter as a whole anticipates that the addressees' good behavior will neither bring commendation from the governor nor silence the critics.

On the contrary, 1 Peter implies that recognition of Christians' good deeds will only occur within the Christian communities; only their connection with Christ—God's honored—will issue in honor for believers, honor that, like their good deeds, will only be acknowledged within their communities of faith—until the eschaton, that is, when all slander will cease. As for outsiders to the communities, the most the letter can hope for prior to the eschaton is that those who currently calumniate the believers will find their efforts frustrated. In the end, the antagonists will certainly be forced to recognize their error and to render glory to God. In an ironic twist, the opponents

---

[8]See above, pp. 83-94.
[9]See above, p. 100.
[10]See above, pp. 83-94, 159-69.

who seek to deny honor to 1 Peter's addressees will themselves finally be ignominiously exposed as ignorant and be obliged to render honor to the final arbiter of claims to honor—God. In the meantime, believers are to understand themselves as a members of liminal communities within a hostile society—as πάροικοι, as παρεπίδημοι (2:11), as God's slaves (2:16)—and to conduct themselves honorably within that society, subjecting themselves to all of its institutions, including the emperor and his governors, and rendering τιμή to all people, especially the emperor (2:17). Such behavior is to be carried out alongside their special obligations to fear God and to love one another within the liminal communities of faith (2:17).[11]

1 Peter 2:18-25

In the previous chapter, I examined how 1 Pet 2:18-20 uses slavery, the liminal social status par excellence, as a metaphorical designation of its embattled addressees.[12] These verses invoke slaves who do right and suffer unjustly at the hands of cruel masters as models for the intended readers, who are suffering amid a hostile society. In the course of the argument, 1 Peter twice uses the word χάρις with reference to God's approval: Verse 19 begins with the words τοῦτο γὰρ χάρις, and v. 20 concludes, in a similar fashion, with the words τοῦτο χάρις παρὰ θεῷ. Both of these noun clauses are apodoses of conditional sentences whose protases are virtually synonymous: the condition of v. 19 is enduring pain while suffering unjustly, while the condition of v. 20b is enduring suffering for doing good. Furthermore, situated between these two conditional sentences and contrasted with them is the conditional sentence of v. 20a. Within v. 20, the concluding clause, τοῦτο χάρις παρὰ θεῷ, is set in opposition to the opening question, which begins with the words ποῖον γὰρ κλέος. Two kinds of repute are thus contrasted: κλέος and χάρις. The former, whose legitimacy 1 Peter questions, is public fame or renown and is gained on the basis of enduring

---

[11]See above, pp. 161-63, 168-69.
[12]See above, pp. 151-54.

beatings for doing wrong;[13] the other, which v. 20b explicitly says comes from God (παρὰ θεῷ), is divine approval and is won by enduring suffering for doing good.[14] If we take our cue from (1) the contrast between v. 20a and v. 20b and (2) the synonymity between v. 20b and v. 19, then we must read the clause τοῦτο γὰρ χάρις in v. 19 as synonymous with the clause τοῦτο χάρις παρὰ θεῷ and understand them both as references to the recognition or approval that is granted by God to the one who endures unjust suffering.[15] The χάρις to which 1 Peter refers both in v. 19 and in v. 20, therefore, is God's approval given to those who suffer slanderous abuse at the hands of a hostile society.

Conspicuously absent from 1:18-20 is any reference to time. The aphoristic nature of the pronouncements in vv. 19-20 concerning χάρις is to be compared and contrasted with 1 Peter's use of χάρις in 1:10 and 1:13. There, χάρις is a virtual synonym of σωτηρία, ἔπαινος, δόξα, and τιμή and denotes the eschatological action of God to vindicate, to commend, to honor God's faithful people. In 2:19-20, the same divine action in vindicating/commending is expressed, but here the temporal reference is entirely absent. If anything, the implication would appear to be that God's approval

---

[13]The word κλέος is a hapax legomenon in the NT. For the definition, see BAGD, 434, and the literature cited there, esp. Job 28:22; Josephus *Ant.* 4 §§ 105, 115; *1 Clem.* 5:6; 54:3.

[14]The clause τοῦτο χάρις παρὰ θεῷ, as Michaels points out, is reminiscent of the idiom often translated, "to find or have favor (χάρις) with someone," as in Exod 33:12, 16; Prov 12:2 (Michaels, *1 Peter*, 142). My rendering—χάρις from God—calls attention to God's activity as the giver of such χάρις. See, e.g., the NSRV rendering of Prov 12:2 ("The good obtain favor from the Lord") and of 1 Pet 2:20 ("... you have God's approval").

[15]Cf. Kelly's definition of χάρις in v. 19 as "an act which is intrinsically attractive and thus wins God's approval" (*Epistles of Peter*, 116; cf. Michaels, *1 Peter*, 139). It seems to me that χάρις in v. 19, as in v. 20, refers not to the human action but to the divine response. The human action that wins God's approval, both in v. 19 and in v. 20, is expressed in the conditional clause rather than the result clause. Goppelt objects to the kind of interpretation I am proposing, arguing that χάρις here is not God's response to the one who suffers; rather, "such a person is surrounded and borne along by 'grace,' by God's bestowal of himself, which accepts that person in love" (*1 Peter*, 199). Goppelt's account of these verses seems to me to be formulated in such a general, theological fashion—so as to avoid the implication that humans can achieve God's approval—that the sociopolitical dimension of the argument is obscured.

(χάρις) is a present reality for the suffering addressees: Not merely at the eschaton but now, whenever a believer does good and suffers for it, God's approval is granted. In this regard, 2:19-20 is similar to 2:7, where τιμή seems to be viewed as already granted to believers in Christ.

In any case, what is most important about 2:18-20 is its insistence that honor is not a matter of societal approbation but of divine approval. In 1 Peter's symbolic universe, God is both the arbiter of claims to honor and the source of honor for God's people. In the absence of societal acknowledgement of praiseworthy behavior, 2:19-20 says, God will both recognize it and grant the appropriate commendation. Against the claims of the society at large, therefore, these verses inscribe an alternative way of calculating honor within the liminal communities of the addressees. The behaviors for which the readers are being reviled are precisely the behaviors that God enjoins and calls good, and the vilification such behaviors evoke in the larger society results not in loss of honor (despite the intention of the antagonists) but in God's approval.

Moreover, according to 1 Pet 2:21a, the addressees' experience of suffering is no aberration; rather, they were called by God to precisely such a life. And the warrant for this claim, as stated in 2:21b-25, is the exemplary suffering of Christ.[16] Christ suffered on behalf of his followers, thereby leaving them a model (ὑπογραμμός), *in order that* (ἵνα) they should follow in his footsteps. Here is 1 Peter's clearest statement of the exemplary nature of Christ's suffering. No mention is made here of the paradigmatic nature of the second part of Christ's experience, namely, his glorification; rather, all the emphasis in this paragraph falls on the necessity of unjust suffering—both Christ's and that of his followers.

---

[16]At least parts of 1 Pet 2:22-25 almost certainly derive from a preexisting hymn or creed celebrating the redemptive suffering of Christ. See Rudolf Bultmann, "Bekenntnis- und Liedfragmente im ersten Petrusbrief," *Exegetica: Aufsätze zur Erforschung des Neuen Testaments* (by Rudolf Bultmann, ed. Erich Dinkler; Tübingen: Mohr-Siebeck, 1967) 295-97; Boismard, *Quatre hymnes*, 111-32; and Goppelt, *1 Peter*, 207-10. For arguments to the contrary, see, e.g., Best, *1 Peter*, 120; and Michaels, *1 Peter*, 136-37.

The exemplary aspects of Christ's suffering are spelled out in vv. 22-23. Christ did not commit sin; no guile was found on his lips; when reviled, he did not revile in return; when suffering, he did not make threats but, instead, entrusted himself to God. Later in the letter, 1 Peter alludes to several of these exemplary behaviors of Christ without explicitly citing them as such: In 3:9-10, the addressees are told not to revile when they are reviled and not to speak guile;[17] in 4:19, they are instructed to entrust themselves to God amid their suffering. The warrant for these exhortations is already given in the example of Christ's manner of suffering described in 2:22-23.

Verses 24-25 continue recounting Christ's suffering, but no longer as a pattern to be followed. These verses focus on the effects on the addressees of Christ's unique, redemptive suffering. As such, 2:24-25 recalls 1:3-5, 18-21, 23-25 and 2:9-10 and anticipates 3:18-22. Furthermore, 2:24-25 appears to express both an implicit imperative and the assurance of God's empowerment to obey that imperative. Christ is said to have borne our (ἡμῶν) sins on the tree "in order that we might die to sins and live to righteousness." If this purpose clause implies a proscription against behaviors that are contrary to the divine will, it expressly says that the purpose of Christ's death was that his followers might not engage in such behaviors. That is to say, whereas the emphasis in vv. 21-23 falls on the behavior of the addressees, in v. 24, the emphasis shifts to Christ's redemptive activity on their behalf. Indeed, v. 24 continues, the addressees *were* healed by Christ's suffering. Verse 25, moreover, affirms that the readers have already responded appropriately to Christ; whereas they once strayed like sheep, they have since returned to God. In light of v. 24, the emphasis in v. 25 would appear to fall not on the human activity of responding to God (which the addressees certainly have done) but on God's action of performing the tasks of the ποιμήν and of the ἐπίσκοπος.

First Peter 2:18-25, therefore, establishes the centrality of Christ in the letter's project of symbolic-universe maintenance. If badly treated slaves symbolize the suffering of Christian existence amid a hostile society, the suffering Christ functions both as the

---

[17] See above, pp. 163-64.

pattern to be followed in living out that suffering existence and as the means by which the readers were initiated into the relationship with God and with Christ that empowers them to fulfill their calling. Although 1 Peter has earlier hinted that the suffering-followed-by-glory sequence that characterized Christ's experience will be replicated in the experience of Christ's followers, it is only the suffering of Christ—more specifically, Christ's manner of suffering—that is explicitly held up as exemplary in this section. Whereas the believer's honor, praise, and the like are closely associated with Christ earlier in the letter, and whereas 2:18-25 insists once again that Christian life must follow the pattern of suffering followed by glory/honor/commendation (in this case, χάρις), the believer's honor is here only obliquely connected to Christ. This connection resides in the letter's juxtaposition of (1) the assurance that enduring unjust suffering after the model of Christ will meet with God's approval and (2) the statement that Christ refused to respond in kind when reviled but, instead, entrusted himself to God, who judges righteously. Because the reader already knows that Christ's trust in God was not misplaced—since God did in fact vindicate Christ and give him δόξα after his sufferings—the reader may infer that conformity to Christ's example of patient suffering and trusting God will result in a similarly favorable outcome for Christ's followers.

1 Peter 3:13–4:6

After the lengthy parenetic section that opens chap. 3, Christ is next mentioned in the paragraph beginning at 3:13. Reinforcing the categorical distinction between the people of God and their antagonists that was established in 1 Pet 2:4-10, 1 Pet 3:12-13 states that those who oppose God's people are themselves opposed by God, while God is favorably disposed toward and receptive to those who do good. If, therefore, the addressees should suffer on account of righteousness, they will be blessed (v. 14). When reviled, they should neither fear their antagonists nor be troubled (quoting Isa 8:12); rather, they should reverence Christ as Lord and always be prepared to respond to challenges concerning their hope and to do so with gentleness and fear, thereby maintaining a good conscience (vv. 14-15). Moreover, they are to follow these directives in order that (ἵνα) when they are accused (καταλαλέω) of being wrongdoers, the challenge to their honor will backfire and those who revile (ἐπηρεάζω) their good behavior in Christ will themselves be put to shame (καταισχυνθῆναι) (v. 16).

Whether 1 Peter actually anticipates that a believer's gentle response to a challenge will in fact result in the challenger's being publicly shamed in the present is not clear. Several factors, however, point to another interpretation. The statement in v. 17—that it is better to suffer for doing right, if that is God's will, than for doing wrong—would appear to indicate that ongoing suffering for doing right is to be expected, even when one responds appropriately to slanderous accusations. Furthermore, we have already seen that such unwarranted suffering for doing good is precisely what Christians are called to according to 1 Pet 2:19-23. Moreover, 2:12, as we have seen, appears not to expect the silencing of slander prior to the eschatological "day of visitation." Finally, the phrase ἐν Χριστῷ in 3:16 is instructive: What is being reviled is not "your good behavior" but, literally, "your good in-Christ behavior." That is to say, the behavior in question is deemed good by virtue of its orientation to Christ and is only recognizable as good by those who are themselves in Christ (cf. 5:10, 14). Hence, it appears that 1 Pet 3:16 does not anticipate public humiliation of the calumniators and exoneration of the accused, at least not as a rule (although the occasional exception is certainly not ruled out). What is in view, rather, is the recognition by those who acknowledge the critical principle of doing the good in Christ—that is, those within the liminal communities of Christ's followers—that, societal evaluations notwithstanding, it is the non-Christian accusers who are truly shamed in such encounters.

Having concluded this hortatory section with the statement that it is better to suffer for doing good, should that be God's will, than for doing wrong (v. 17), 1 Peter once again invokes Christ as the warrant for its parenesis (v. 18). Christ's suffering is explicitly mentioned, as was the case in 2:21; but 1 Pet 3:18 differs from 2:21 in that the former does not say that Christ's manner of suffering is to be emulated by his followers. On the contrary, Christ suffered *once* (ἅπαξ) concerning sins. Even more emphatically than in 2:24-25, 1 Pet 3:18 underscores the realization in the lives of the addressees of the redemptive effects of Christ's suffering. Whereas 2:24 states the purpose of Christ's suffering in terms of the person's dying to sins and living to righteousness, and 2:25 affirms that the addressees have themselves returned to God, in 3:18, the purpose of Christ's death is expressed solely in terms of Christ's activity on his followers: Christ is the actor who suffered "in order that he might bring you to God." Where we might have expected, in light of 2:21-23, to find an appeal to Christ's suffering as exemplary for his followers, 3:18 instead cites Christ's suffering as his unrepeatable redemptive act on behalf of his followers. Verses 19-22 continue to explicate the salvation-producing effects of Christ's unique suffering.

Then, in 4:1, the letter shifts yet again from the indicative mood to the imperative, this time citing the christological warrant prior to issuing the exhortation. "Therefore" (οὖν), that is, in light of the preceding recital of Christ's suffering and its effects, "because Christ has suffered in the flesh" (reading the participle παθόντος as causal), "arm yourselves . . ." Until this point, the logic of the argument in 4:1 has been clear; now, however, difficulties arise. The interpretation of the remainder of this notoriously difficult verse turns on several exegetical issues, most notably, the meaning of τὴν αὐτὴν ἔννοιαν, the significance of ὅτι, and the referent of ὁ παθών. Without attempting an exhaustive treatment of all the matters in question, the following reading of 4:1 seems to me to make the most sense in light of both the immediate context and the larger argument of 1 Peter.

In the first place, τὴν αὐτὴν ἔννοιαν should be understood in its most simple, literal sense, as "the same thought" or "the same insight." Since nothing is said of the mental state of Christ in the immediate context, perhaps the reader is to think of the statement in 2:23 that Christ trusted God amid his suffering. What is more likely, however, is that the "thought" is not Christ's at all but an insight to be drawn from the letter's recitation in 3:18-22 of Christ's suffering and its results. Indeed, since the preceding verses present no thought of Christ to which τὴν αὐτὴν ἔννοιαν might refer, it appears that ὅτι should be understood as introducing the content of the ἔννοια, namely, "that the one who has suffered in the flesh has done with sin." This aphorism is general enough to apply both to Christ and to his followers. Indeed, the multivalence of the ὅτι clause should give pause to anyone who attempts to assign one and only one referent to ὁ παθών. With reference back to 3:18, Christ could be said to have "done with sin" in the sense that his once-for-all (ἅπαξ) suffering "concerning sins" (περὶ ἁμαρτιῶν) was the decisive solution to the problem of sin, after which Christ had no need to deal further with sins.[18] With reference forward to 4:2-5, Christ's followers can be said to have "done with sin" both in the sense that they have already ceased participation in "the same flood of dissipation" (ἡ αὐτὴ τῆς ἀσωτίας ἀνάχυσις) that characterizes their antagonists (v. 4) and in the sense that they must have already determined to live no longer by passions but by the will of God (v. 2).[19] One might object that this interpretation threatens to assign a purgative effect to human suffering. To this objection, two responses may be made. (1) We have already seen that 1:6-7 comes very close to assigning to suffering the function of purifying the faith of the sufferer; and we shall shortly see that 4:12 actually does interpret the intended readers' experience as a fiery trial that tests them.[20] It would not, therefore, be uncharacteristic of 1 Peter to assign a purifying effect to human suffering in 4:1. (2) On the other hand, the aphoristic formulation of 4:1b should not be understood as expressing an unambiguous relation between suffering in the flesh and having done with sin, as if the latter were always—as in Christ's case and in the case of purgative suffering—the product of the former. In a sense, the aphorism sets up a correspondence between Christ and his followers in terms of suffering, which both experience(d), and of having done with sin, which both—though in quite different ways—have experienced and/or will experience.

This interpretation has the advantage of making sense of the citation of Christ as warrant in that it understands Christ's suffering as prototypical, if not exemplary. Whereas both 3:17-18 and 4:1a

---

[18] So Michaels, *1 Peter*, 228.

[19] Cf. Goppelt, *I Peter*, 282-83.

[20] Best argues that 4:1b refers to the purifying effects of suffering on the human being (*I Peter*, 151-52).

invoke the christological warrant without holding up Christ's suffering as the example to be followed, my reading of the ὅτι clause in 4:1b construes Christ's suffering not merely as uniquely redemptive (as in 3:18) but also as prototypical, thus making clearer the connection between the warrant and the imperative than is the case in 3:17-18. Christ suffered in the flesh and so finished with sin; believers are to arm themselves with this thought amid their suffering and to continue seeking to be entirely rid of sin. The believer's experience is aligned with Christ in that his prototypical suffering, by which he had done with sin, has opened up the possibility for them to be done with sin. Suffering for taking the first steps in this direction (see 4:4), therefore, must not become the occasion for returning to the behaviors forsaken at conversion; rather, in the midst of such suffering, one must arm oneself with the thought that the one who suffers has done with sin so as to live no longer by passions but by God's will. Verse 5 then reassures the readers that their accusers will themselves be judged by God, that those who have called them to account (3:15) will themselves be called to account by God (4:5).

In this section, 1 Peter continues its sustained elaboration of the implications for its readers of Christ's suffering. Christ's suffering was the unique, unrepeatable act by which redemption was accomplished. At the same time, Christ's suffering is somehow prototypical in that Christ's followers find themselves suffering amid a hostile society that reviles them for forsaking one set of behaviors and adopting another. What society calls "wrongdoing," however, Christ's followers call "doing good in Christ." Christ's suffering has constituted them as liminal communities within a largely hostile society and has empowered them to conduct themselves in the midst of their antagonists in a manner befitting Christ's followers; Christ, therefore, functions as the touchstone for what really is good conduct and what is not, for what really puts one to shame and what brings honor. And 1 Peter once again assures the addressees that their accusers will themselves be judged by the only one whose decision really counts—God. In this way, 1 Peter continues to insists on the legitimacy of the Christian symbolic universe in the face of the suffering that adherence to this universe is bringing the addressees.

And the suffering Christ continues to play the prominent role in 1 Peter's construal of its symbolic universe.

1 Peter 4:12-19

These eight verses present 1 Peter's most sustained and direct treatment of the suffering of its addressees. The reader cannot help but notice the allusions in 4:12 to earlier portions of the letter. Echoing 2:19-21 and 3:13-17, 1 Pet 4:12 insists that suffering is nothing strange for Christians and therefore should not surprise them when it occurs. Furthermore, whereas 1:6-7 associates the addressees' suffering with purifying fire (without going so far as to say that their suffering would perform a purifying function for them), and 4:1b presents a connection between suffering and having done with sin, in 4:12, the letter unambiguously calls the addressees' suffering a "fiery trial" (πύρωσις) whose purpose is to test them (πρὸς πειρασμὸν ὑμῖν). As is the case in 1:6-7 and in 4:1b, however, the letter does not here develop this notion of suffering as trial. Instead, as it does elsewhere, 1 Peter embarks in 4:13 on a christological rationale for suffering.

The readers are instructed in 4:13 to rejoice insofar as they presently share (κοινωνέω) in the sufferings of Christ, in order that they might rejoice at the future revelation of Christ's δόξα.[21] Verses 14 and 16 then specify what kind of suffering is participation in Christ's suffering, namely, being reviled for the name of Christ (v. 14) or suffering simply for being a Christian (v. 16). Whereas 1 Peter has already said that Christians have been called to suffer and that their life of suffering is to be modeled on the example of suffering set by Christ, 4:13 (in connection with vv. 14, 16) goes one step further than previous pronouncements by explaining that, by suffering, the addressees are actually participating in Christ's sufferings. Moreover, although this verse does not explicitly say that those who share in Christ's sufferings now will also share in his glory when it is revealed, it strongly implies as much. We have

---

[21] I read χαίρετε as an imperative that commands how the readers are to respond to suffering in contradistinction (ἀλλά) to the negated imperative of 4:12.

already seen that the pattern suffering-followed-by-glory is characteristic of both Christ's life and that of his followers, and that believers' vindication/commendation/δόξα will occur at the revelation of Jesus Christ. Now, in 4:13, the intended readers are told to rejoice in recognition of the fact that their suffering is a *sharing* in Christ's suffering; it follows, therefore, that their rejoicing at the future revelation of Christ's glory will be a response to their *sharing* in his glory.

Furthermore, 4:14 takes another step beyond what 1 Peter has said earlier. Whereas we have seen that τιμή and χάρις, which are ultimately eschatological realities, are to some extent already the present experience of suffering believers (2:7, 19-20), and that those who suffer on account of righteousness are blessed (3:14), in 4:14, we read that the one who is reproached for the name of Christ is blessed because the spirit of δόξα and of God already rests upon him or her. Since God is both the arbiter of claims to honor and the source of honor for Christ's followers, God's spirit is at the same time the spirit of glory. And it is by the divine spirit of glory that honor is safeguarded within the communities of believers despite the accusations and challenges brought by non-Christians. According to 4:14-16, whatever the larger society thinks, in the eyes of God and God's people, reproach for the name of Christ does not result in loss of honor; the one who suffers for being a Christian, therefore, should not be ashamed (μὴ αἰσχυνέσθω). On the contrary, such a person should glorify God in the face of hostilities.

Finally, 1 Pet 4:17 unexpectedly introduces the notion that unjust suffering—suffering for being a Christian—is to be interpreted as the beginning of God's eschatological judgment.[22] The idea is not, however, developed to any great extent. On the contrary, the letter immediately shifts attention toward the far greater judgment that awaits those who do not obey the gospel, citing Prov 11:31 (vv. 17b-18), and then concludes with the exhortation that those who suffer according to God's will should persist in doing good and entrust themselves to God, their faithful creator. The perceptive reader would certainly recognize in this admonition an echo of the

---

[22] See above, pp. 143-46.

statement in 2:23 that, amid his suffering, Christ entrusted himself to God, who judges righteously.

1 Peter 5:1-14

In 1 Pet 5:1, the letter's implied author is said to be a witness of the sufferings of Christ and "a sharer in the glory that is about to be revealed." In light of the recurrence throughout the letter (whether explicitly or implicitly) of the pattern of suffering followed by glory and of the temporal coincidence of the believer's glorification with the revelation of Christ and his glory, there is no doubt that the implied author is not unique in being a sharer in the δόξα about to be revealed. Indeed, this author's self-designation as "fellow elder" (5:1) indicates that the formulation in 5:1 should be seen as a particular expression of what 5:4 says of all elders, namely, that when Christ the chief shepherd is manifested, they will obtain "the unfading crown of glory" (τὸν ἀμαράντινον τῆς δόξης στέφανον) (cf. 1:4-5, 7). Although the first four verses of chap. 5 are directed specifically to elders, moreover, the fact that what they have to say about the relationships among suffering, honor, and Christ are of a piece with what 1 Peter says elsewhere indicates that these verses are simply the application to elders of the symbolic connection between suffering and honor that governs the entire letter. For 1 Peter, that is, *everyone* who presently shares (κοινωνέω) in Christ's sufferings (4:13) is also a sharer (κοινωνός) in the glory—presumably Christ's—that is about to be revealed (cf. 1:7, 13; 4:13, 14).

That 1 Pet 5:1 and 4 represent specific applications of a universal truth is further evidenced in v. 5b, where all the addressees are instructed to humble themselves toward one another. That is to say, all believers are to emulate the example (τύπος) of the elders, who are told to reject the conventional way of "tending the flock" within a hierarchical society and to leave the bestowal of prestige to God. The reward promised in 5:5 to such behavior is the reception of God's χάρις (cf. 1:13; 2:19-20). Humility with respect to God is also enjoined, in 5:6; and here the result of humbling oneself is that "in due time" (ἐν καιρῷ) God will exalt (ὑψόω) that person. Just as believers are called to endure unjust suffering caused by outsiders to their communities of faith, they are also called to lives of humility and deference toward each other within their communities; and to both the call to suffering and the call to humility 1 Peter explicitly attaches the promise that God will vindicate and honor those who heed the call. As always in this letter, God is the only one who can bestow honor, and God does so against the claims and expectations of Greco-Roman society.

Appropriately, the closing words of the letter body (5:6-10) are about suffering and glory and the roles played in 1 Peter's symbolic universe by God and by Christ. God is the one who will exalt the humble (v. 6). Hence, just as they were earlier instructed to entrust themselves to God (4:19), here the readers are told to cast all their cares on God, because God cares for them (5:7). Whereas suffering has been conceived of as purgative and even as God's judgment earlier in the letter, yet another interpretation of suffering is offered in v. 8. Here suffering is said to be the work of the devil, who, like a lion, seeks prey to devour. The final act, however, will be God's. The same God, v. 10 says, who originally called the addressees into the eternal δόξα in Christ Jesus (cf. 3:16)—the God of all χάρις—will, after they have suffered a little while (cf. 1:6), personally (αὐτός) restore, establish, and strengthen them.

Conclusions

Having explicated in chapter 4 the liminal communal identity that 1 Peter constructs for it addressees, I assayed in this section to examine how 1 Peter's legitimation of the Christian symbolic universe employs the figure of Christ to deal with the threats to the addressees' honor emanating from outside their communities. Christ is invoked both as the prototype or template for Christian life and as the example for his followers. His suffering was uniquely redemptive, to be sure, but it also set the pattern that Christian life must follow, and Christ's disposition during suffering sets the example for the faithful, who are to follow in his steps.

Christ is the means by which God has saved the addressees, and Christ continues to function as their example and as the touchstone for how they should conduct themselves in society.

Those who are "in Christ" should continue to exhibit "good behavior in Christ"—that is, behavior that God deems good, regardless of the evaluation of the larger society—despite the reproach such behavior will inevitably bring from non-Christians. Just as Christ endured unjust suffering without reviling in return, without speaking guile, without threatening his antagonists, so should his followers. And just as Christ entrusted himself to God, the righteous judge, so should his followers.

Indeed, it is God who is the primary actor throughout 1 Peter. God is the one who raised and glorified Christ; and God is the one who caused the addressees to be reborn and who will save them and give them glory, praise, honor, and grace. God is the creator and the eschatological judge. In the face of the hostile attacks from their opponents, the addressees are instructed to continue to do good, knowing full well that what God considers good is at odds with what the society at large considers good, which means that the addressees can hold out little hope that the slander will subside any time prior to the eschaton. Despite the ongoing reproach, however, the Petrine addressees are assured that such attacks on their honor cannot succeed, because God is the true source of honor and the only arbiter of claims to honor. God will, in the eschatological judgment, put their calumniators to shame and will exonerate, commend, vindicate, and honor them.

That is to say, the replication in their experience of Christ's endurance of unjust suffering will be followed by the replication in their lives of Christ's experience of being glorified by God. Indeed, their present suffering is nothing less than their participation in Christ's sufferings, and just as Christ's glorification followed upon his sufferings, so will their sharing in his glory follow upon their sharing in his sufferings. Moreover, although this eschatological vindication, like the final judgment and shaming of the accusers, lies in the future, already in the present God's vindication and commendation is experienced, at least to some extent. Indeed, God's spirit of glory already rests on those who are reproached for bearing the name of Christ.

First Peter thus legitimates the addressees' symbolic universe by providing an alternative way of calculating honor within their alternative, liminal communities of faith. In the face of slanderous attacks by outsiders, the addressees know that only God determines what behavior is praiseworthy, that only God can evaluate such challenges to honor, and that only God can truly bestow honor. Despite—even, because of—the withholding of recognition of their honor by the society at large, therefore, the addressees are assured that God's honor is, and will be, granted to those who conduct themselves as Christians and, consequently, suffer the attacks that such a lifestyle will inevitably bring. The honor denied by the larger society is granted by God and recognized as such within the liminal communities of faith whose members accept 1 Peter's understanding of reality.

CHAPTER 6

CONCLUSION

The objective of this study, as stated at the beginning, has been to ascertain how 1 Peter's references to the suffering and glorification of Christ were intended to function as constitutive parts of the letter's response to the suffering of its addressees. In light of the letter's concern for the social situation of its addressees—reflected both in the rhetorical situation of social hostility that occasioned the letter and in 1 Peter's prescriptions for behavior within the larger society and within the addressees' communities—it seemed appropriate to look to the social sciences for assistance in pursuing this objective. In particular, I adopted Berger and Luckmann's construal of the sociology of knowledge as the interpretive framework for this study. In terms of the sociology of knowledge, the task of this investigation was restated as follows: to uncover the function of the Christ symbolism within 1 Peter's legitimation of the symbolic universe of its addressees.

Before explicating 1 Peter's answer to the problem facing its addressees, however, the problem itself had to be addressed. In chapter 3, I undertook this task in three stages.

(1) I argued that although the authorship, date, and provenance of 1 Peter are impossible to determine precisely, the evidence favors what appears to be the majority position among scholars, namely, that 1 Peter is a pseudonymous letter that originated in Rome sometime during the period 75-105 CE.

(2) I then embarked on a two-part examination of 1 Peter's rhetorical situation, that is, the situation the letter rhetorically constructs as the occasion for its composition. I first sought to

identify the geographical location, ethnic composition, and social stratum of 1 Peter's addressees, understanding "addressees" not as any actual, historical persons who might have received and read the letter but as 1 Peter's rhetorically constructed intended readers. The letter, I argued, was directed to Christian communities in the four provinces of northwestern Asia Minor named in the adscript. Moreover, these Christian communities were composed not of Jews or even of non-Jewish adherents to synagogues but of gentiles who had converted to Christianity. There may well have been numerous Jews and God-fearers in the *actual* Christian communities of northwestern Asia Minor, but 1 Peter does not address itself to them.

In my examination of the social status of the addressees, I could find no evidence in support of John Elliott's thesis that the addressees were παρεπίδημοι and πάροικοι in the legal, technical sense of those words, that is, that they were literally displaced foreigners now temporarily (παρεπίδημοι) or permanently (πάροικοι) residing in northwestern Asia Minor. Elliott's thesis fails at two points. In the first place, the meaning of the word πάροικος as a first-century technical term was not "resident alien," as Elliott insists, but "noncitizen." Second, and more important, πάροικοι is not, in any case, used by 1 Peter in its legal, technical sense. On the contrary, πάροικοι—like παρεπίδημοι, διασπορά, and ἐκλεκτοί—is drawn from the LXX and metaphorically applied to 1 Peter's addressees. Hence, 1 Peter's designation of its addressees as πάροικοι and παρεπίδημοι does not identify their legal status as displaced aliens (or as noncitizens of the Empire), although it certainly does reflect something of the letter's view of their precarious position in society (on which more was said in chapter 4). Very little indeed can be discovered from the letter about the socioeconomic condition of the addressees, other than that they were suffering at the hands of their non-Christian neighbors.

(3) I then undertook to identify the origin and nature of the suffering the addressees were experiencing. Although the details are difficult to come by, the addressees' suffering appears to have been the result of their withdrawal from certain aspects of public life that they considered to be incommensurate with their new faith. Given the interweaving of Roman civic and religious life on the one hand

and the monotheistic, exclusivist, and conversionist nature of Christianity on the other, it is understandable that converts to Christianity would have withdrawn from some aspects of Greco-Roman social life and that such withdrawal would have provoked the ire of their non-Christian neighbors. Indeed, the few references to Christianity to be found in the extant Roman literature of the time are entirely hostile toward the new religion.

More specifically, 1 Peter assumes that its readers were being verbally abused by their antagonists. They were being called to account for their changed behavior in the wake of their conversion to Christianity and were being accused of wrongdoing. The letter may even reckon with the likelihood of judicial proceedings being brought against them. Moreover, the essence of the problem was that such verbal attacks against the addressees constituted a threat to their honor. In Greco-Roman society, accumulation of honor and avoidance of disgrace were of paramount concern, and social transactions between individuals were governed by elaborate codes of honor and shame. The pervasive challenge to honor emanating from outsiders to their communities, therefore, posed a profound problem for 1 Peter's addressees. In a society in which one's place was determined by one's socially conferred honor, these Christians were being denied honor by the society at large. Nothing less than their place within that society was under attack. First Peter, therefore, must provide its readers with a legitimation of their symbolic universe that will deal with this problem of suffering. If they are to remain Christians without sacrificing the honor on which social life depends, they must be supplied with a means to respond to the challenges to their honor that they are routinely facing in their interactions with outsiders to their communities.

In the next two chapters, I turned attention to 1 Peter's answer to this problem of the threat to the addressees' honor. In chapter 4, I argued that 1 Peter rhetorically constitutes the Christian communities as alternative social entities that can mediate to their individuals the plausibility structures for the Christian symbolic universe (especially 1 Peter's legitimation of that symbolic universe) and within which honor can be recognized despite the challenges brought from outsiders. Victor Turner's theory of liminality provided the interpretive lens through which the ambiguous elements in this symbolic construction appeared to gain coherence. Temporally, the addressees live in a literally liminal time between the eschatological events of Christ's death and resurrection and the eschatological consummation that will be signaled by the final revelation of Christ's glory. Through a variety of metaphors, drawn mostly from the LXX but also from the everyday world of Hellenistic society, 1 Peter constructs for its addressees a liminal identity that is appropriate to their temporal liminality. Social-structurally, they live in a metaphorically liminal place that is neither fully integrated into society nor fully abstracted from it. Within their communities, they live in a kind of institutionalized liminality amid the larger, hostile society. They are elect sojourners of the diaspora, resident aliens, living stones being built into a spiritual house, obedient children, newborn babies, free persons who are slaves to God.

As members of liminal communities, moreover, they are called to an intracommunity ethic that corresponds to Turner's notion of normative communitas. First Peter presupposes that the relationships within the addressees' communities will to some extent exhibit the hierarchical social structure of the larger society, and yet the letter severely attenuates this structure by means of its intracommunity ethic of sibling love, compassion, and humility. Relationships with outsiders to the community, on the other hand, are to be characterized by the submission to the Emperor and his governors and the respect for all people that Greco-Roman society expected of its members.

First Peter's construction of a liminal identity for its addressees, however, is but one aspect of the letter's response to the problem of their suffering. If they accept 1 Peter's construction as their own self-identity, then their suffering can be seen as a function of their ambiguous relationship to the society at large. The problem of suffering, however, remains. The construction of a liminal self-identity does not so much answer the problem of suffering as it provides the context within which 1 Peter's answer can work. If the problem of suffering is the threat to honor, the liminal Christian communities provide the addressees with the social collectives within which their honor can be recognized despite the larger society's contrary evaluation.

In chapter 5, I turned attention to the alternative means by which 1 Peter proposes that honor be calculated within these alternative communities. Although the letter says in 4:17 that the addressees' suffering is the beginning of God's judgment, and implies in 4:1-2 (in conjunction with 1:6-7 and 4:12) that suffering has a purifying function, neither of these ideas is well integrated into the rest of the letter because neither flows from the christological answer to the problem of suffering that pervades 1 Peter. It is the symbol of the Christ who suffered and was consequently glorified that provides the pivot around which 1 Peter's response turns.

Christ functions as both the paradigm for the sufferer who will be honored/ glorified by God and as the model for faithful endurance of unjust suffering. Throughout 1 Peter, God is depicted as the sole source of honor and the only one who can accurately evaluate claims to honor, and Christ is presented as the embodiment of the relation between suffering and honor. Just as Christ was honored by God in consequence of his suffering, so God will bestow honor on Christ's followers as a result of their suffering. Just as Christ trusted God to dispense honor against the claims of his opponents, so must Christ's followers. Christian suffering, in fact, is a participation in Christ's suffering and, as such, bears within it the promise of participation in Christ's glory. Moreover, although imminent future glory/honor/ praise is assured the addressees in consequence of their suffering, already God's approval is said to be theirs and already the spirit of God and of glory is said to rest upon them. Hence, the letter says, the slanderous accusations of outsiders will result in loss of honor not for the addressees but for their accusers. Such evaluations, of course, can only be made within the Christian communities, for which Christ is the touchstone for what is honorable behavior and what is shameful. First Peter assures its addressees that eschatological glory/honor/praise as the direct action of God awaits them in the very near future and that this eschatological honor is already to some extent a present reality.

BIBLIOGRAPHY

TEXTS AND TRANSLATIONS

Apocalypsis Henochi Graece. Ed. Matthew Black. PVTG 3. Leiden: Brill, 1970.

The Apostolic Fathers. Trans. Kirsopp Lake. 2 vols. LCL. Cambridge: Harvard University Press; London: William Heinemann, 1912-13.

Aristotle: Politics. Trans. Harris Rackham. LCL. Cambridge: Harvard University Press; London: William Heinemann, 1932.

Biblia Hebraica Stuttgartensia. Ed. K. Elliger and W. Rudolph. Stuttgart: Deutsche Bibelgesellschaft, 1977.

Cicero, vol. 9. Trans. H. Grose Hodge. LCL. Cambridge: Harvard University Press; London: William Heinemann, 1927.

Cicero: De Officiis. Trans. Walter Miller. LCL. Cambridge: Harvard University Press; London: William Heinemann, 1913.

Cicero: In Catilinam; Pro Murena; Pro Sulla; Pro Flacco. Trans. Louis E. Lord. LCL. Cambridge: Harvard University Press; London: William Heinemann, 1937.

Clément d'Alexandrie: Le Protreptique. 3d ed. Trans. and ed. Claude Mondésert with André Plassart. SC 2. Paris: Cerf, 1976.

Dio Chrysostom. Trans. J. W. Cohoon and H. Lamar Crosby. 5 vols. LCL. Cambridge: Harvard University Press; London: William Heinemann, 1932-51.

Diodorus of Sicily. Trans. C. H. Oldfather et al. 12 vols. LCL. Cambridge: Harvard University Press; London: William Heinemann, 1933-67.

Epictetus. Trans. W. A. Oldfather. 2 vols. LCL. Cambridge: Harvard University Press; London: William Heinemann, 1925-28.

Eusebius: The Ecclesiastical History. Trans. Kirsopp Lake, J. E. L. Oulton, and H. J. Lawlor. 2 vols. LCL. Cambridge: Harvard University Press; London: William Heinemann, 1926-32.

Ioannis Stobaei: Anthologii. Ed. Curtius Wachsmuth and Otto Hense. 5 vols. Berlin: Apud Weidmannos, 1884-1912.

Josephus. Trans. H. St. J. Thackeray, Ralph Marcus, and Louis H. Feldman. 9 vols. LCL. Cambridge: Harvard University Press; London: William Heinemann, 1926-65.

Juvenal and Persius. Rev. ed. Trans. G. G. Ramsay. LCL. Cambridge: Harvard University Press; London: William Heinemann, 1940.

Novum Testamentum Graece. 26th ed. Ed. Kurt Aland et al. Stuttgart: Deutsche Bibelgesellschaft, 1979.

The Old Testament Pseudepigrapha. Ed. James H. Charlesworth. 2 vols. Garden City: Doubleday, 1983-85.

Orientis Graeci Inscriptiones Selectae. Ed. Wilhelm Dittenberger. 2 vols. Hildesheim: Goerg Olms, 1903-5. Reprint, 1960.

Philo. Trans. F. H. Colson and G. H. Whitaker. 10 vols. LCL. Cambridge: Harvard University Press; London: William Heinemann, 1929-62.

Plato. Trans. Harold North Fowler, W. R. Lamb, and R. G. Bury. 9 vols. LCL. Cambridge: Harvard University Press; London: William Heinemann, 1914-55.

Plato: The Republic. Trans. Paul Shorey. 2 vols. LCL. Cambridge: Harvard University Press; London: William Heinemann, 1935-37.

Pliny. Trans. Betty Radice. 2 vols. LCL. Cambridge: Harvard University Press; London: William Heinemann, 1969.

Plutarch's Moralia. Trans. Frank Cole Babbitt et al. 15 vols. LCL. Cambridge: Harvard University Press; London: William Heinemann, 1927-76.

S. Dionysius Areopagita. Ed. J.-P. Migne. *Patrologiae Cursus Completus*, Series Graeca, vol. 3. Paris: Migne, 1857.

The Sentences of Pseudo-Phocylides with Introduction and Commentary. By P. W. van der Horst. SVTP 4. Leiden: Brill, 1978.

Septuaginta. Ed. Alfred Rahlfs. 2 vols. in 1. Stuttgart: Deutsche Bibelgesellschaft, 1979.

S. Thasci Caecili Cypriani Opera Omnia. Ed. G. Wilhelm Hartel. CSEL 3. Vindobonae: Apud C. Geroldi Filium, 1868-71.

Suetonius. Trans. J. C. Rolfe. 2 vols. LCL. Cambridge: Harvard University Press; London: William Heinemann, 1914-1951.

Tacitus. Trans. Clifford H. Moore and John Jackson. 4 vols. LCL. Cambridge: Harvard University Press; London: William Heinemann, 1925-37.

The Testaments of the Twelve Patriarchs: A Critical Edition of the Greek Text. By Marinus de Jonge, in cooperation with H. W. Hollander et al. PVTG 1/2. Leiden: Brill, 1978.

Thucydides. Trans. Charles Forster Smith. 4 vols. LCL. Cambridge: Harvard University Press; London: William Heinemann, 1921-30.

SECONDARY LITERATURE

Achtemeier, Paul J. *1 Peter: A Commentary on 1 Peter*. Hermeneia. Minneapolis: Fortress, 1996.

———. "Newborn Babes and Living Stones: Literal and Figurative in 1 Peter." *To Touch the Text: Biblical and Related Studies in Honor of Joseph A. Fitzmyer, S.J.*, ed. Maurya P. Horgan and Paul J. Kobelski, 207-36. New York: Crossroad, 1989.

———. Review of *A Home for the Homeless: A Sociological Exegesis of 1 Peter, Its Situation and Strategy*, by John H. Elliott. *JBL* 103 (1984) 130-33.

Adam, Alfred. "Das Sintflutgebet in der Taufliturgie." *WD* n.s. 3 (1952) 20-21.

Attridge, Harold W. *The Epistle to the Hebrews: A Commentary on the Epistle to the Hebrews*. Hermeneia. Philadelphia: Fortress, 1989.

Aune, David E. *The New Testament in Its Literary Environment*. LEC 6. Philadelphia: Westminster, 1987.

Balch, David L. "Early Christian Criticism of Patriarchal Authority: I Peter 2:11-3:12." *USQR* 39 (1984) 161-73.

———. "Hellenization/Acculturation in 1 Peter." *Perspectives on First Peter*, ed. Charles H. Talbert, 79-101. NABPRSSS 9. Macon: Mercer University Press, 1986.

———. *Let Wives Be Submissive: The Domestic Code in I Peter*. SBLMS 26. Atlanta: Scholars Press, 1981.

Balz, Horst. "μάταιος." *Exegetical Dictionary of the New Testament*, ed. Horst Balz and Gerhard Schneider, 2. 396. Grand Rapids: Eerdmans, 1991.

Barraclough, Geoffrey. *Main Trends in History*. Main Trends in the Social and Human Sciences. New York/London: Holmes & Meier, 1979.

Bauckham, Richard J. "The Martyrdom of Peter in Early Christian Literature." *Aufstieg und Niedergang der römischen Welt*, pt. 2, vol. 26/1, ed. Wolfgang Haase, 539-95. Berlin/New York: de Gruyter, 1992.

Bauer, Walter, William F. Arndt, F. Wilbur Gingrich, and Frederick W. Danker. *A Greek-English Lexicon of the New Testament and Other Early Christian Literature*. 2d ed. Chicago/London: University of Chicago Press, 1979.

Beare, Francis Wright. *The First Epistle of Peter: The Greek Text with Introduction and Notes*. 3d ed. Oxford: Blackwell, 1970.

Beasley-Murray, G. W. *Baptism in the New Testament*. London: Macmillan, 1962.

Beker, J. Christiaan. *Suffering and Hope: The Biblical Vision and the Human Predicament*. Philadelphia: Fortress, 1987; 2d ed., Grand Rapids: Eerdmans, 1994.

Benko, Stephen. *Pagan Rome and the Early Christians*. Bloomington: Indiana University Press, 1984.

Berger, Adolf, and Barry Nicholas. "Law and Procedure, Roman." *The Oxford Classical Dictionary*, 2d ed., ed. N. G. L. Hammond and H. H. Scullard, 583-90. Oxford: Clarendon, 1970.

Berger, Peter L. *A Rumor of Angels: Modern Society and the Rediscovery of the Supernatural*. Expanded ed. New York: Doubleday, Anchor, 1990.

———. *The Sacred Canopy: Elements of a Sociological Theory of Religion*. New York: Doubleday, 1967; Anchor, 1969.

Berger, Peter L., and Thomas Luckmann. *The Social Construction of Reality: A Treatise in the Sociology of Knowledge*. New York: Doubleday, 1966; Anchor, 1967.

Best, Ernest. *I Peter.* NCB. London: Oliphants, 1971.

Beyer, Hermann Wolfgang. "βλασφημέω, βλασφημία, βλάσφημος." *Theological Dictionary of the New Testament*, vol. 1, ed. Gerhard Kittel, 621-25. Grand Rapids: Eerdmans, 1964.

———. "ἐπισκέπτομαι, ἐπισκοπέω, ἐπισκοπή." *Theological Dictionary of the New Testament*, vol. 2, ed. Gerhard Kittel, 599-622. Grand Rapids: Eerdmans, 1964.

Bigg, Charles. *A Critical and Exegetical Commentary on the Epistles of St. Peter and St. Jude.* ICC. New York: Scribner's, 1901.

Bitzer, Lloyd F. "The Rhetorical Situation." *Philosophy and Rhetoric* 1 (1968) 1-14.

Blass, Friedrich, Albert Debrunner, and Robert W. Funk. *A Greek Grammar of the New Testament and Other Early Christian Literature.* Chicago/London: University of Chicago Press, 1961.

Boismard, M.-É. "Pierre (Première épître de)." *Dictionnaire de la Bible, Supplément*, vol. 7, ed. Henri Cazelles and André Feuillet, 1415-55. Paris: Letouzey & Ané, 1966.

———. *Quatre hymnes baptismales dans la première épître de Pierre.* Paris: Cerf, 1961.

———. "Une liturgie baptismale dans la Prima Petri." Pts. 1, 2. *RB* 63 (1956) 182-208; 64 (1957) 161-83.

Boissevain, Jeremy. "Towards a Social Anthropology of the Mediterranean." *Current Anthropology* 20 (1979) 81-93.

Bornemann, Wilhelm. "Der erste Petrusbrief--eine Taufrede des Silvanus?" *ZNW* 19 (1919-20) 143-65.

Bradley, Keith R. *Discovering the Roman Family.* New York/Oxford: Oxford University Press, 1991.

———. *Slaves and Masters in the Roman Empire: A Study in Social Control.* New York/Oxford: Oxford University Press, 1987.

Broughton, T. R. S. "Roman Asia Minor." *An Economic Survey of Ancient Rome*, ed. Tenney Frank, 4. 499-916. Baltimore: Johns Hopkins Press, 1938.

Brox, Norbert. *Der erste Petrusbrief.* EKKNT 21. Zurich: Benziger Verlag; Neukirchen-Vluyn: Neukirchener Verlag, 1979; 3d ed., 1989.

———. "Zur pseudepigraphischen Rahmung des ersten Petrusbriefes." *BZ* n.s. 19 (1976) 76-96.

Bultmann, Rudolf. "Bekenntnis- und Liedfragmente im ersten Petrusbrief." *ConNT* 11 (1947) 1-14. Reprint, *Exegetica: Aufsätze zur Erforschung des Neuen Testaments*, by Rudolf Bultmann, ed. Erich Dinkler, 285-97. Tübingen: Mohr-Siebeck, 1967.

Burton, Ernest De Witt. *Syntax of the Moods and Tenses in New Testament Greek.* 3d ed. Chicago: University of Chicago Press, 1900. Reprint, Grand Rapids: Kregel, 1976.

Carney, T. F. *The Shape of the Past: Models and Antiquity.* Lawrence, KS: Coronado, 1975.

Carter, Warren. *Households and Discipleship: A Study of Matthew 19-20.* JSNTSup 103. Sheffield: JSOT Press, 1994.

Chase, F. H. "Peter, First Epistle of." *A Dictionary of the Bible, Dealing with Its Language, Literature, and Contents Including the Biblical Theology,* ed. James Hastings, 3. 779-96. Edinburgh: Clark, 1898. Reprint, Peabody: Hendrickson, 1988.

Clements, R. E. *The World of Ancient Israel: Sociological, Anthropological and Political Perspectives.* New York: Cambridge University Press, 1989.

Cohen, Shaye J. D. "Crossing the Boundary and Becoming a Jew." *HTR* 82 (1989) 13-33.

———. "Was Judaism in Antiquity a Missionary Religion?" *Jewish Assimilation, Acculturation and Accommodation: Past Traditions, Current Issues and Future Prospects,* ed. Menachem Mor, 14-23. Lanham/New York/London: University Press of America, 1992.

Conzelmann, Hans, and Andreas Lindemann. *Arbeitsbuch zum Neuen Testament.* 10th ed. Tübingen: Mohr-Siebeck, 1991.

Corley, Kathleen E. "1 Peter." *Searching the Scriptures,* vol. 2, *A Feminist Commentary,* ed. Elisabeth Schüssler Fiorenza, 349-60. New York: Crossroad, 1994.

Coser, Lewis. *The Functions of Social Conflict.* New York: Free Press, 1956.

Cranfield, C. E. B. *I & II Peter and Jude: Introduction and Commentary.* Torch Bible Commentaries. London: SCM, 1960.

Cross, F. L. *I. Peter: A Paschal Liturgy.* London: Mowbray, 1954.

Cullmann, Oscar. *Peter--Disciple, Apostle, Martyr: A Historical and Theological Study.* Trans. Floyd V. Filson. Library of History and Doctrine. 2d ed. Philadelphia: Westminster, 1962.

Dalton, William Joseph. *Christ's Proclamation to the Spirits: A Study of 1 Peter 3:18-4:6.* AnBib 23. Rome: Pontifical Biblical Institute, 1965; 2d ed. 1989.

Danker, Frederick W. Review of *A Home for the Homeless: A Sociological Exegesis of 1 Peter, Its Situation and Strategy,* by John H. Elliott. *Int* 37 (1983) 84-88.

Daube, David. "Participle and Imperative in 1 Peter." *The First Epistle of St. Peter: The Greek Text with Introduction, Notes and Essays,* by Edward Gordon Selwyn, 467-88. London: Macmillan, 1946; 2d ed., 1947.

Davids, Peter H. *The First Epistle of Peter.* NICNT. Grand Rapids: Eerdmans, 1990.

Davis, John. *People of the Mediterranean: An Essay in Comparative Social Anthropology.* Library of Man. London: Routledge & Kegan Paul, 1977.

Delaney, Carol. "Seeds of Honor, Fields of Shame." *Honor and Shame and the Unity of the Mediterranean,* ed. David D. Gilmore, 35-48. Washington: American Anthropological Association, 1987.

Delling, Gerhard. "χρόνος." *Theological Dictionary of the New Testament,* vol. 9, ed. Gerhard Friedrich, 581-93. Grand Rapids: Eerdmans, 1974.

de Ste Croix, G. E. M. "Why Were the Early Christians Persecuted?" *Past and Present* 26 (November 1963) 6-38.

———. "Why Were the Early Christians Persecuted?--A Rejoinder." *Past and Present* 27 (April 1964) 28-33.

Edelman, Murray. *Politics as Symbolic Action: Mass Arousal and Quiescence.* Institute for Research on Poverty Monograph Series. Chicago: Markham, 1971.

Edmundson, George. *The Church in Rome in the First Century: An Examination of Various Controverted Questions Relating to Its History, Chronology, Literature and Traditions.* London/New York: Longmans Green, 1913.

Elliott, John H. "Disgraced Yet Graced: The Gospel according to 1 Peter in the Key of Honor and Shame." *BTB* 25 (1995) 166-78.

———. *The Elect and the Holy: An Exegetical Examination of I Peter 2:4-10 and the Phrase βασίλειον ἱεράτευμα.* NovTSup 12. Leiden: Brill, 1966.

———. "1 Peter, Its Situation and Strategy: A Discussion with David Balch." *Perspectives on First Peter*, ed. Charles H. Talbert, 61-78. NABPRSSS 9. Macon: Mercer University Press, 1986.

———. *A Home for the Homeless: A Social-Scientific Criticism of 1 Peter, Its Situation and Strategy*, with a new introduction. Minneapolis: Fortress, 1990.

———. *A Home for the Homeless: A Sociological Exegesis of 1 Peter, Its Situation and Strategy.* Philadelphia: Fortress, 1981.

———. "Peter, First Epistle of." *The Anchor Bible Dictionary*, ed. David Noel Freedman, 5. 269-78. New York/London/Toronto/Sydney/Aukland: Doubleday, 1992.

———. Review of *Gemeinde im 1. Petrusbrief: Untersuchungen zum Selbstverständnis einer christlichen Gemeinde an der Wende vom 1. zum 2. Jahrhundert*, by Friedrich Schröger. *CBQ* 45 (1983) 705-6.

———. *What Is Social-Scientific Criticism?* GBS. Minneapolis: Fortress, 1993.

Eyben, Emiel. "Fathers and Sons." *Marriage, Divorce, and Children in Ancient Rome*, ed. Beryl Rawson, 114-43. Oxford: Clarendon, 1991.

Feldman, Louis H. "Was Judaism a Missionary Religion in Ancient Times?" *Jewish Assimilation, Acculturation and Accommodation: Past Traditions, Current Issues and Future Prospects*, ed. Menachem Mor, 24-37. Lanham/New York/London: University Press of America, 1992.

Feldmeier, Reinhard. *Die Christen als Fremde: Die Metapher der Fremde in der antiken Welt, im Urchristentum und im 1. Petrusbrief.* WUNT 64. Tübingen: Mohr-Siebeck, 1992.

Fenn, Richard K. *The Death of Herod: An Essay in the Sociology of Religion.* Cambridge: Cambridge University Press, 1992.

———. "Sociology and Social History: A Preface to a Sociology of the New Testament." *JSP* 1 (1987) 95-114.

Ferguson, Everett. "Canon Muratori: Date and Provenance," *Studia Patristica* 18 (1982) 677-83.

Finley, M. I. *Ancient Slavery and Modern Ideology*. New York: Penguin, 1980.

Fredriksen, Paula. "Judaism, the Circumcision of Gentiles, and Apocalyptic Hope: Another Look at Galatians 1 and 2." *JTS* n.s. 42 (1991) 532-64.

Frend, W. H. C. *Martyrdom and Persecution in the Early Church: A Study of a Conflict from the Maccabees to Donatus*. New York: New York University Press, 1967.

Frier, B. "Roman Life Expectancy: Ulpian's Evidence." *Harvard Studies in Classical Philology* 86 (1982) 213-51.

Furnish, Victor Paul. "Elect Sojourners in Christ: An Approach to the Theology of I Peter." *PSTJ* 28/3 (Spring 1975) 1-11.

Gadamer, Hans Georg. *Truth and Method*. Trans. and rev. Joel Weinsheimer and Donald G. Marshall. 2d ed. New York: Crossroad, 1989.

Gager, John G. *The Origins of Anti-Semitism: Attitudes toward Judaism in Pagan and Christian Antiquity*. New York/Oxford: Oxford University Press, 1985.

Garnsey, Peter. "Legal Privilege in the Roman Empire." *Studies in Ancient Society*, ed. M. I. Finley, 141-65. Past and Present Series. London/Boston: Routledge & Kegan Paul, 1974.

Garnsey, Peter, and Richard Saller. *The Roman Empire: Economy, Society and Culture*. Berkeley/Los Angeles: University of California Press, 1987.

Garrett, Susan R. "Sociology of Early Christianity." *The Anchor Bible Dictionary*, ed. David Noel Freedman, 6. 89-99. New York/London/Toronto/Sydney/ Aukland: Doubleday, 1992.

Gaudemet, J. "Familie I (Familienrecht)." *Reallexikon für Antike und Christentum*, vol. 7, ed. Theodor Klauser, 286-358. Stuttgart: Hiersemann, 1969.

Gauthier, Philippe. "Métèques, périèques et *paroikoi*: Bilan et points d'interrogation." *l'Etranger dans le monde grec*, ed. Raoul Lonis, 23-46. Nancy: Presses Universitaries de Nancy, 1988.

Geertz, Clifford. *The Interpretation of Cultures: Selected Essays*. New York: Basic, 1973.

Gilmore, David D. "Anthropology of the Mediterranean Area." *Annual Review of Anthropology* 11 (1982) 175-205.

———. "Introduction: The Shame of Dishonor." *Honor and Shame and the Unity of the Mediterranean*, ed. David D. Gilmore, 2-21. Washington: American Anthropological Association, 1987.

———, ed. *Honor and Shame and the Unity of the Mediterranean*. Washington: American Anthropological Association, 1987.

Goodman, Martin. *Mission and Conversion: Proselytizing in the Religious History of the Roman Empire*. Oxford: Clarendon, 1994.

Goppelt, Leonhard. *A Commentary on I Peter*. Ed. Ferdinand Hahn. Trans. and aug. John E. Alsup. Grand Rapids: Eerdmans, 1993. German original, *Der erste Petrusbrief*. MeyerK 12/1. Göttingen: Vandenhoeck & Ruprecht, 1978.

———. *Theology of the New Testament*. Vol. 2, *The Variety and Unity of the Apostolic Witness to Christ*. Ed. Jürgen Roloff. Trans. John E. Alsup. Grand Rapids: Eerdmans, 1982. German original, Göttingen: Vandenhoeck & Ruprecht, 1976.

Greenlee, J. Harold. *A Concise Exegetical Grammar of New Testament Greek*. 4th ed. Grand Rapids: Eerdmans, 1979.

Grudem, Wayne A. *The First Epistle of Peter: An Introduction and Commentary*. TNTC. Leicester, England: InterVarsity; Grand Rapids: Eerdmans, 1988.

Grundmann, Walter. "δῆμος, ἐκδημέω, ἐνδημέω." *Theological Dictionary of the New Testament*, vol. 2, ed. Gerhard Kittel, 63-65. Grand Rapids: Eerdmans, 1964.

Guthrie, Donald. *New Testament Introduction*. 3d ed. Downers Grove: InterVarsity, 1970.

Hagner, Donald Alfred. *The Use of the Old and New Testaments in Clement of Rome*. NovTSup 34. Leiden: Brill, 1973.

Hahneman, Geoffrey Mark. *The Muratorian Fragment and the Development of the Canon*. Oxford Theological Monographs. Oxford: Clarendon, 1992.

Harnack, Adolf von. "Bishop Lightfoot on the Genuineness and Date of the Ignatian Epistles." *The Expositor* 3d ser., no. 15 (March 1886) 175-92.

———. *Geschichte der altchristlichen Litteratur bis Eusebius*. Pt. 2, vol. 1, *Die Chronologie der altchristlichen Litteratur bis Eusebius*. Leipzig: Hinrichs'sche Buchhandlung, 1897.

Harrison, P. N. *Polycarp's Two Epistles to the Philippians*. Cambridge: Cambridge University Press, 1936.

Hauck, Friedrich. *Die Briefe des Jakobus, Petrus, Judas und Johannes*. NTD 10. 5th ed. Göttingen: Vandenhoeck & Ruprecht, 1949.

Heussi, Karl. *Die römische Petrustradition in kritischer Sicht*. Tübingen: Mohr, 1955.

Hiers, Richard H. "Day of Christ." *The Anchor Bible Dictionary*, ed. David Noel Freedman, 2. 76-79. New York/London/Toronto/Sydney/Aukland: Doubleday, 1992.

———. "Day of Judgment." *The Anchor Bible Dictionary*, ed. David Noel Freedman, 2. 79-82. New York/London/Toronto/Sydney/Aukland: Doubleday, 1992.

Hill, David. "On Suffering and Baptism in I Peter." *NovT* 18 (1976) 181-89.

Holmberg, Bengt. *Sociology and the New Testament: An Appraisal*. Minneapolis: Fortress, 1990.

Bibliography

Hommel, H. "Metoikoi." *Paulys Real-Encyclopädie der classischen Altertumswissenschaft*, rev. and ed. Georg Wissowa et al., 15/2. 1413-58. Stuttgart: J. B. Metzlersche Verlagsbuchhandlung, 1932.

Hopkins, Keith. "Élite Mobility in the Roman Empire." *Studies in Ancient Society*, ed. M. I. Finley, 103-20. Past and Present Series. London/Boston: Routledge & Kegan Paul, 1974.

Humbert, G. "Peregrinus." *Dictionnaire des antiquités grecques et romaines*, ed. Ch. Daremberg and Edmond Saglio, 14/1. 389-92. Paris: Librairie Hachette, n.d.

Hunzinger, Claus-Hunno. "Babylon als Deckname für Rom und die Datierung des 1. Petrusbriefes." *Gottes Wort und Gottes Land: Hans-Wilhelm Hertzberg zum 70. Geburtstag am 16. Januar 1965 dargebracht von Kollegen, Freunden und Schülern*, ed. Henning Graf Reventlow, 67-77. Göttingen: Vandenhoeck & Ruprecht, 1965.

Jones, A. H. M. *The Criminal Courts of the Roman Republic and Principate*. Oxford: Blackwell, 1972.

―――. *Studies in Roman Government and Law*. Oxford: Blackwell, 1960.

Kelly, J. N. D. *The Epistles of Peter and of Jude*. BNTC. London: Black, 1969. Reprint, Peabody: Hendrickson, n.d.

Kennedy, George A. *New Testament Interpretation through Rhetorical Criticism*. Studies in Religion. Chapel Hill/London: University of North Carolina Press, 1984.

Kilpatrick, G. D. "1 Peter 1:11 ΤΙΝΑ ʾΗ ΠΟΙΟΝ ΚΑΙΡΟΝ." *NovT* 28 (1986) 91-92.

Knox, John. "Pliny and I Peter: A Note on I Pet 4:14-16 and 3:15." *JBL* 72 (1953) 187-89.

Koester, Helmut. *Introduction to the New Testament*. 2 vols. FFNT. Philadelphia: Fortress, 1982.

―――. *Synoptische Überlieferung bei den Apostolischen Vätern*. TU 65. Berlin: Akademie-Verlag, 1957.

Kübler, B. "Peregrinus." *Paulys Real-Encyclopädie der classischen Altertumswissenschaft*, rev. and ed. Georg Wissowa et al., 19/1. 639-55. Stuttgart: J. B. Metzlersche Verlagsbuchhandlung, 1937.

Kümmel, Werner Georg. *Introduction to the New Testament*. Trans. Howard Clark Kee. 17th ed. Nashville: Abingdon, 1973.

Lamau, Marie-Louise. *Des chrétiens dans le monde: Communautés pétriniennes au Ier siècle*. LD 134. Paris: Cerf, 1988.

Leaney, A. R. C. *The Letters of Peter and Jude: A Commentary on the First Letter of Peter, a Letter of Jude and the Second Letter of Peter*. CBC. Cambridge: Cambridge University Press, 1967.

Lightfoot, J. B. and J. R. Harmer, trans. and eds. *The Apostolic Fathers: Greek Texts and English Translations of Their Writings*. Ed. and rev. Michael W. Holmes. 2d ed. Grand Rapids: Baker, 1992.

Lohse, Eduard. "Parenesis and Kerygma in 1 Peter." *Perspectives on First Peter*, ed. Charles H. Talbert, 37-59. NABPRSSS 9. Macon: Mercer University Press, 1986. German original, "Paraenese und Kerygma im 1.Petrusbrief." *ZNW* 45 (1954) 68-89.

MacMullen, Ramsay. *Enemies of the Roman Order: Treason, Unrest, and Alienation in the Empire*. Cambridge: Harvard University Press, 1966.

———. *Paganism in the Roman Empire*. New Haven/London: Yale University Press, 1981.

———. *Roman Social Relations: 50 B.C. to A.D. 284*. New Haven/ London: Yale University Press, 1974.

Magie, David. *Roman Rule in Asia Minor to the End of the Third Century after Christ*. 2 vols. Princeton: Princeton University Press, 1950.

Malherbe, Abraham J. *Moral Exhortation: A Greco-Roman Sourcebook*. LEC 4. Philadelphia: Westminster, 1986.

Malina, Bruce J. *The New Testament World: Insights from Cultural Anthropology*. Rev. ed. Louisville: Westminster/John Knox, 1993.

———. Review of *The Origins of Christian Morality: The First Two Centuries*, by Wayne A. Meeks. *TToday* 52 (July 1995) 269-70.

Malina, Bruce J., and Jerome H. Neyrey. "Honor and Shame in Luke-Acts: Pivotal Values of the Mediterranean World." *The Social World of Luke-Acts: Models for Interpretation*, ed. Jerome H. Neyrey, 25-65. Peabody: Hendrickson, 1991.

Mann, Michael. *The Sources of Social Power*. Vol. 1, *A History of Power from the Beginning to A.D. 1760*. Cambridge/New York/New Rochelle/Melbourne/Sidney: Cambridge University Press, 1986.

Marrou, H. I. *A History of Education in Antiquity*. Trans. George Lamb. Madison: University of Wisconsin Press, 1956. French original, 1948.

Marshall, I. Howard. *1 Peter*. IVPNTCS. Downers Grove/Leicester, England: InterVarsity, 1991.

Martin, Dale B. *Slavery as Salvation: The Metaphor of Slavery in Pauline Christianity*. New Haven/London: Yale University Press, 1990.

Martin, Ralph P. "The Composition of I Peter in Recent Study." *Vox Evangelica: Biblical and Historical Essays by Members of the Faculty of the London Bible College*, ed. Ralph P. Martin, 29-42. London: Epworth, 1962.

Martin, Troy W. *Metaphor and Composition in 1 Peter*. SBLDS 131. Atlanta: Scholars Press, 1992.

Meeks, Wayne A. *The First Urban Christians: The Social World of the Apostle Paul*. New Haven/London: Yale University Press, 1983.

———. "A Hermeneutics of Social Embodiment." *Christians among Jews and Gentiles: Essays in Honor of Krister Stendahl on His Sixty-fifth Birthday*, ed. George W. E. Nickelsburg with George W. MacRae, 176-86. Philadelphia: Fortress, 1986.

Bibliography

———. *The Moral World of the First Christians.* LEC 6. Philadelphia: Westminster, 1986.

Michaels, J. Ramsey. *1 Peter.* WBC 49. Waco: Word, 1988.

Michel, Otto. "οἶκος, οἰκία, οἰκεῖος." *Theological Dictionary of the New Testament,* vol. 5, ed. Gerhard Friedrich, 119-59. Grand Rapids: Eerdmans, 1967.

Millauer, Helmut. *Leiden als Gnade: Eine traditionsgeschichtliche Untersuchung zur Leidenstheologie des ersten Petrusbriefes.* Europäische Hochschulschriften 23/56. Bern: Herbert Lang, 1976.

Mitton, C. L. "The Relationship between 1 Peter and Ephesians." *JTS* n.s. 1 (1950) 67-73.

Neill, Stephen. *The Interpretation of the New Testament, 1861-1961: The Firth Lectures, 1962.* Corrected ed. Oxford/New York: Oxford University Press, 1966.

Neill, Stephen, and Tom Wright. *The Interpretation of the New Testament, 1861-1986.* 2d ed. Oxford/New York: Oxford University Press, 1988.

Nock, A. D. *Conversion: The Old and the New in Religion from Alexander the Great to Augustine of Hippo.* London/New York/Toronto: Oxford University Press, 1933. Reprint, Lanham: University Press of America, 1988.

O'Connor, Daniel Wm. *Peter in Rome: The Literary, Liturgical, and Archeological Evidence.* New York/London: Columbia University Press, 1969.

Oertel, F. "Katoikoi." *Paulys Real-Encyclopädie der classischen Altertumswissenschaft,* rev. and ed. Georg Wissowa et al., 11/1. 1-26. Stuttgart: J. B. Metzlersche Verlagsbuchhandlung, 1921.

Patterson, Orlando. *Slavery and Social Death: A Comparative Study.* Cambridge/London: Harvard University Press, 1982.

Perdelwitz, Richard. *Die Mysterienreligionen und das Problem des I. Petrusbriefes: Ein literarischer und religionsgeschichtlicher Versuch.* Religionsgeschichtliche Versuche und Vorarbeiten 11/3. Giessen: Töpelmann, 1911.

Perelman, Chaïm, and L. Olbrechts-Tyteca. *The New Rhetoric: A Treatise on Argumentation.* Trans. John Wilkinson and Purcell Weaver. Notre Dame: University of Notre Dame Press, 1969.

Peristiany, J. G., ed. *Honour and Shame: The Values of Mediterranean Society.* Chicago: University of Chicago Press, 1966; Midway Reprint, 1974.

Peristiany, J. G., and Julian A. Pitt-Rivers, eds. *Honor and Grace in Anthropology.* Cambridge Studies in Social and Cultural Anthropology 76. Cambridge: Cambridge University Press, 1992.

Perkins, Pheme. *Peter: Apostle for the Whole Church.* Studies on Personalities of the New Testament. Columbia: University of South Carolina Press, 1994.

Pitt-Rivers, Julian A. "Honour and Social Status." *Honour and Shame: The Values of Mediterranean Society,* ed. J. G. Peristiany, 21-77. Chicago: University of Chicago Press, 1966; Midway Reprint, 1974.

Rawson, Beryl. "Adult-Child Relationships in Roman Society." *Marriage, Divorce, and Children in Ancient Rome*, ed. Beryl Rawson, 7-30. Oxford: Clarendon, 1991.

Reicke, Bo. *The Epistles of James, Peter, and Jude: Introduction, Translation, and Notes.* AB 37. Garden City: Doubleday, 1964.

Richard, Earl. "The Functional Christology of First Peter." *Perspectives on First Peter*, ed. Charles H. Talbert, 121-39. NABPRSSS 9. Macon: Mercer University Press, 1986.

Ricoeur, Paul. *Interpretation Theory: Discourse and the Surplus of Meaning.* Fort Worth: Texas Christian University Press, 1976.

Robinson, John A. T. *Redating the New Testament.* Philadelphia: Westminster, 1976.

Rostovtzeff, Michael. *The Social and Economic History of the Roman Empire.* 2d ed. Revised by P. M. Fraser. 2 vols. Oxford: Clarendon, 1957.

Rowland, Christopher. *The Open Heaven: A Study of Apocalyptic in Judaism and Early Christianity.* New York: Crossroad, 1982.

Saller, Richard. "Corporal Punishment, Authority, and Obedience in the Roman Household." *Marriage, Divorce, and Children in Ancient Rome*, ed. Beryl Rawson, 144-65. Oxford: Clarendon, 1991.

Sanders, E. P. *Jesus and Judaism.* Philadelphia: Fortress, 1985.

Schaefer, Hans. "Paroikoi." *Paulys Real-Encyclopädie der classischen Altertumswisenschaft*, rev. and ed. Georg Wissowa et al., 18/4. 1695-1707. Stuttgart: J. B. Metzlersche Verlagsbuchhandlung, 1949.

Schelkle, Karl Hermann. *Die Petrusbriefe; Der Judasbrief.* HTKNT 13/2. Freiburg/Basel/Vienna: Herder, 1961.

Schmidt, Karl Ludwig. "διασπορά." *Theological Dictionary of the New Testament*, vol. 2, ed. Gerhard Kittel, 98-104. Grand Rapids: Eerdmans, 1964.

Schmidt, Karl Ludwig, Martin Anton Schmidt, and Rudolf Meyer. "πάροικος, παροικία, παροικέω." *Theological Dictionary of the New Testament*, vol. 5, ed. Gerhard Friedrich, 841-53. Grand Rapids: Eerdmans, 1967.

Schneider, Jane. "Of Vigilance and Virgins: Honor, Shame and Access to Resources in Mediterranean Societies." *Ethnology* 9 (1971) 1-24.

Schoedel, William R. "Polycarp, Epistle of." *The Anchor Bible Dictionary*, ed. David Noel Freedman, 5. 390-92. New York/London/Toronto/Sydney/Aukland: Doubleday, 1992.

———. *Polycarp, Martyrdom of Polycarp, Fragments of Papias.* The Apostolic Fathers: A New Translation and Commentary 5. London/Camden/Toronto: Nelson & Sons, 1967.

Schottroff, Luise. *Lydia's Impatient Sisters: A Feminist Social History of Early Christianity.* Trans. Barbara Rumscheidt and Martin Rumscheidt. Louisville: Westminster John Knox, 1995.

Bibliography

Schrage, Wolfgang. "Der erste Petrusbrief." *Die "katholischen" Briefe: Die Briefe des Jakobus, Petrus, Johannes und Judas*, by Horst Balz and Wolfgang Schrage, 60-121. NTD 10. 12th ed. Göttingen: Vandenhoeck & Ruprecht, 1980.

Schrenk, Gottlob. "ἐκδικέω, ἔκδικος, ἐκδίκησις." *Theological Dictionary of the New Testament*, vol. 2, ed. Gerhard Kittel, 442-46. Grand Rapids: Eerdmans, 1964.

―――. "ἐκλεκτός." *Theological Dictionary of the New Testament*, vol. 4, ed. Gerhard Kittel, 181-92. Grand Rapids: Eerdmans, 1967.

Schröger, Friedrich. *Gemeinde im 1. Petrusbrief: Untersuchungen zum Selbstverständnis einer christlichen Gemeinde an der Wende vom 1. zum 2. Jahrhundert*. Schriften der Universität Passau, Reihe Katholische Theologie 1. Passau: Passavia Universitätsverlag, 1981.

Schürer, Emil. *The History of the Jewish People in the Age of Jesus Christ (175 B.C.-A.D. 135)*. Rev. ed. Rev. and ed. Geza Vermes, et al. 3 vols. Edinburgh: Clark, 1973-87.

Schüssler Fiorenza, Elisabeth. *In Memory of Her: A Feminist Theological Reconstruction of Christian Origins*. 10th anniversary ed. New York: Crossroad, 1994.

Schutter, William L. *Hermeneutic and Composition in I Peter*. WUNT 2/30. Tübingen: Mohr-Siebeck, 1989.

Scroggs, Robin. "The Sociological Interpretation of the New Testament: The Present State of Research." *NTS* 26 (1979-80) 164-79. Reprint, *The Text and the Times: New Testament Essays for Today*, 46-68. Minneapolis: Fortress, 1993.

Selwyn, Edward Gordon. *The First Epistle of St. Peter: The Greek Text with Introduction, Notes and Essays*. London: Macmillan, 1946; 2d ed., 1947.

Sherwin-White, Adrian N. *The Roman Citizenship*. 2d ed. Oxford: Clarendon, 1973.

―――. "The Roman Citizenship: A Survey of Its Development into a World Franchise." *Aufstieg und Niedergang der römischen Welt*, pt. 1, vol. 2, ed. Hildegard Temporini, 23-58. Berlin/New York: de Gruyter, 1972.

―――. *Roman Law and Roman Society in the New Testament*. Oxford: Oxford University Press, 1963. Reprint, Grand Rapids: Baker, 1992.

Simmel, Georg. *Conflict*. Trans. Kurt H. Wolff. Glencoe: Free Press, 1955.

Smallwood, E. Mary. *The Jews under Roman Rule, from Pompey to Diocletian: A Study in Political Relations*. SJLA 20. 2d ed. Leiden: Brill, 1981.

Soards, Marion L. "1 Peter, 2 Peter, and Jude as Evidence for a Petrine School." *Aufstieg und Niedergang der römischen Welt*, pt. 2, vol. 25/5, ed. Wolfgang Haase, 3827-49. Berlin/New York: de Gruyter, 1988.

Spicq, Ceslas. *Les épîtres de Saint Pierre*. SB. Paris: Gabalda, 1966.

Steiger, Wilhelm. *Exposition of the First Epistle of Peter*. Trans. Patrick Fairbairn. Edinburgh: Clark, 1836. German original, 1832.

Stern, M. "The Jewish Diaspora." *The Jewish People in the First Century: Historical Geography, Political History, Social, Cultural and Religious Life and Institutions*, ed. S. Safrai and M. Stern, 1. 143-55. CRINT. Philadelphia: Fortress, 1974.

Stibbs, A. M., and A. F. Walls. *The First Epistle General of Peter: An Introduction and Commentary*. TNTC. London: Tyndale; Grand Rapids: Eerdmans, 1959.

Stowers, Stanley Kent. *Letter Writing in Greco-Roman Antiquity*. LEC 5. Philadelphia: Westminster, 1986.

Streeter, Burnett Hillman. *The Primitive Church: Studied with Special Reference to the Origins of the Christian Ministry*. London: Macmillan, 1929.

Strobel, August. "Zum Verständnis von Mt 21:1-13." *NovT* 2 (1958) 210-19.

———. "Zum Verständnis von Rom. 13." *ZNW* 47 (1956) 67-93.

Sundberg, Albert C., Jr. "Canon Muratori: A Fourth-Century List," *HTR* 66 (1973) 1-41.

Talbert, Charles H. "Once Again: The Plan of 1 Peter." *Perspectives on First Peter*, ed. Charles H. Talbert, 141-51. NABPRSSS 9. Macon: Mercer University Press, 1986.

Tàrrech, Armand Puig. "Le milieu de la premiére épître de Pierre." *Revista Catalana de Teologia* 5 (1980) 95-129, 331-402.

Tcherikover, Victor. *Hellenistic Civilization and the Jews*. Trans. S. Applebaum. Philadelphia: Jewish Publication Society; Jerusalem: Magnes Press, Hebrew University, 1959.

Theissen, Gerd. "Sociological Research into the New Testament: Some Ideas Offered by the Sociology of Knowledge for a New Exegetical Approach." *Social Reality and the Early Christians: Theology, Ethics, and the World of the New Testament*, trans. Margaret Kohl, 1-29. Minneapolis: Fortress, 1992.

Thiede, Carsten Peter. "Babylon, der andere Ort: Anmerkungen zu 1 Petr 5,13 und Apg 12,17." *Biblica* 67 (1986) 532-38. Reprint, *Das Petrusbild in der neueren Forschung*, ed. Carsten Peter Thiede, 221-29. Wuppertal: Brockhaus, 1987.

———. *Simon Peter: From Galilee to Rome*. Grand Rapids: Zondervan, Academie, 1988.

Thurén, Lauri. *The Rhetorical Strategy of 1 Peter, with Special Regard to Ambiguous Expressions*. Åbo, Finland: Åbo Academy Press, 1990.

Trebilco, Paul R. *Jewish Communities in Asia Minor*. SNTSMS 69. Cambridge: Cambridge University Press, 1991.

Turner, Victor. "Betwixt and Between: The Liminal Period in *Rites de Passage*." *Proceedings of the 1964 Annual Spring Meeting of the American Ethnological Society*, ed. June Helm, 4-20. N.p.: American Ethnological Society, 1964. Reprint, *The Forest of Symbols: Aspects of Ndembu Ritual*, by Victor Turner, 93-111. Ithaca/London: Cornell University Press, 1967.

———. *Dramas, Fields, and Metaphors: Symbolic Action in Human Society*. Symbol, Myth, and Ritual Series. Ithaca/London: Cornell University Press, 1974.

———. *The Forest of Symbols: Aspects of Ndembu Ritual*. Ithaca/London: Cornell University Press, 1967.

———. *Process, Performance and Pilgrimage: A Study in Comparative Symbology*. Ranchi Anthropology Series 1. New Delhi: Concept, 1979.

———. *The Ritual Process: Structure and Anti-Structure*. Symbol, Myth, and Ritual Series. Ithaca: Cornell University Press, 1969.

———. "Variations on a Theme of Liminality." *Secular Ritual*, ed. Sally F. Moore and Barbara G. Myerhoff, 36-52. Assen/Amsterdam: Van Gorcum, 1977.

Van Gennep, Arnold. *The Rites of Passage*. Trans. Monika B. Vizedom and Gabrielle L. Caffee. London: Routledge & Kegan Paul, 1960. French original, 1908.

Van Unnik, W. C. "The Critique of Paganism in 1 Peter 1:18." *Neotestamentica et Semitica: Studies in Honour of Matthew Black*, ed. E. Earle Ellis and Max Wilcox, 129-42. Edinburgh: Clark, 1969.

———. "The Teaching of Good Works in I Peter." *NTS* 1 (1954-55) 92-110.

Vatz, Richard E. "The Myth of the Rhetorical Situation." *Philosophy and Rhetoric* 6 (1973) 154-61.

Von Rad, Gerhard. *Old Testament Theology*. Trans. D. M. G. Stalker. 2 vols. New York/Hagerstown/San Francisco/London: Harper & Row, 1962-65.

Wiedemann, Thomas E. J. *Slavery*. Oxford: Clarendon, 1987.

Wilken, Robert L. *The Christians as the Romans Saw Them*. New Haven/London: Yale University Press, 1984.

Wilson, Bryan R. "An Analysis of Sect Development." *American Sociological Review* 24 (1959) 3-15.

———. *Magic and the Millennium: A Sociological Study of Religious Movements of Protest among Tribal and Third-World Peoples*. New York: Harper & Row, 1973.

———. *Sects and Society: A Sociological Study of the Elim Tabernacle, Christian Science, and Christadelphians*. Berkeley: University of California Press, 1961.

Wilson, Robert R. *Sociological Approaches to the Old Testament*. GBS. Philadelphia: Fortress, 1984.

Windisch, Hans. *Die katholischen Briefe*. HNT 15. 2d ed. Tübingen: Mohr-Siebeck, 1930.

Windisch, Hans, and Herbert Preisker. *Die katholischen Briefe*. HNT 15. 3d ed. Tübingen: Mohr-Siebeck, 1951.

Winter, Bruce W. *Seek the Welfare of the City: Christians as Benefactors and Citizens*. Grand Rapids: Eerdmans; Carlisle, England: Paternoster, 1994.

Wittgenstein, Ludwig. *The Blue and Brown Books*. 2d ed. Oxford: Blackwell, 1969.

———. *Zettel*. Ed. G. E. M. Anscombe and G. H. von Wright. Trans. G. E. M. Anscombe. Berkeley: University of California Press, 1967.

INDEX OF ANCIENT TEXTS

SEPTUAGINT (RAHLFS EDITION)

Genesis
15:13	79
23:4	79, 80, 143
26:3	79
49:1	131

Exodus
2:15	79
2:22	79
6:1	79
6:6	79
18:3	79
19:6	142, 158
33:12	191
33:16	191

Leviticus
25:23	80

Numbers
24:14	131

Deuteronomy
4:30	131
23:8	79
28:25	76
30:4	76

Joshua
7:19	160

1 Chronicles
16:13	77

1 Esdras
5:7	79

2 Esdras
8:35	79
11:9	76

Esther
8:12t	77, 78

Judith
5:9	79
5:19	76

Tobit
14:6-7	160

2 Maccabees
1:27	76

3 Maccabees
6:36	79
7:19	79

4 Maccabees
18:7	103

Psalms
2:11	162
18:12	151
18:14	151
26:9	151
33	157
33:5	79
33:9	157

33:13-17	164	**Psalms of Solomon**	
33:14	157	8:28	76
34:10	162	9:2	76
49:13-14	159	12:3	79
49:23	159	17:17	79
50:17-19	159	17:34-35	160
50:17-21	168		
38:13	80	**Hosea**	
54:16	79	1:6	142
55:9	158	1:9	142
70:15	158	2:25	142
88:4	77	3:5	131
104:6	77	5:11	63
104:43	77	6:6	168
105:5	77		
106:22	158	**Micah**	
117:22	139	4:1	131
118:54	79	4:1-2	160
119:5	79	6:6-8	168
138:1 (A)	76		
140:2	159, 168	**Habakkuk**	
146:2	76	3:16	78, 79

Proverbs
Zechariah
3:9   162   2:11   160
11:31   200
12:2   191   **Isaiah**
24:21   163   2:2-3   160
                        2:20   63
Job   3:18   68
28:22   191   8:12   194
                        8:14   139, 188
Wisdom   10:3   159
3:9   77   28:16   102, 139, 187, 188
14:22   63   29:13   162
19:10   79   40   67
                        40:6-8 67
Sirach   43   143, 158
Prologue 34 79   43:3   158
1:11-30 162   43:4   158
16:8   78   43:8   158
18:4   158   43:8-13 159
41:5   78   43:9   158
44:6 (B) 78   43:14   158
46:1   77   43:21   158
                        43:20   77, 78
                        43:20-21 142

Index of Ancient Texts

43:21	142, 158	25:19	131
43:22-24	158	37:24	131
45:13-25	160	41:17	76
45:23	160		
48:20	151	*Lamentations*	
49:6	76	2:22	78, 79
49:6-7	160		
65:9	77	*Ezekiel*	
65:15	77	8-9	144
65:23	77	8:17	144
		9:6	144
Jeremiah		9:9	144
6:15	159	38:16	131
10:15	159		
10:25	63	*Daniel*	
13:14 (א)	76	10:14	131
15:7	76	10:14 (θ′)	131
23:20	131	12:2	76

New Testament

Matthew		13:15	62
22:14	77	13:16	62
24:22	77	13:17	79
24:24	77	13:26	62
24:31	77	14:15	63
		15:23	45
Mark		16:14	62
13:20	77	17:4	62
13:22	77	17:17	62
13:27	77	17:30	63
		18:7	62
Luke			
18:7	77	*Romans*	
24:18	79	1:1	151
		8:33	77
John		11	67
7:35	76	12:1-2	168
		13:1-4	88, 161
Acts		13:1-7	162
7:6	79		
7:29	79	*1 Corinthians*	
9:31	162	3:8-9	67
10:2	62	3:16-17	144
10:22	62	6:19	144
10:35	62	7:22	151

9:3	90-91
9:7-11	67
11:2-16	176
14:33-36	176
15:23	67
15:37-39	67
15:42-44	67

2 Corinthians
6:16	144
7:11	91
9:6-10	67
11:2	103

Galatians
1:10	151
6:10	144

Ephesians
2:19	79, 144
2:21	144
4:18	63
5:21	162
5:22	148
6:1	148
6:4	149
6:5	148
6:6	151

Philippians
1:1	151
2:5-11	160
4:18	168

Colossians
3:12	77
3:18-25	148
3:21	149

1 Thessalonians
4:5	63

1 Timothy
2:1-2	50
2:1-3	162
3:15	144

2 Timothy
2:10	77

Titus
1:1	77
2:5	103
3:1	88
3:1-3	162
3:8	88

Hebrews
1:2	131
3:6	144
11:9	79
11:13-16	80
13:16	168

James
1:1	76, 151

1 Peter
1:1	57, 64, 67, 74-77, 80, 81, 103, 136, 141, 142, 143, 146
1:1-2	2, 181
1:1–2:10	8
1:2	77, 124, 183
1:2-12	137
1:3	2, 66, 67, 133, 150, 181, 183
1:3-4	133
1:3-5	18, 193
1:3-9	127, 133, 145, 181-83
1:3-12	133
1:3–2:10	4
1:3–4:11	2
1:3–5:11	2
1:4	14, 175, 181, 185
1:4-5	201
1:5	127-31, 133, 181-82, 184
1:5-9	133, 184
1:6	1, 6, 87, 131, 133, 181-82, 184, 202
1:6-7	6, 182, 185, 197, 199, 209
1:6-8	2

1:7	67, 133, 160, 181-83, 184-85, 187, 201	2:1	156-57, 164, 170, 187
1:8	46, 128, 133, 182	2:2	2, 150
1:9	128-29, 133, 182, 184	2:2-3	67, 156
1:10	127, 183, 184, 191	2:4	139, 158, 168, 185, 186, 187
1:10-11	183	2:4-6	185
1:10–2:3	183-86	2:4-7	185
1:11	127-29, 130, 132, 133, 183, 184	2:4-10	138, 158, 186-88, 194
1:11-12	185	2:5	64, 124, 138-42, 143-44, 159, 168, 186
1:12	2, 127, 132, 183	2:6	185, 187
1:13	109, 133-34, 137, 145, 183, 184, 191, 201	2:6-7	133
1:13-14	133	2:6-8	139, 187
1:13-17	109	2:7	142, 187, 188, 192, 200
1:13-21	153	2:7-8	159, 168, 187
1:14	61, 67, 110, 150, 154, 157, 160	2:8	142, 158, 188
1:14-16	66	2:9	78, 139, 141-43, 154, 157-59, 168, 188
1:14-17	110, 140, 145, 147, 183, 184	2:9-10	61, 142, 188, 193
1:14-18	61	2:9-17	168
1:14-19	62, 64, 83	2:10	2, 133, 142, 154, 188
1:15	63, 110	2:11	13, 66, 75, 78-81, 143, 153, 154, 190
1:15-16	138	2:11-17	153, 162, 188-90
1:16	133, 149	2:11–3:12	8
1:17	62, 75, 78-79, 81, 110, 132, 137-38, 141, 142, 149, 153, 160, 163, 164, 184	2:11–4:11	8
		2:12	18, 23, 63, 66, 87-88, 90, 92, 100-3, 142, 143, 145, 153, 157-61, 168, 188, 189, 195
1:18	61, 62, 63, 67, 110, 154, 166	2:12-15	90-91, 100, 165
		2:13	161, 162, 164, 174
1:18-19	66, 133, 150, 153	2:13-14	88, 153, 174
1:18-20	184, 191	2:13-17	50, 66, 162
1:18-21	110, 193	2:14	88-89, 92, 100, 153, 157, 161, 189
1:18-22	109		
1:19	67, 124, 184, 185, 186	2:14-15	88
1:19-20	191	2:15	23, 88, 100, 155, 157, 161, 162, 189
1:20	131, 132, 191		
1:21	134, 145, 185	2:16	68, 151, 153, 154, 155, 157, 162, 164, 190
1:22	110, 157, 162, 170, 171-72, 176	2:17	149, 153, 162, 164, 171, 174, 176, 190
1:22–2:3	186		
1:23	2, 67, 150	2:18	102, 110, 152, 153, 165, 174
1:23-25	67, 150, 156, 193		
1:24-25	67	2:18-20	165, 190, 192
2	164	2:18-25	165, 167, 190-94

2:19	87, 153, 190-91	3:13-17	88, 90-91, 165, 166, 199
2:19-20	68, 69, 153, 191-92, 200, 201	3:13-18	23
2:19-21	199	3:13–4:6	194-99
2:19-23	195	3:14	87, 164, 165, 194, 200
2:19-25	152-53	3:14-15	164, 195
2:20	87, 102, 128, 165, 190-91	3:14-17	153
2:21	6, 8, 163, 192, 195	3:15	4, 8, 10, 51, 87, 90-91, 100, 134, 198
2:21-23	193, 196	3:15-16	66
2:21-24	153	3:15-20	18
2:21-25	192	3:16	4, 63, 87, 88, 100-2, 145, 157, 164, 187, 188, 195, 202
2:22	157, 164		
2:22-23	193		
2:22-25	192	3:16-17	90
2:23	46, 157, 163-64, 196, 201	3:17	1, 87, 92, 157, 162, 163, 164, 195
2:24	193, 196	3:17-18	197, 198
2:24-25	193, 196	3:18	8, 153, 195-96, 197, 198
2:25	2, 133, 193, 196		
3	194	3:18-22	193, 196
3:1	110, 165, 166, 174	3:19-22	196
3:1-2	18, 63, 103, 165	3:21	2, 5, 124, 133
3:1-4	68	3:24	6
3:1-6	68, 166, 169, 174	4:1	87, 153, 196, 197, 198, 199
3:1-7	102		
3:3	68, 69	4:1-2	145, 209
3:3-5	103	4:2	132, 162, 163, 197
3:3-6	165	4:2-4	66, 161
3:5-6	61, 103	4:2-5	197
3:6	164, 165	4:3	61, 63, 69
3:7	68, 103, 110, 165, 167-68, 174, 176	4:3-4	4, 61, 62, 64, 83, 110, 155, 161
3:7-8	176	4:4	63, 87, 90, 101, 103, 157, 161, 197, 198
3:8	128, 163, 171, 173, 176		
3:9	101, 110, 153, 157, 163-64	4:5	129-30, 145, 160, 198
		4:7	128-31
3:9-10	193	4:8	162, 172
3:9-11	170	4:8-11	172, 176
3:10	157	4:9	172
3:10-12	164	4:9-11	124
3:11	157, 164, 165	4:10	140, 172
3:12	157, 164	4:10-11	49
3:12-13	194	4:11	2
3:13	100, 157, 164, 194	4:12	1, 2, 3, 6, 87, 145, 197, 199, 209
3:13-14	1		
3:13-16	100	4:12-14	161

Index of Ancient Texts

4:12-17	42	5:3	173
4:12-19	146, 199-201	5:4	201
4:12–5:11	2	5:5	68, 172, 173, 174, 201
4:12–5:14	2, 8	5:5-6	172, 175, 176
4:13	6, 87, 129, 133, 160, 199-200, 201	5:6	129-30, 173, 201, 202
		5:6-10	202
4:13-16	153	5:7	202
4:14	4, 6, 87, 92, 101, 157, 199, 200, 201	5:8	67, 166, 202
		5:9	87, 134, 149, 171
4:14-16	91, 200	5:10	14, 16, 87, 129-31, 160, 195, 202
4:15	88, 92, 101, 161		
4:15-16	4, 8, 66, 87, 166	5:12	9, 45
4:16	92, 101, 129, 145, 161, 187, 188, 199	5:13	43, 52
		5:14	195
4:16-17	145		
4:17	6, 128-30, 140, 143-45, 149, 155, 200, 209	*2 Peter*	
		1:1	151
4:17-18	146, 160, 200	3:1	43
4:18	145	3:3	131
4:19	87, 145-46, 162, 163, 165, 193, 202		
		Jude	
5	201	18	131
5:1	46, 129, 133, 172, 201		
5:1-4	68, 172	*Revelation*	
5:1-5	49, 176	1:6	158
5:1-14	201-2	5:10	158
5:2	172	11:13	160
5:2-3	172, 176	17:14	77

OTHER PSEUDEPIGRAPHA

Assumption of Moses
4:2   77

1 Enoch
1:1   77
1:8   77
38:2-5   77
39:6-7   77
48:1   77
58:1-4   77
62-63   160
90:30-33   160

Epistle of Aristeas
250   175

Pseudo-Phocylides
207   149

Sibylline Oracles
3:669-731   160
5   46

Testament of Asher
7:2   76

Testament of Levi
11:2   79

OTHER EARLY-JEWISH LITERATURE

Josephus
Antiquities of the Jews
4 § 105   191
4 § 115   191
14 § 110   62

Philo
De Cherubim
120-121   79

Philo
De Confusione Linguarum
77-82   79
79   80
80   78

Philo
De Decalogo
165-167   148

Philo
De Ebrietate
55   175

Philo
De Praemiis et Poenis
115   76

Philo
De Specialibus Legibus
2.225-227   148
2.233   148

OTHER EARLY-CHRISTIAN LITERATURE

Acts of Saint Cyprian
1   86

Epistle of Barnabas
12:9   131
16:5   131

1 Clement
1:1   77
2:4   77
5:6   191
6:1   77
46:3-4   77
46:8   77
49:5   77
54:3   191
58:2   77
59:2   77
60:4–61:2   50

2 Clement
14:2   131

Clement of Alexandria
Protrepticus
9.88.3   76

Eusebius
Ecclesiastical History
3.39.17   53

Shepherd of Hermas, Visions
1.3.4   77
2.1.3   77
2.2.5   77
2.4.2   77
3.8.3   77

Ignatius
Letter to the Philadelphians
11:2   45

Ignatius
Letter to the Romans
10:1   45

Index of Ancient Texts 235

Ignatius
Letter to the Smyrnaeans
12:1   45

Martyrdom of Polycarp
16:1   77

Polycarp
Letter to the Philippians
1:3   53

8:1   53
10:2   53
14   45

Pseudo-Dionysius
Epistles
8   92

CLASSICAL GREEK AND LATIN LITERATURE

Aristotle
Politica
1253b.7-8   148
1254a.22-24   148
1254b.13-21   148
1260a.9-14   148

Cicero
De Imperio Cn. Pompeii
14   59

Cicero
De Officiis
2.9, 11   99

Cicero
Pro Flacco
28.66-69   85

Dio Chrysostom
Orationes
46.12   74

Diodorus Siculus
Bibliotheca Historica
13.47.4   73, 74

Epictetus
Discourses
2.10.7   147
3.22.1-8   99

Epictetus
Encheiridion
30   147

Hierocles
On Duties (=Stobaeus)
4.22.24   147

Juvenal
Satires
14.96-106   85

Plato
Leges
690A   147
781A   175

Plato
Respublica
425B   147
431C   148
433D   148
455D   175
457A   175

Pliny the Younger
Epistulae
10.96.2   51
10.96.4   82
10.96.7   60
10.96.8   84
10.96.9   82-83, 84
10.97   51

Plutarch
  Moralia
1105A   75, 76

Pseudo-Plutarch
  De Liberis Educandis
(*Moralia*) 7E 149

Suetonius
  Nero
16.2   84

Tacitus
  Annales
15.45   84

Tacitus
  Historiae
5.1-13   85
5.4-5   85

Thucydides
  History of the Peloponnesian War
2.45   175

INDEX OF MODERN AUTHORS

Achtemeier, Paul J. 14-15, 20, 21, 68, 78, 81, 152
Adam, Alfred 2
Arndt, William F. 102, 103, 127, 128, 129, 131, 191
Attridge, Harold W. 131
Aune, David E. 136
Balch, David L. 10, 12-15, 18, 19, 20-21, 51, 68, 86, 91, 103, 104, 112-18, 147, 158, 159, 160, 166-68, 176
Balz, Horst 43, 63
Barraclough, Geoffrey 28, 29
Bauckham, Richard J. 42
Bauer, Walter 102, 103, 127, 128, 129, 131, 191
Beare, Francis Wright 2, 4, 5, 43, 45, 47, 50, 53, 63, 109, 132, 140, 159
Beasley-Murray, G. W. 2
Beker, J. Christiaan 14
Benko, Stephen 86
Berger, Adolf 90, 91
Berger, Peter L. 30-38, 111, 205
Best, Ernest 43, 47, 52, 54, 63, 89, 91, 137, 139, 140, 151, 192, 197
Beyer, Hermann Wolfgang 92, 102
Bigg, Charles 44, 49, 84, 187
Bitzer, Lloyd F. 55-56
Blass, Friedrich 110, 128, 130
Boismard, M.-É. 3, 5, 44, 52, 53, 192
Boissevain, Jeremy 94
Bornemann, Wilhelm 2
Bradley, Keith R. 147, 148, 151
Broughton, T. R. S. 58, 59, 73
Brox, Norbert 4, 8-9, 19, 43, 47, 52-54, 58, 76, 109-10, 127-28, 159

Bultmann, Rudolf 192
Burton, Ernest De Witt 110
Carney, T. F. 28
Carter, Warren 148, 149, 151, 152
Chase, F. H. 45
Clements, R. E. 24
Cohen, Shaye J. D. 85
Conzelmann, Hans 53
Corley, Kathleen E. 104
Coser, Lewis 11-12
Cranfield, C. E. B. 47
Cross, F. L. 3-4, 49
Cullmann, Oscar 42
Dalton, William Joseph 41, 44, 45, 46, 47, 50
Danker, Frederick W. 67, 69, 102, 103, 127, 128, 129, 131, 191
Daube, David 110
Davids, Peter H. 44, 46, 48
Davis, John 94
Debrunner, Albert 110, 128, 130
Delaney, Carol 97
Delling, Gerhard 132
de Ste Croix, G. E. M. 84, 86, 90, 93
Edelman, Murray 37
Edmundson, George 46
Elliott, John H. 10-13, 14, 15, 17-21, 24-28, 41, 42, 44, 45, 47, 52, 54, 58, 59, 60, 61, 62, 64-78, 81-83, 98, 105, 112-18, 136, 139-41, 144, 147, 153, 157-59, 206
Eyben, Emiel 149
Feldman, Louis H. 85
Feldmeier, Reinhard 10, 15-18, 20, 43, 63, 70, 72, 73-74, 80, 116-18, 137, 140, 152, 157-59

Fenn, Richard K. 29-30
Ferguson, Everett 53
Finley, M. I. 148, 153
Fredriksen, Paula 62, 85
Frend, W. H. C. 86
Frier, B. 150
Furnish, Victor Paul 137
Funk, Robert W. 110, 128, 130
Gadamer, Hans Georg 25-26
Gager, John G. 85
Garnsey, Peter 82, 86, 98-99, 149-50, 152
Garrett, Susan R. 24
Gaudemet, J. 149
Gauthier, Philippe 72
Geertz, Clifford 29, 33, 37, 38-39, 56
Gilmore, David D. 94, 95, 97
Gingrich, F. Wilbur 102, 103, 127, 128, 129, 131, 191
Goodman, Martin 84, 85
Goppelt, Leonhard 4, 7-8, 19, 21, 42, 43, 44, 45, 47, 49, 50, 51, 52, 53, 54-55, 60, 61, 62, 63, 69, 76, 77, 84-85, 86, 88, 89, 91-92, 93, 98, 103, 109, 128, 129, 131, 137, 139, 140, 151, 157, 159, 187, 188, 191, 192, 197
Greenlee, J. Harold 110
Grudem, Wayne A. 44, 45, 47, 49, 50
Grundmann, Walter 75, 80
Guthrie, Donald 44, 45, 49, 50, 58
Hagner, Donald Alfred 46, 47
Hahneman, Geoffrey Mark 53
Harmer, J. R. 48
Harnack, Adolf von 1, 2, 48
Harrison, P. N. 48
Hauck, Friedrich 2
Heussi, Karl 53
Hiers, Richard H. 130
Hill, David 5-6, 19
Holmberg, Bengt 24, 28
Hommel, H. 72
Hopkins, Keith 82, 98
Humbert, G. 72
Hunzinger, Claus-Hunno 53
Jones, A. H. M. 73, 82, 90, 91
Kelly, J. N. D. 44-45, 47, 49, 52, 53, 54, 61, 62, 76, 87, 88, 89, 90, 91, 92, 109, 128, 132, 139, 140, 151, 159, 187, 188, 191
Kennedy, George A. 55
Kilpatrick, G. D. 127
Knox, John 50
Koester, Helmut 48, 50
Kübler, B. 72
Kümmel, Werner Georg 19, 43, 45, 47, 49, 52, 53
Lamau, Marie-Louise 65, 68-69
Leaney, A. R. C. 3, 50
Lightfoot, J. B. 48
Lindemann, Andreas 53
Lohse, Eduard 4-5, 19, 21
Luckmann, Thomas 30-38, 111, 205
MacMullen, Ramsay 59, 69, 85, 86, 99
Magie, David 59
Malherbe, Abraham J. 149
Malina, Bruce J. 29, 95, 96, 97
Mann, Michael 28-29
Marrou, H. I. 148
Marshall, I. Howard 44, 45
Martin, Dale B. 148
Martin, Ralph P. 5
Martin, Troy W. 10, 15-16, 61, 76, 99, 103-4, 137, 149
Meeks, Wayne A. 24, 25, 27, 29, 99
Michaels, J. Ramsey 19, 42, 43, 44, 46, 47-48, 49, 50, 51, 52, 60, 61, 62, 63, 69, 76, 77, 88, 91, 127, 128, 129, 131, 132, 133, 137, 139, 140, 153, 157, 159, 162, 163, 175, 182, 185, 187, 191, 192, 197
Michel, Otto 140, 141, 144
Millauer, Helmut 6-7, 19, 54
Mitton, C. L. 47
Neill, Stephen 42
Neyrey, Jerome H. 95
Nicholas, Barry 90, 91
Nock, A. D. 86
O'Connor, Daniel Wm. 42
Oertel, F. 72
Olbrechts-Tyteca, L. 55-56, 64
Patterson, Orlando 151-52

Index of Modern Authors

Perdelwitz, Richard 1-4
Perelman, Chaïm 55-56, 64
Peristiany, J. G. 94-95, 96
Perkins, Pheme 42
Pitt-Rivers, Julian A. 94-95, 96, 97
Preisker, Herbert 2-3, 4
Rawson, Beryl 148, 149
Reicke, Bo 5, 48, 59, 60
Richard, Earl 13-14, 19, 21
Ricoeur, Paul 26
Robinson, John A. T. 44, 45, 46, 49, 50, 52
Rostovtzeff, Michael 71, 72, 73
Rowland, Christopher 130
Saller, Richard 82, 86, 98, 99, 149, 150, 151, 152
Sanders, E. P. 160
Schaefer, Hans 70-73
Schelkle, Karl Hermann 47, 50, 62, 87
Schmidt, Karl Ludwig 70-71, 75, 76, 78, 79, 80
Schmidt, Martin Anton 70-71, 75, 78, 79, 80
Schneider, Jane 94, 97
Schoedel, William R. 48
Schottroff, Luise 176
Schrage, Wolfgang 43
Schrenk, Gottlob 77, 78, 89
Schröger, Friedrich 65
Schürer, Emil 59, 62
Schüssler Fiorenza, Elisabeth 104
Schutter, William L. 19, 43, 44, 47-48, 53, 59, 62, 63, 69, 84, 86, 87-92, 99
Scroggs, Robin 24
Selwyn, Edward Gordon 1, 3-4, 19, 44, 45, 46, 47, 48, 49, 50, 61, 62, 63, 69, 76, 77, 87, 88, 109-10, 128, 140, 151, 157, 159, 187
Sherwin-White, Adrian N. 73, 82, 90
Simmel, Georg 11-12
Smallwood, E. Mary 60, 86
Soards, Marion L. 54
Spicq, Ceslas 44, 47, 49, 52, 62
Steiger, Wilhelm 61
Stern, M. 60
Stibbs, A. M. 46
Stowers, Stanley Kent 136
Streeter, Burnett Hillman 2, 53
Strobel, August 3, 162
Sundberg, Albert C., Jr. 53
Talbert, Charles H. 112-18
Tàrrech, Armand Puig 64-67, 74, 81-82, 105, 150, 153
Tcherikover, Victor 60, 72
Theissen, Gerd 24
Thiede, Carsten Peter 42, 44
Thurén, Lauri 44, 45, 47, 49, 57, 114-18, 159
Trebilco, Paul R. 85
Turner, Victor 21, 39, 118-26, 150, 156, 169, 176-77, 207-8
Van Gennep, Arnold 119, 121, 123
Van Unnik, W. C. 63, 159, 160
Vatz, Richard E. 55-56
Von Rad, Gerhard 160
Walls, A. F. 46
Wiedemann, Thomas E. J. 151, 152
Wilken, Robert L. 82-83, 84, 85, 86
Wilson, Bryan R. 11-12, 117
Wilson, Robert R. 24
Windisch, Hans 2, 3, 4, 151
Winter, Bruce W. 75, 89
Wittgenstein, Ludwig 25-26
Wright, Tom 42

www.ingramcontent.com/pod-product-compliance
Lightning Source LLC
Chambersburg PA
CBHW031252230426
43670CB00005B/152